CHRIST AND HIS BRIDE:
Their Love Story

The Song of Songs
A verse-by-verse study of Song of Solomon

DIXIE MCCLINTOCK

and

JUDY RUSK

Faith Journey Publishing

Christ and His Bride: Their Love Story

Copyright 2024 by Faith Journey Publishing

All rights reserved. No portion of this book may be reproduced, stored in a retrieval system, or transmitted in any form or by any means—electronic, mechanical, photocopy, recording, or otherwise—without prior written permission of the publisher, except as provided by United States of America copyright law. For permission requests, please address Faith Journey Publishing, LLC.

Published 2024
Printed in the United States of America
ISBN: 979-8-9858168-3-9

Editor: Mari Fitz-Wynn
Copy editor: Abigayle Markwardt
Cover design: Leah Morrison
Formatting: Kimball H. McNeal

For information, contact:
Faith Journey Publishing, LLC
contact@faithjourneypublishing.com

Contents

Introduction	Song of Solomon	1
Chapter One	Song of Solomon 1:1-17	5
Chapter Two	Song of Solomon 2:1-17	34
Chapter Three	Song of Solomon 3:1-11	59
Chapter Four	Song of Solomon 4:1-16	72
Chapter Five	Song of Solomon 5:1-16	94
Chapter Six	Song of Solomon 6:1-13	121
Chapter Seven	Song of Solomon 7:1-13	138
Chapter Eight	Song of Solomon 8:1-14	153
Conclusion		180
Appendices		182
About the Authors		189

Heavenly Father,

In dedication and devotion to Your glory, we give You thanks and praise for the Song of Solomon, the beautiful allegory of Your Son's love for His bride, and of her burgeoning love for Him. May the study of this love story be a life-changing experience for all who read it.

INTRODUCTION

For a number of years, co-author Judy Rusk studied weekly with my mother, Nema McClintock, in a ladies' Bible study in our home. That's how Judy and I met. When Mother was no longer able to continue teaching due to health concerns, Judy and I began studying the Bible together.

In January of 2012, Judy and I finished her first study of the Song of Solomon. I knew the time had come to write this book. (Twenty years ago, I had taught the Song of Solomon to different groups and had entertained the idea of writing a commentary on it.)

When I asked Judy if she wanted to join me in this writing project, she quickly answered, "No," but God had changed her mind by the next week. She believed the Lord wanted her to branch out into new territories. The Lord even gave her a dream confirming that thought.

We have purposed this study of the Song of Solomon not as a marriage manual or a history but only in reference to Christ and His Bride, her development and transformation, His beauty of character and actions, their love, and their work. We hope you will come to understand how much the Lord wants you and every believer, male or female, to be part of His Bride. We want to share what the Lord has shown us thus far, in the hope you will hear His love song to you and draw nearer to Him.

There are three primary speakers in this dramatic song or play:
- The Shulamite maiden
- The shepherd-king bridegroom represented by Solomon
- A group called the Daughters of Jerusalem

Speakers may change in the middle of a verse in the Song of Solomon. Therefore, this book requires careful attention as to who is speaking at any one time. A key to determining this is given by their address: "beloved" is what the bride calls Solomon, and "love" is what he calls her.

The KJV will be the translation primarily used in this study, unless otherwise noted. We will capitalize the Bride of Christ, so she will be easily distinguishable from the Shulamite maiden. When referring to Christ, the pronouns He, Him, and His are also capitalized, and the word Bridegroom to distinguish from Solomon the bridegroom.

We suggest you read the Song of Solomon's eight short chapters to get a general overview of the book before you start this verse-by-verse study.

DEFINITION OF THE BRIDE

Salvation in Christ Jesus is the first necessary qualification to be His Bride, but it is not the only one. The Bride of Christ must have two washings: one by blood and one by water. Christ's blood cleanses the *spirit* and is the washing for salvation: Jesus Christ "loved us, and washed us from our sins in His own blood..." (Revelation 1:5)

The second washing, by the water of the Word and the Holy Spirit, is not for salvation or the spirit, but for the purification and transformation of the soul. "Christ also loved the church, and gave Himself for it; that He might sanctify and cleanse it with the washing of water by the Word, that He might present it to Himself a glorious church, not having spot, or wrinkle, or any such thing; but that it should be holy and without blemish." Ephesians 5:25-27 NKJV (John 15:3, Romans 12:2, John 7:37-39, Psalm 119:9-11)

This second washing, done by Christ through His Holy Spirit, His Word, and with a believer's cooperation, is to prepare His Bride for the day of their marriage when she dons her beautiful white wedding dress, representing the works she has done in His name. (Ephesians 2:10, Revelation 19:8) The Bride of Christ is an active participant in her preparation for their marriage. "Alleluia: for the Lord God omnipotent reigns. Let us be glad and rejoice, and give honor to Him: for the marriage of the Lamb is come, and His wife hath made herself ready. To her was granted that she should be arrayed in fine linen, clean and white: for the fine linen is the righteousness of saints," (Revelation 19:7-8).

Not all believers allow the Lord to cleanse them through the teaching and application of the Word of God. Some seem to have little interest in developing a living, growing relationship with Christ; and do not give much attention to getting to know Him, or learning and applying the Word in their lives. They show paltry interest in their spiritual development. They may be in the body of Christ, but are not of the Bride, simply because they choose not to be.

Membership in the body of Christ is based on believing God's truth—those who have responded to the call to salvation. The formation of the Bride of Christ is based on truth *and* love. Those who fall in love with Jesus, who become passionately joined spirit and soul to Him, who not only allow but enthusiastically desire the Holy Spirit's transformation of them, no matter what it involves, will be exalted as the Bride of Christ.

His Bride will be fully mature, a spiritual adult, not a baby. Those desiring to be part of His Bride seek to be filled with all the fullness of God—that is, the love found in Christ Jesus, which encompasses love of God, love of man, love of the brethren, and love of their enemies. (Romans 12:1-2, 1 Corinthians 3:18, Luke 10:27, Ephesians 4:12-16, 22,

Ephesians 3:17-19, John 15:12, Matthew 5:44)

Those who do not allow the Holy Spirit to mature them to the Bride level will still enjoy their status as wedding guests at the marriage supper of the Lamb and His Bride. (Matthew 22:2-4, 9, 25:10, Revelation 19:7, 9)

Some might argue Jesus treats all believers the same, meaning He would not elevate one group above another or separate some for special honor. We would remind them of all the hundreds of disciples who followed Jesus; He chose twelve to be apostles or leaders, and from those, He chose three to be what has been termed "the inner circle." (1 Corinthians 15:5, Matthew 10:2-4, 17:1, 26:36-38)

In 1 Corinthians 3:6-8,11-15, it is also clear that not only do differences in service or ministry occur, but differences in rewards are given in proportionate measures. Salvation itself comes by the grace and goodness of God, not us, and it cannot be earned, as taught in Ephesians 2:8-9. However, what measure of rewards and level of honor we desire for our eternal future are earned.

At the end of each letter written to the churches recorded in Revelation 2 and 3, a reward, sometimes more than one, is promised to those who are overcomers. Many of the parables Jesus taught also had this overcomer-reward theme. Being an overcomer is one of the noteworthy characteristics of the Bride of Christ.

If it sounds as if Judy and I are making a distinction between the body of Christ and the Bride, that's correct; we are. As Eve was formed from a part, but not the whole of Adam, Judy and I believe the Bride of Christ will be formed from a part of the body of Christ.

Those who are washed in His blood through their confession of faith in His atonement *and* who then allow Jesus by His Spirit to wash them by the water of the Word and cleanse them day by day will make up the Bride of Christ. This second washing is also demonstrated by an active, daily life of loving communion with Jesus, whole-heartedly trusting Him, applying His Word, walking honestly in its principles, and taking instruction and direction from His indwelling Holy Spirit. The Bride consists of those who love Jesus passionately, trust Him implicitly, and who want and actively seek an abiding, deep-and-growing-deeper relationship with Him. This is depicted in the love story of Solomon and his Shulamite bride.

Even if you're not sure about this particular premise about the Bride of Christ, keep reading. What matters is that you want your love for Jesus to grow, and deepen, and you intend to let the Holy Spirit accomplish that in you.

CHAPTER 1 (1:1-17)

Judy-1:1 The song of songs, which is Solomon's.

Solomon

God had promised King David of Israel that a son born to him would be a man of rest. "And I will give him rest from all his enemies round about: for his name shall be Solomon, and I will give peace and quietness unto Israel in his days." (1 Chronicles 22:9) This son of David and Bathsheba was also named Jedidiah, which means "beloved of the LORD." (2 Samuel 12:24-25)

At a crucial time in Israel, Solomon was anointed king, succeeding his father. "And the LORD magnified Solomon exceedingly in the sight of all Israel, and bestowed upon him *such* royal majesty as had not been on any king before him in Israel." (1 Chronicles 29:25) Under Solomon's rule, Israel rose to her peak in land and glory. Solomon's accomplishments included building a temple of great splendor in Jerusalem to honor the Lord.

However, Solomon's zeal for God diminished in his later years. Without a godly leader, a country is divided. In Proverbs 11:14, Solomon himself wrote that without wise leadership, a nation is in trouble; but with good counselors, there is safety. What a picture this is of one man's life who was well-educated, given wisdom and a great ability to write. Solomon loved God, knew and kept His words, and was blessed in every way, until during his later years when he let pagan wives turn his heart away from the one true God. (1 Kings 4:29-32, 11:1-10)

Song of Solomon

Of the three books of the Bible penned by Solomon, Ecclesiastes explains the futility of trying to live a happy life apart from God. Solomon also wrote three thousand proverbs, about nine hundred of which are in the book of Proverbs—instructions on how to live a godly life in an ungodly world. In Proverbs 4:3-6, the king wrote, "For I was my father's son, tender and only beloved in the sight of my mother. He taught me also and said unto me, 'Let your heart retain my words; keep my commandments and live. Get wisdom, get understanding: forget it not, neither decline from the words of my mouth. Forsake her not, and she shall preserve you: love her, and she shall keep you.' " (Proverbs 1:1, Ecclesiastes 1:1, 12)

Solomon also wrote one thousand and five songs, but this is the one, The Song of Solomon, God chose to include and honor as a book in the Bible. In it, and through Solomon, the Lord wrote His extraordinary love song to us. (1 Kings 4:32)

Dixie-1:1 The song of songs, which is Solomon's.

Songs

In Bible times, songs were widely used forms of historical record and were also utilized as educational devices. They allowed information to be disseminated and learned by the masses, adults, and children. Beginning with the exodus from Egypt, Moses, the great prophet and leader of the Hebrews, wrote several songs, including one recorded in Exodus 15:1-19, which gives praise for Jehovah's deliverance of the children of Israel from their slavery in Egypt. (Deuteronomy 31:19-22, 32:1-44, Psalm 90)

King David, Solomon's father, was quite an accomplished musician and penned many songs under the inspiration and anointing of the Holy Spirit of God, including 2 Samuel 22, and many psalms. David composed Psalm 72 as a prayer specifically for his son, Solomon. Psalm 127, perhaps written by a temple musician, is also designated as a song for Solomon.

Song of Songs

Of the many songs the prolific Solomon wrote, only this one—circa 965 B.C. — nearly one thousand years before Christ's advent, was termed the Song of Songs. There was no better song, in Solomon's estimation, than the love story he had written. Unknowingly, he prophetically told of a greater love story, that of Christ and His Bride, which, in God's estimation, is truly the greatest love story of a man for a woman. He gave Solomon the privilege of telling it.

The Song of Solomon symbolizes the inner struggles of the Bride to move from mediocrity to a rich, vibrant relationship of love in all its fullness and relates the constant and loving patience of her Bridegroom as He encourages her in that pursuit. Through this book, God the Father stirs those who would be of the Bride to let go of the things that hold them back from totally loving His beloved Son.

In the spiritual and prophetic interpretation of the Song of Solomon, Jesus Christ is the Bridegroom (Matthew 9:15, 25:1-13), as John the Baptist referred to Him (John 3:28-29); His Bride, a part of Grace Age believers; the father of the Bridegroom is Father God; and the father of the Bride is the Apostle Paul. (2 Corinthians 11:2) Parts of the wedding ceremony and celebration are pictured in Psalm 45 and Revelation 19:7-9.

Meditation One: Write your own love song or love letter to the Lord Jesus in a journal or notebook. Instead of facts, tell Him of your love for Him. Begin "My beloved Jesus…"If you find this meditation difficult, just write, "I love You, Lord Jesus," and then ask the Holy Spirit to make your words true. (Mark 9:24) Leave enough space to allow additional thoughts. At the end of this study, reading this letter will point out changes in you that you perhaps hadn't realized. (2 Corinthians 3:18) Use your notebook or journal for your thoughts, questions, and future meditations.

Judy-1:2 Let him kiss me with the kisses of his mouth: for thy love is better than wine.

Thy love

The Shulamite maiden has answered the call to come to this wonderful shepherd. She has embraced him and what he has to offer her. In the same way, the Bride has received the salvation of the new covenant, a binding agreement of Jesus' eternal faithfulness, which includes promises of real truth she can depend on, and so much more! "Yea I have loved thee with an everlasting love: therefore with loving kindness have I drawn thee." (Jeremiah 31:3) "But it is good for me to draw near to God: I have put my trust in the Lord GOD, that I may declare all thy works." (Psalm 73:28)

What a privilege to draw near to the God of the Universe and put all my trust in Him. "Let us draw near with a true heart in full assurance of faith…" (Hebrews 10:22) "Now the just shall live by faith; but if any draw back, my soul shall have no pleasure in him." (Hebrews 10:38)

Dixie-1:2 Let him kiss me with the kisses of his mouth: for thy love is better than wine.

A Gentile bride

The Shulamite is a young Gentile woman, probably from Lebanon. There are seven references to Lebanon in the Song of Solomon (3:9, 4:8 twice, 4:11, 15, 5:15, 7:4). It seems to me there is little value in referencing Lebanon so many times, unless it is a key to her beginnings. The Bride of Christ is primarily Gentile. In 2 Corinthians 11:2, Paul tells the Corinth church, primarily Gentile believers, that they are engaged to Christ. (John 10:16, Acts 11:18, 14:27)

The Book of Ruth is also an allegory of Christ and His Bride. Its love story tells of a Gentile widow from Moab and her suitor and husband-to-be, Boaz, ancestor of King Solomon of Israel. (It might be beneficial to take some time to read the Book of Ruth, which only has four chapters, to see if you can spot the similarities between the accounts of Boaz and Ruth and Christ and His Bride.)

In the Book of Ruth, God's hand is in the *circumstances* that draw these two to each other. In the Song of Solomon, we are given a more intimate look at the *relationship* between the shepherd-king and his chosen one. Both books present fascinating aspects of the love story of Christ and His Bride.

The kisses of his mouth

There are many kinds of kisses: kisses of welcome, forgiveness and reconciliation, adoration, friendship, and those given by family, friends, and even enemies like Judas. However, the kisses this young woman desires are those of romantic love.

At the beginning of this song, the Shulamite maiden knows Solomon as a shepherd, but not yet as a king. They have met before, probably several times, and they have fallen in love with each other. (verse 7) His love is acknowledged in this verse and hers in the next.

The Lord has always expressed His love for us first. The apostle John taught: "We love him, because he first loved us." (1 John 4:19) God's love was not based on what we were or what we could contribute to Him.

As Moses wrote to the children of Israel, "The Lord did not set his love upon you, nor choose you, because ye were more in number than any people; for ye were the fewest of all people…" (Deuteronomy 7:7) The disciples of Christ were few in number, but John said Jesus loved them to the end, and quoted Him as saying, "…the Father hath loved me, so have I loved you…" (John 15:9)

As the Shulamite girl talks with the women working with her (verse 5), she speaks of her beloved and how wonderful he is. Her thoughts and words are focused on him. She desires his kisses (1:2) and refers to him as the one "whom my soul loves" (1:7). Yearning to be more than an acquaintance of his, she's not satisfied with the status quo. This is the expression of her heart's longing for a closer relationship. The young maiden wants his kisses, those outward demonstrations of his heart's desire for her. This is not parallel to the kiss of salvation, because she asks for many kisses.

This handsome shepherd has come to visit her again. It's a surprise. She turns and, seeing him, realizes he has overheard her words, so she speaks directly to him. (We know that because the pronouns change from "him" to "thy." She tells him why she desires his kisses: 'Your love is better than wine.' Wine speaks of pleasure and enjoyment. He has become more than that to her.

In a land where water was limited and wine important for survival, she declares his love even more necessary. The best of her world doesn't compare to one kiss from him. She knows the effects of wine are fleeting, but the love of this man would change her life forever.

Those who are of the Bride of Christ also have thoughts of love for their Beloved. They view Jesus as Who He is, a real Person, the One with Whom they desire sweet communion. They have experienced and recognized the manifestations of His love in their lives, the kisses of His grace, those personal, "this-is-a-kiss-from-my-Beloved" blessings. As they understand His great love for them more fully, their love for Him will increase and deepen. (1 John 4:19) They won't be able to keep quiet about their growing feelings for Him. They will want to share that with others, as the maiden does in this verse.

Kisses

Jesus promised that those who kept His commandments, showing their love for Him, would experience manifestations of Him in their lives—in a sense, kisses from Him. (John 14:21)

Kathleen, a young college girl with very limited resources, had learned to rely on the Lord. She asked Him to provide dry milk for her meals. That same day, a neighbor asked Kathleen to watch her children for a few hours while she went to the doctor. When the woman returned, she didn't have any money to give Kathleen but offered two boxes of dry milk as payment, a sweet kiss for Kathleen from the Beloved.

A dear friend who lives in North Carolina became an empty nester when she sent her last son off to college in another state. She was so lonely the first few days after he left. Naturally, this mother wanted to hear her son's voice, but he had forgotten to take his phone charger in the hurry of packing. By this time, his phone was dead, and she knew she couldn't get in touch. Just then, she heard the Lord direct her to call her son. It made no sense, but recognizing the voice of the Holy Spirit, she picked up the phone and dialed her son's number. He answered! He had found a student with the same kind of phone and charger. As soon as he had finished using the borrowed charger, his phone rang! He was so happy to hear his mother's voice, and she felt the same way hearing her son. She was so glad she obeyed. This was another example of a kiss from the Beloved to both of them.

Later, at the end of her son's first semester, she would drive eight hours to pick him up at his college. The problem confronting her was that she needed nearly $400 for the final payment on his semester's tuition. After praying, she started getting her things together for the trip. Dressed in a red and black outfit, as she packed, she heard a voice in her spirit say, "Wear the brown jeans." In her mind, my friend countered, "I don't want to wear brown. I want to wear this red outfit." It's more Christmasy, was her thought. She heard the voice again: "Wear the brown jeans." This time, realizing it was the Lord, she took off the red outfit and put on the brown jeans. Something was in the pocket. She pulled out some cash—$390, just what she needed to finish paying her son's tuition—another kiss from her Beloved.

About a year ago, I asked the Lord about the way I was spending my time taking people who couldn't drive to their doctor's appointments, opportunities to be helpful that involved considerable time out of my day. I wanted to be sure I wasn't overdoing it and neglecting other things. One Sunday morning, after our Sunday School class, Ann approached me and said rather nervously, "Dixie, this is a new practice for me; I believe the Lord has given me a word for you. I'm going to be obedient and tell it to you. You can judge it as to its truth." I smiled and said, "Okay." She said the Lord had told her He was pleased with me and that I was His girl. She went on to say, "I don't know whether that means anything to you or not, but that's what He said to me."

I told her what I had prayed, and she was thrilled to know the Lord had indeed spoken to her and she had heard clearly. Both of us received kisses from the Beloved that day.

Think about the kisses you have received from the Lord. Begin to ask for more kisses from your Beloved, as the Shulamite did. Let your love for Him grow. Ask how you can give Him kisses in return. I'm sure our Bridegroom would love to receive kisses from us. As a father listened to his three-year-old child finishing his bedtime prayer, he heard the child say, "I love You, Jesus." He then saw his sweet little boy put his tiny hands to his lips, and blow Jesus a kiss. Did you know the word "worship" means "to kiss toward"? Have you ever blown Jesus a kiss? Try it.

> **Meditation Two:** Write an account of each kiss received from the Beloved this week or in the last thirty days. Then, watch for an opportunity to share them with others. You don't need to preach to people, but perhaps you can show them what they're missing by not being in a growing relationship with the Lord Jesus. (Note His kisses in your journal throughout this study.)

Judy-1:3 Because of the savour of thy good ointments thy name is as ointment poured forth, therefore do the virgins love thee.

Thy name

Like the people we know, the mere mention of their names reveals something of their personality to us. When we hear the word God, His very Name reveals His attributes: Most High God, Almighty God, Everlasting God, the One who reveals Himself, The Lord our Righteousness. God has many revelatory titles such as Lord our Provider, The Lord is Present, The Lord our Healer, The Lord our Banner, The Lord who sees me wherever I am, and The Lord my Peace. The Lord my Shepherd is also known as The Holy One. He is my ever-present help in times of trouble, my Shield and Defender, my Rock, and my High Tower. God is my Fortress, Promise Keeper, Creator, Savior, Sustainer, Keeper of my heart, Author and Finisher of my faith. He has revealed Himself as the Giver of Grace, my Father, my Wonderful Counselor, Word of God, Living Word, Lord of Lords, King of kings, and many more.

Dixie-1:3 Because of the savour of thy good ointments, thy name is as ointment poured forth, therefore do the virgins love thee.

Gifts

The shepherd has given the Shulamite maiden gifts, the savor of his good ointments, and those presents have made this young woman love him more. Membership in the body of Christ includes the indwelling Holy Spirit and brings a multitude of gifts: love, joy, peace, righteousness, comfort, blessings, access to the throne of God, etc. All of these and more are a part of the abundant life, of which the Lord Jesus spoke in John 10:10.

These also include the gifts of the Holy Spirit, listed in the chapters of 1 Corinthians 12-14, Romans 12, 1 Peter 4, and Ephesians 4. All of the spiritual gifts, and their ministry to us and through us, bring a greater personal awareness of God's love and grace and a realization of the great honor of being a partner in the Lord's work on Earth. (1 Corinthians 3:9) Every believer should have a sense of savoring the marvelous blessings the Lord has given and continues to give each day. Savoring them implies thinking and meditating on their richness and being thankful for them on a daily basis. This increasing awareness of His goodness fosters a climate in which love for the Lord blossoms in the believer: "… therefore do the virgins love thee."

Thy name is as ointment poured forth

Those ancient balms were fragrant, pleasurable, and often used for healing. The mere mention of her beloved's name brings a soothing presence, peace, refreshment, and spurs thoughts of love for him. Do you find that true in your life? Does hearing Jesus' name bring a smile and a sense of calm to your mind?

The mention of the name of Jesus brings help, power, peace, joy, and much more to His Bride. The recitation of His names and titles brings strength to the weak and the weary. When we need comfort, confidence, or even a new way to praise Him, we can meditate on His names and titles: Lover of my soul, Lion of Judah, Lamb of God, Baptizer with the Holy Spirit, Son of God, Messiah, the Christ, and Conquering King.

Jesus is also known as Daystar, Bright and Morning Star, Head of the Church, Fullness of the Godhead, True Vine, and Bread of Life. His other titles include, The Way, the Truth, and the Life, Good Shepherd, and the Resurrection. He is the Righteous Judge, Light of the World, First Fruits of them that sleep. The Great High Priest, the Once-and-For-All-Sacrifice for sin, The Alpha, and the Omega, Jesus is my Advocate, Mediator, Intercessor, the One Who fills and directs my life, and my soon-coming-King. Holy is His Name.

Therefore do the virgins love thee

In this verse, "virgins" are those who have not given themselves sexually to anyone. The Shulamite maiden thinks no one could help but love Solomon because he is so wonderful, and any young woman would respond with love if she knew him. The Bride of Christ is confident that others would love Jesus, too, if they knew Him better; because He is so amazing and magnificent.

Meditation Three: In your journal, include some of your favorite names and titles of Christ listed in these sections, and use them to praise Him. Saying them out loud changes the atmosphere around you.

Judy-1:4 Draw me, we will run after thee: the king hath brought me into his chambers: we will be glad and rejoice in thee, we will remember thy love more than wine: the upright love thee.

We will run

The maiden says, "We will run after thee," meaning her and her companions. She wants them to be blessed as she has been. The Bride wants everyone to know the same joy, excitement, and peace that have become hers. Her plea to other believers: "O taste and see that the LORD is good: blessed is the one that trusts in Him." (Psalm 34:8) The Beloved is One Who loves her as she is, despite the world's criticism that makes her feel unworthy to be the recipient of such love. Isn't that always the way it is? For the LORD sees not as man sees; for man looks on the outward appearance, but the LORD looks on the heart. (1 Samuel 16:7)

A poem in *Streams in the Desert*, written by Mrs. Charles E. Cowman, reminds me of this. One who is ahead on the journey of life is instructed to encourage others, and tell them of the joys and pitfalls ahead. For instance, the Bride might say to her friends: "You will have weary times, but I'll call back with reminders that He went with me. Since I'm ahead of you, and because your faith is young, I can warn you of possible dangers, and encourage you to keep going. He was there for me when the roots were torn, thunder crashed, and earthquakes shook the ground. He held me tight and comforted me as I continued the journey of life. My face glowed in triumph and my feet never hesitated. He will hear you when you cry out, even though you may not see Him. Oh, carry on, dear friend, His name is Faithful and True. His name alone will bring a thrill to your heart to see you through."

Meditation Four: Read Psalm 50:23 Tell the Beloved Jesus how wonderful He is. Mention when you first became aware of His love, goodness, mercy, power, etc., and express your thanks to Him. Add your thoughts to your Meditation One love letter.

Dixie-1:4 Draw me, we will run after thee: the king hath brought me into his chambers: we will be glad and rejoice in thee, we will remember thy love more than wine: the upright love thee.

Draw me

What the Shulamite maiden has seen in the shepherd makes her want to know more. By this request of "draw me," she acknowledges her need for his help. God has been drawing people to Himself and His Son since the beginning of time. He is the initiator. Surprisingly, not just the Holy Spirit, but the Father God is also a teacher, and He presents a series of lessons each person must learn to advance to the next level of spiritual development. Jesus taught, "No man can come to Me, except the Father Who has sent Me draw him... It is written in the prophets, and they shall be all taught of God." (John 6:44-45)

What are the lessons that the Father teaches to sinners, so that they will be drawn to Christ?

- **First lesson:** God is. (Psalm 19:1-3, Romans 1:19-20, Psalm 53:1)

  Every person must acknowledge the existence of God. If he does not, his choice stops him from spiritual progress. In my opinion, it takes very little faith to believe there is a supreme Creator-God. It is evident from creation, not from the Bible, religious dogma, or church statements, but from creation itself: God exists. The testimony of creation surrounds everyone; therefore, everyone can believe the truth that confronts them each day, in the rising and setting of the sun, the glow of the moon, the shine of the stars, the changing seasons, and the things that support life on this planet. Creation speaks and demonstrates: a Creator-God designed and instigated all this for you. (Romans 1:19-20)

- **Second lesson:** God is powerful.

- **Third lesson:** He is the sovereign Creator-God. Mankind is to worship Him, giving Him glory for His greatness. (Romans 1:21)

- **Fourth lesson:** God is good. Mankind is to be thankful to Him for what He has done for them. (Romans 2:4, 1:21) These lessons begin bringing them into truth, opening their eyes to the reality of God's great grace in their lives, eventually leading to a relationship with the Father through Christ and to the fulfillment of the first commandment: love God with all your being. (Psalm 50:23, Luke 10:27)

- **Fifth lesson:** God is the Judge of people's actions, and they are accountable to Him. (Romans 2:3, 5-6, 8-10) This realization should influence their behavior and treatment of others, thus bringing them closer to the fulfillment of the second commandment: love your neighbor as yourself. (Luke 10:27)

The lessons do not end there, so you may want to search for other principles to add to this list. At some point, if the sinner is humble and does not reject these lessons, he realizes none of his good works are enough to make him acceptable to this perfect and powerful

God, and he understands his sinful self cannot measure up to a holy God's evaluation. However, by this time, he has been taught about Jesus, the sinless Son of God, Who took the sinner's place in the court of God's justice, accepted the sinner's judgment and sentence as if it were His own, and paid sin's penalty of death and hell for all sinners. (Isaiah 53, Romans 4:24-25, 5:6-8, 2 Corinthians 5:21, John 3:16)

The purpose of these lessons is to draw the sinner to God the Father by his receiving Jesus as Lord and Savior. [Jesus said], "Every man, therefore, that has heard, and has learned of the Father, comes unto Me." (John 6:45) Each lesson the Father teaches, if the student learns it and applies it, prepares a building site for laying the foundation and cornerstone of Jesus Christ in the person's life. "Ye are God's building. According to the grace of God which is given unto [the Apostle Paul], as a wise master builder, I have laid the foundation, and another builds thereon... For other foundation can no man lay than that is laid, which is Jesus Christ." (1 Corinthians 3:9-11 NKJV) "Neither is there salvation in any other: for there is none other name under heaven given among men, whereby we must be saved." (Acts 4:12)

> **Meditation Five:** Think back over your life. Can you remember when you learned these different lessons about God and His principles? Take a few minutes to thank Him for what He did to bring you to His Son and salvation, and thank Him for His Holy Spirit Who continues your training. (Philippians1:6)

Once we have come into the family of God and membership in the body of Christ, the Holy Spirit in us begins to draw each person into a closer, deeper, intimate relationship with Jesus. The Holy Spirit is our trainer, the preparer of the Bride for her marriage. (John 14:26, 15:26, 16:13) He teaches and guides believers each step of the way, if they will let Him. He desires all believers to be part of the Bride of Christ and will do everything possible to achieve that result. However, they must cooperate with the Holy Spirit and yield to His will. They must allow Him to wash them in the water of the Word and permit Him to effect changes in them. (Ephesians 5:26, 2 Corinthians 3:17-18)

We will run after thee

The four stages of motor development in a person are: sitting, standing, walking, and running. The Bride is ready to run after her Beloved, to pursue Him, be close to Him, and follow Him wherever He leads. "Let us run...the race set before us...." (Hebrews 12:1) "I do not count myself to have [attained]; but one thing I do, forgetting those things which are behind and reaching forward to those things which are ahead, I press toward the goal for the prize of the upward call of God in Christ Jesus. Therefore let us, as many as are mature,...walk by the same rule, let us be of the same mind." (Philippians 3:13-15 NKJV)

The Bride of Christ knows her future is wrapped up in being with Jesus. He is the key to her happiness and joy.

The king hath brought me into his chambers

Here is the answer to her request in verse four: "Draw me." To be in the living quarters of the king's palace is an honor this maiden never expected to have. To the Bride, the promise of James 4:8 is fulfilled: "Draw nigh to God, and he will draw nigh to you." The Beloved tenderly says to her, "I draw you with bands of love… I have loved you with an everlasting love; therefore, with loving kindness I have drawn you." (Hosea 11:4, Jeremiah 31:3)

We will be glad and rejoice in thee, we will remember thy love more than wine: the upright love thee

The Bride, like the Shulamite, speaks as if all those who are with her feel as she does. How happy she is to be in her Beloved's Presence! She is filled with thoughts of Him, of His loving ways and words. Like wine, those treasured thoughts go down to the very depths of her soul. Her rejoicing is in Him, not herself. The word "upright" describes the Bride and all those pure in heart who will follow the Beloved. Her love is untested, but genuine. As she continues to follow Him, her love will deepen and mature.

~**Principle**: Good or bad, to whom or to what you are drawn will influence others. As you draw closer the Lord, and as you share what the Lord is doing in your life, others will follow. My mother frequently shared with me what she received from the Lord. That sharing encouraged me to want the same kind of closeness with the Lord.

Judy-1:5-6 I am black, but comely, O ye daughters of Jerusalem, as the tents of Kedar, as the curtains of Solomon. Look not upon me, because I am black, because the sun hath looked upon me: my mother's children were angry with me; they made me the keeper of the vineyards; but mine own vineyard have I not kept.

Choices

The maiden says she's black but lovely, lacking assurance in who she is now, not fully understanding what she can become. Her choices will affect others in a positive way.

> The following story is a beautiful example of this. There were two little girls in an orphanage in Ukraine, both with Down syndrome, and one had a hole in her heart. The other had a cleft palate and could not take a bottle comfortably. The children were insecure and alone. If not adopted, the girls would eventually be assigned to a mental institute and be housed there for the rest of their lives. These two precious little ones had no hope, home, or last name.

"But God…." (Romans 5:8, Ephesians 2:4-5, Philippians 4:19) God's presence always changes the picture. He directed a young couple I know to go to Ukraine and adopt the two children. Then God guided the new parents to the right doctors. Both children had successful surgeries, one on her heart and the other on her mouth. At the time of their adoption, the little girls were both very small for their ages, but now they are eating, growing, and laughing. Most importantly, they are loved, and they know it. Secure, accepted, and with a new name, the children are now sisters and part of a wonderful family. I can't help but add: there's no doubt in my mind both girls already understand Jesus loves them. Their happy, smiling Christmas photo says it all.

Daughters of Jerusalem

In Matthew 13:3-8, a sower went forth to sow. The seed of the Word that falls on good ground brings forth a harvest, but there's a battle, as some seeds fall by the wayside and the fowls come and devour them. Some seeds fall upon stony places where they have no depth of earth. When the sun comes up, they are scorched and, because they have no root, they wither away. Some seeds fall among thorns, and weeds spring up and choke them.

The Bride has heard the Word, and with joy receiving it, she must now apply it appropriately. We don't always understand how important this step is, but here again, the world is watching our lives. Our choices affect others.

Keeper of the vineyards

The maiden's black because she's been working in the sun. She has suffered from her experiences in the world, just as Jesus predicted: "In this world you will have tribulation…" (John 16:33) She's been cast aside and not taught as the Bible instructs in Deuteronomy 6:5-7, which teaches parents how to rear their children: "You shall love the LORD thy God with all your heart and with all your soul and with all your might. And these words which I command thee this day shall be in your heart: and you shall teach them diligently unto your children, and shall talk of them when you sit in your house and when you walk by the way and when you lie down and when you rise up."

In the Old Testament, one generation passed their knowledge of God on to the next generation. It's a responsibility that is still ours today, because God's mercy is everlasting, and His truth endures to all generations. (Psalm 100:5, 102:18)

The psalmist writes in Psalm 71:18, "Now also when I am old and gray-headed, O God, forsake me not; until I have shewed thy strength unto this generation and thy power to every one that is to come." In Psalm 145:4, it states: "One generation shall praise Thy works to another and shall declare thy mighty acts." It's just that important!

As a child, I was always taken to church, but none of the family ever spoke of the Scriptures outside church. Thankfully, we eventually moved south to the "Bible Belt," where the Lord is spoken of freely and openly. I like hearing what's going on spiritually in people's lives, and now I love to share what God is doing in my life. When my boys were born, I was determined to teach them everything I learned about the Bible, hoping they would eventually go far beyond my knowledge of the Scriptures.

Mine own vineyard have I not kept

Like the Shulamite maiden, realizing she's neglected herself, the Bride admits, "My own vineyard have I not kept." She now has to dig that fallow ground of her heart a little deeper to protect the seeds of His Word that have been sown, to keep them from being snatched away. (Jeremiah 4:3) She must keep the weeds from choking the spiritual life in her and prevent the cares of the world from robbing her of the great joy that has come to her. (Matthew 13:1-23) As a believer, the Bride of Christ stands on a threshold, torn between looking back to what she was and looking forward to what she can become. Potentially, with so much to lose or gain, she is at a crucial decision point.

Dixie-1:5-6 I am black, but comely, O ye daughters of Jerusalem, as the tents of Kedar, as the curtains of Solomon. Look not upon me, because I am black, because the sun hath looked upon me: my mother's children were angry with me; they made me the keeper of the vineyards; but mine own vineyard have I not kept.

I am black

In Solomon's stunning presence, this maiden realizes that she does not measure up. She begins to tell her companions a little about her background. Having spent too much of her time in the sunny vineyards of her siblings, her skin has darkened. The Shulamite testifies she has neglected her vineyard, and her life, ignoring the really important issues.

This could be a description of the members of the body of Christ, busy doing religious things, but neglecting their relationship with Christ. They know virtually nothing of the sweetness of communion with Him. They don't listen to Him. In fact, these believers may not even know Jesus would speak personally to them.

Does the thought occur there is something missing in their spiritual life? That's what happened to me. One day as I was reading John 10:10, "I am come that they might have life, and that they might have it more abundantly," I realized that I had life in Christ, but in no way could it be characterized as "abundant life." Praying to the Lord for it, I set out to pursue this life, knowing it was centered in Jesus. Deliberately dedicating time to honor the companionship His response has exceeded my expectations. With each passing day, this journey is more than I ever imagined; it keeps getting better, deeper, richer, and fuller as I continue with my Beloved.

The tents of Kedar...curtains of Solomon

Kedar was Ishmael's second son and Abraham's grandson by Hagar, the Egyptian servant girl of Sarah, Abraham's wife. Kedar's descendants were of a nomadic Arabian tribe, living in tents made from the skins of the herds of black goats they kept. (Genesis 25:13, Psalm 120:5-7, Isaiah 60:7) The Shulamite uses this reference to the tents of Kedar to symbolize her past of unrest, dissatisfaction, and unsettled future.

In contrast, even though equating herself with being sunburned, dark like the tents of Kedar, the maiden describes herself as lovely as the curtains of Solomon. While recognizing she has little to offer this noble shepherd, if based on outward appearance (tents), the young woman knows her inner beauty (curtains) is genuine, ready to be discovered by a discerning man.

The Bride of Christ is made of those who were sinners (Isaiah 64:6), now forgiven and called "saints," meaning "set apart" for God. (1 Corinthians 1:1-2, 2 Corinthians 1:1). Note: I think it is important for believers to let go of the title "sinner" and to begin to live under the inspiring title of "saint." Becoming a follower of Jesus Christ has made us new creations. (2 Corinthians 5:17) We do a disservice to the Lord and His sacrifice, when we continue to live under that old banner of "sinner."

The Holy Spirit in the Scriptures makes clear the distinction between saint and sinner. (1 Peter 4:18, Romans 5:8, 5:19, Galatians 2:16-18) We are in Christ, now "holy ground," a holy temple of the Spirit of God, an extraordinary place where God meets with us. (Exodus 3, 1 Corinthians 6:19-20) We must let go of our past and live in the truth. Self-flagellation, beating ourselves up about life prior to salvation in Christ, is similar to digging up a dead body at the cemetery. The old man—your past with its sin and shame—is dead and buried. Don't keep digging it up.

Learn to let go of the beggar's cape, symbolic of your old life, as blind Bartimaeus did in faith, knowing he would never need to beg again. Accept your transformation as a new creation of beauty and holiness. (Mark 10:50-52) Leave the grave clothes behind, as Lazarus did when he was raised from the dead, and as Jesus did at the garden tomb, and walk in newness of life and light. (John 11:44, Luke 24:12, Romans 6:4)

The *spirit* of the Bride is lovely with the righteousness of Christ (2 Corinthians 5:21, Isaiah 61:1-3). The *soul* of the Bride of Christ is in the process of being changed and transformed. (John 15:3, 1 John 1:9, Ephesians 5:25-26, Romans 12:2, 2 Corinthians 3:18) It is essential for her to walk in the beauty of spirit, and to speak the language of the Spirit every day. In this way, soul will become one with spirit, and every spot, wrinkle, and blemish will be eliminated.

> **Meditation Six:** Ask forgiveness for not seeing and accepting yourself as the Lord has taught. Repeat through the day: "I am a new creation in Christ, and my Beloved loves me."

They made me the keeper of the vineyards; but mine own vineyard have I not kept

When you're trying to please others, being what they want you to be, they end up displeased, even angry with you. Here, the maiden admits her failure. This young woman hasn't pleased those who assigned her work. She's neglected her development in trying to do what they required or wanted. Though a prince's daughter, we do not see a royal attitude. (7:1) She shows no evidence or even an essence of the confidence that should accompany one with her privileged background.

The Bride of Christ has long been too busy doing religious work, governed by the "this-is-how-a-Christian-looks" lessons and sermons. She hasn't pleased those in charge, for they always see her lack, her failure. She desires to be like Mary of Bethany, sitting and learning at the feet of Jesus, but they want her to be Martha, serving them, signing up as a volunteer for every church event and program. (Luke 10:38-42) The Bride of Christ is awakening to her condition, and beginning to realize her error and neglect of her advancement. This is one of the primary steps in changing and becoming the person God wants her to be.

Judy-1:7 Tell me, O thou whom my soul loveth, where thou feedest, where thou makes thy flock to rest at noon: for why should I be as one that turneth aside by the flocks of thy companions?

Thou whom my soul loves

We use the word "love" so casually these days…saying, "I love ice cream," and then turning to a spouse, saying, "I love you." The same word shouldn't be used in both circumstances. This young woman's statement reminds me of Peter saying he loved Jesus. (John 21:15) Three times Jesus asked Peter if he loved Him, and three times Peter said, "Yes," but the depth of love Jesus was looking for didn't come until later. In Jesus' day, there were different words for love, like *phileo*, a friendship-type love, and *agape*, a sacrificial love. The degree of our commitment to the Lord is shown in our response. As we grow spiritually, we move from soulish love, centered on self, to spirit love, centered on the loved one. The Bride loves Jesus to a degree, but, as she gets to know Him better, her love will increase, becoming sacrificial and more like His love.

Tell me

The maiden asks where to find her shepherd, where he feeds his sheep, and where he rests at noon, for why should she be as one following the flocks of his companions? She's asking why should she be in the back of the crowd when she could be next to him. This verse is understandable if we remember when the Lord was calling to each of us. It took time for us to believe He truly cared and would keep us as the apple of His eye and hide us under the shadow of His wings. (Psalm 17:8)

Dixie-1:7 Tell me, O thou whom my soul lovest, where thou feedest, where thou make thy flock to rest at noon: for why should I be as one that turneth aside by the flocks of thy companions?

Tell me

First, there was "Kiss me," then, "Draw me," and now, "Tell me." (1:2,4) The Bride is that part of the body of Christ who actually wants more knowledge of Him, from Him, and more closeness and intimacy with Him. She has come to realize if she asks Him, she will receive—more than can be imagined or dreamed. "Blessed are those which do hunger and thirst after righteousness: for they shall be filled." (Matthew 5:6)

> My mother taught a three-hour Bible class each week in her home. Her preparation included study in the mornings, interspersed with afternoons of work uprooting poison ivy and honeysuckle vines in the woods back of our house. One day, while working there, she asked the Lord a specific question about a part of the lesson she had not understood when studying that morning. He supplied the answer, giving clarity immediately. My mother addressed another question to Him, and He answered that one, too. I can still remember her amazement and joy when she realized He wanted to converse, to give her understanding in His Word, and that she could receive immediate teaching. Do you believe He will respond to your request for more knowledge? Why wouldn't He, even if it's not immediate? He wants you to learn. Have faith in Him.

Thou whom my soul loves

Isn't that a beautiful phrase? The Bride's growing freedom to speak a love language to her Beloved Jesus demonstrates the more she recognizes His greatness, the more lavish her adoration becomes.

Thy flock to rest

The maiden knows this shepherd takes good care of his sheep. He directs them to green pastures and provides still water, for sheep are scared of moving water and will not drink from it. The shepherd must dam a part of the stream to form a small, quiet pond so the sheep can drink. He also allows them to rest in the heat of the day when the sun would be its hottest. Remember Psalm 23:2-3? The Shulamite maiden wants to be near her beloved. So does the Bride, and she knows the answer is found, not with more service, but in a closer relationship—that is, fellowship with Christ.

Why should I be as one that turns aside by the flocks of thy companions?

The Shulamite does not want to follow others. She wants to be with her beloved. The Bride of Christ has learned from others about her Shepherd-King but is no longer content with an indirect connection based on others' closeness to Him. She wants and needs her own close relationship with Him. His Bride desires Him and no other. She is on the doorstep of passion.

Meditation Seven: Like the Bride, say, "Beloved, kiss me, draw me, tell me more. I want my spiritual eyes, ears, and heart to be more open to You every moment." (Note the date in your journal and include details as to how your prayer is being fulfilled.)

Judy-1:8 If thou know not, O thou fairest among women, go thy way forth by the footsteps of the flock, and feed thy kids beside the shepherds' tents.

If thou know not

Follow those who follow Me and they will lead you to Me. "He that walketh with wise men shall be wise: but a companion of fools shall be destroyed." (Proverbs 13:20)

Dixie-1:8 If thou know not, O thou fairest among women, go thy way forth by the footsteps of the flock, and feed thy kids beside the shepherds' tents.

If thou know not

"Have I been so long with you and yet you don't know Me?" (John 14:9 MSG) Jesus asked one of His disciples. Ignorance is a problem and an important one to remedy.

Fairest among women

Remember the story of Snow White and the question the evil witch asks: "Mirror, mirror on the wall, who is fairest of them all?" In Jesus' eyes, His Bride, whom He has made "snow white" by His blood, and who seeks to know Him in a greater way, is the fairest of them all. (Isaiah 1:18)

Go thy way forth by the footsteps of the flock

Don't wander off. Stay close to those who already intimately know Me, they'll help you find your way to Me. When I was five years old, our family moved to Birmingham, Alabama, because of my father's job, and we lived in a nice trailer park for several years. The Meyers, an elderly pastor and his wife, lived next to us. They invited us to their small church. They gave my mother her first Scofield Reference Study Bible as a gift. She began studying it, and the more she learned, the hungrier she became. Eventually, Mother was asked to teach the teens' Sunday School class in that same church.

When I was nine, we moved to Chattanooga, Tennessee. Mother continued to study and teach. Later, upon her retirement from work, she started a Bible study group in her home, which lasted for nearly twenty years. Pastor Meyers and his wife were shepherds, leading my mother (and consequently, the rest of the family) to a true life in Christ. Without their help, our lives might have been very different.

Feed thy kids

As we seek to be drawn closer to our Beloved, it is a great privilege to bring others with us. (Song of Solomon 5:9, 6:1, 2 Timothy 2:1-2) They follow our lead, learning and growing as we nurture them, while also teaching by word and example how to feed His lambs. (John 21:15)

Judy–1:9 I have compared thee, O my love, to a company of horses in Pharaoh's chariots.

Company of horses

Solomon compliments his love's beauty and strength by comparing her to the finest horses of a king. This verse brought my childhood to mind.

I grew up in St. Louis and can remember seeing the famous Clydesdale teams of horses many times at Grant's Farm. They were magnificent creatures, so beautiful and strong in their own right. One Clydesdale could pull 600 pounds but a team of two could pull 1,700 pounds. Together, they pulled 500 pounds more than if they worked apart. In parades, eight horses were used to pull the celebration wagon. Can you imagine what would happen if all eight went in separate directions?

Now, let's apply this to the church of Christ. There are many gifts, but the same Spirit works in them all. The body of Christ needs to be individually strong within, pulling together to accomplish the work of Christ, with each member using his gifts. There is to be no division or schism in the body, but its members should have the same care one for another. If one suffers, all the members suffer with him, or if one is honored, all the other members are to rejoice. (1 Corinthians 12:4,25,26)

Dixie–1:9 I have compared thee, O my love, to a company of horses in Pharaoh's chariots.

My love

Words are so important. Can you imagine what hearing him refer to her as his love would do to this young maiden? "...I will call... her beloved, which was not beloved." (Romans 9:25) What a treasure he gave her, one that she could hold on to, one that she would cherish in the day and remember joyfully in the night!

Company of horses

In today's world, this comparison would not be considered a compliment, but in the culture of King Solomon's time, it would be deemed a very flattering statement. Comparing her to one of Pharaoh's horses would have been impressive, but comparing her to a company of his horses said so much more. Not just any horse was chosen to be in Pharaoh's service. Nothing but the finest, fastest, strongest horses would have been selected to serve Egypt's highest ruler. Obedient and trained to work together, they would be most beautiful, too. Everything about them had to be exceptional. In particular, mares were used both for riding and chariots in the East. They were swifter, could endure more hardship, and were able to go longer without food than either a stallion or a gelding. The beloved's amazing compliment implied that he saw her as a very strong and exceptionally beautiful woman of the highest caliber.

Christ views His Bride as beautiful, and the finest that could be chosen. Though she sees herself as weak and unattractive, He sees her potential for strength and ability. (Ephesians 2:10, Philippians 4:13) His confidence will be rewarded, as we will see in later chapters. Although she has moved at a slower spiritual pace than necessary, He knows she is willing to work with Him for the purpose and achievement of the goals of God.

Judy-1:10 Thy cheeks are comely with rows of jewels, thy neck with chains of gold.

Jewels and gold

In the Old Testament, necklaces of gold generally showed that a person was empowered to rule. Some examples of this are found in Genesis 41:42-44, when Pharaoh of Egypt gave Joseph a gold necklace after promoting him to rulership, and in Daniel 5:7, 16, 29, where King Belshazzar of Babylon rewarded Daniel with a gold chain for being the only one able to read and interpret a mysterious message written supernaturally upon a wall of the king's palace.

Solomon has given jewels to his bride-to-be because he sees the change in her, as she has allowed his love to make a difference in her life. Her beauty is shining through, and he has given her necklaces to add to her loveliness and to encourage her. Maybe the jewels are engagement or pre-wedding presents, as Ezekiel 16:11-12 describes: "I decked thee also with ornaments and I put bracelets upon thy hands, and a chain on thy neck. And I put a jewel on thy forehead and earrings in thine ears and a beautiful crown upon thine head."

Christ sees the beauty in His Bride and gives her gifts, too, but eternal ones of much greater value than Solomon's. They include redemptive grace. "For by grace are ye saved through faith; and that not of yourselves: it is the gift of God…" Included also are the gifts of righteousness, the robe of righteousness, and the garment of salvation. (Ephesians 2:8, Romans 5:17, Job 29:14a, Isaiah 61:10)

There's also the marvelous indwelling of the Holy Spirit and many spiritual gifts. (John 14:16-17, 1 Corinthians 6:19, 1 John 3:24, 1 Corinthians 12-14, Romans 12:3-8, Ephesians 4:7-16, 1 Peter 3:10-11)

Dixie-1:10 Thy cheeks are comely with rows of jewels, thy neck with chains of gold.

Jewels…gold

Women of modest means in ancient cultures wore small silver coins as headband ornaments. (Luke 15:8-10) Richer ladies wore jewels and pearls, gold chains, and other pieces of gold coin about their necks and on their headpieces. Solomon has presented his bride-to-be with lovely betrothal jewels and gold, fit for his queen. (Genesis 24:22, 30, 38, 47-48, 53) Spiritually, the valuables represent wisdom. In Proverbs 1:9, Solomon wrote "My son, hear the instruction of your father and forsake not the law of your mother: for they shall be an ornament of grace unto your head, and chains about your neck." (NKJV) The Bride of Christ has heeded the wisdom of her spiritual parents, those who supervised her instruction in eternal matters, and she has increased in wisdom by doing so. This, with her respect and deference, is an ornament of spiritual grace, which has enhanced her beauty in the King's eyes.

Thy cheeks…thy neck

In this poem of love, the Bride's cheeks would be associated with her speech, perhaps even her attitude; jewels with her deeds. (Luke 6:45, 1 Corinthians 3:11-13) Her neck symbolizes strength, mercy, truth, sound wisdom, and discretion. (Proverbs 3:3, 21-22)

In contrast, a stiff neck indicates rebellion, as stated in Deuteronomy 31:27: "I know thy rebellion, and thy stiff neck: behold…ye have been rebellious against the LORD." In 2 Chronicles 36:11-13, a stiff neck accompanies a hardened heart. King Zedekiah "…stiffened his neck, and hardened his heart from turning unto the LORD God of Israel."

Christ sees the Bride adorned with lovely words and strength of purpose and will. Though it is early in their relationship, her spiritual appearance is already beautiful to Him. Her desire to be close to Him, and no other, blesses and pleases Him. The Lord also desires to present to His Bride additional love gifts. He has given her so much, yet His loving, generous heart yearns to bless her even more. There is no limit to His grace and love.

Judy-1:11 We will make thee borders of gold with studs of silver.

We will make

The Shulamite's companions also want to present gifts to her, which will add to her beauty. They will spare no expense and use their best materials. During my childhood, neighbors and friends would gather pieces of fabric to sew together, resulting in beautiful quilts given with great pride to loved ones.

God knows the end of our lives from the beginning. "For I know the thoughts that I think toward you, saith the LORD, thoughts of peace, and not of evil, to give you an expected end." (Jeremiah 29:11) It's all about trusting Him and continuing to go forward with confidence in building our faith. Hebrews 12:2 advises us to look unto Jesus, the Author and Finisher of our faith. 1 Peter 4:19 encourages us to "...commit the keeping of [our] souls to him in well doing, as unto a faithful Creator." We really can't lose by focusing on Jesus and the example He set before us. The Bible is a book of instructions in life, and there are exceeding great and precious promises to assure our victory. (2 Peter 1:3-4)

These verses in Song of Solomon 1:9-11 remind me again of seeds that have fallen on good ground, taken root, and begun to grow. (Matthew 13:23, Luke 8:15) The Bridegroom says, "Keep going, and what you are, We will enhance." (John 14:12)

Dixie-1:11 We will make thee borders of gold with studs of silver.

We will make

Her companions are happy for her and want to celebrate her engagement with gifts. However different her appearance from theirs, they want to bless her, and so they pledge their best. How important it is for the Bride to have the right kind of friends who will help, not hinder, her spiritual growth.

Borders of gold

Some Eastern women's handkerchiefs, shawls, and head attire had ornate borders or fringes of gold and silver. Spiritually, "gold" is thought to signify agape love and "silver" redemption. (1 Corinthians 3:12, 13:13, 1 Peter 4:8, 1:18, Genesis 23:15, Numbers 3:49-51)

Judy-1:12 While the king sitteth at his table, my spikenard sends forth the smell thereof.

Fragrance

The king has probably lavished her with expensive perfumes, and she wore some on this special evening just to please him. Her fragrance was noted by him.

As we follow in the Beloved's steps, becoming more and more like Him, we grow to be a sweet fragrance to Him. This fragrance isn't something in the natural realm but is made up of the spiritual qualities of the character and life of a person. This heavenly perfume is pleasing to the Lord and attention-getting to others. We are a fragrance of Christ to God, and to those who are being saved and those who are perishing. (2 Corinthians 2:15)

Have you noticed when you hug someone wearing perfume, the fragrance transfers onto you and lingers? In the same way, we give forth Christ's fragrance because we've embraced Him!

The more we follow in Jesus' ways and allow the Holy Spirit to change us, the more we become a sweet savor of Christ to others. (2 Corinthians 3:18, John 12:3, Matthew 5:15)

Peter wrote about Jesus' extraordinary personality and the fragrance of His life, in that Christ did no sin, neither was guile found in His mouth; when He was reviled, He didn't seek revenge; when He suffered, He threatened not, but committed Himself to God. (1 Peter 2:21-23) This kind of behavior is so very different from the world's. (John 13:35)

> **Meditation Eight:** Since this study started, what changes, if any, in your thoughts and behavior have you noticed? Complete the statement: "I have changed in my thinking or actions concerning…" Thank the Holy Spirit for His continuing work in you.

Dixie–1:12 While the king sitteth at his table, my spikenard sends forth the smell thereof.

At his table

In this verse, the scene has changed. The Shulamite maiden has been invited to dinner with the king, as part of his answer to her request of "draw me," and it exceeds her dreams. (Ephesians 3:20)

The king

This is the first reference to Solomon's kingship. The maiden has known him as shepherd; now she sees him in the much higher position of authority as a national leader. Imagine what a surprise that must have been! She watches him as he sits at his table, eating and conversing with others, and she is pleased with his ways and manner.

The Bride must look at Jesus and see Him as her King, not just the Good Shepherd. He deserves her loyalty, adoration, and reverence. Observing His ways with others will show her what kind of Bridegroom He will be. It is a good reason why we as Christians must consistently and frequently share what the Lord is doing *in, for,* and *through* us. Others will be drawn to a closer relationship with Him, because they will become aware of the fragrance of His resurrected life, desiring what they see us experiencing with Him.

His Bride celebrates Jesus as King above all, agreeing with the Prophet Isaiah's writings as he penned the vision and prophecy of the coronation of Jesus as King of Heaven and Earth. "In the year that King Uzziah died, I saw also the LORD sitting upon a throne, high and lifted up, and His train filled the temple. Above it stood the seraphim… And one cried unto another, and said, Holy, holy, holy, is the LORD of hosts: the whole earth is full of His glory. And the posts of the door moved at the voice of him that cried, and the house was filled with smoke. Then said I, Woe is me! for I am undone; because I am a man of unclean lips, and I dwell in the midst of a people of unclean lips: for mine eyes have seen the King, the LORD of hosts." (Isaiah 6:1-5)

Jesus referred to this prophetic passage from Isaiah as a scene from part of His glorious coronation, which would occur after His resurrection. (John 12:41, Isaiah 6:9-10, Hebrews 1:1-13)

Spikenard

The main ingredient of this costly, aromatic ointment and oil was extracted from the roots of an herb called nard. The maiden wears this as her signature fragrance, perhaps in a pendant, because Solomon mentions it here, and twice in Song of Solomon 4:13-14, describing the beauty of her virginal life as a garden filled with wonderfully fragrant and fruitful plants. The heat of her body warms the ointment and causes it to permeate the atmosphere around her. (Mark 14:3, John 12:3)

It's important to consider our lives in reference to what spiritual fragrance they exude. Are we sweet smells that draw people to us, or do our attitudes, words, and actions repel as a foul odor would? Perhaps we need to slow down and be more deliberate, following the Book of James' admonition, "...be swift to hear, slow to speak, slow to wrath..." so that, by carefully weighing what we do and say, we will cultivate strong habits of kindness and goodness, grace and truth. Consequently, a sweet fragrance of blessing will be released into our atmosphere, and the realms of heaven and His Presence. (James 1:19, John 12:3, Galatians 6:10) If we do not desire to be near the King, there will be no feasting with Him and no sweet perfume from us to Him.

Judy-1:13 A bundle of myrrh is my well-beloved unto me; he shall lie all night betwixt my breasts.

He shall

The word "shall" indicates she is looking forward to her wedding and the night to follow, to a time when they will be one. Likewise, the Bride looks forward to being one with Christ at the resurrection. By that time, she will have reached full maturity. (1 John 3:2) Now she labors, being absolutely sure that the Holy Spirit Who has begun a good work in her will continue it unto the day of Jesus Christ. (Philippians 1:6) What a wonderful understanding—to know that what God has started, He will finish! He never gives up, and neither should we. At the end of our lives, each of us wants to be able to say, "I have fought the good fight, I have finished my course, I have kept the faith..." (2 Timothy 4:7)

However, in the meantime, we are laboring together with God in the same way the disciples did after Jesus' ascension. "And they went forth and preached everywhere, the Lord working with them, and confirming the word with signs following." (1 Corinthians 3:9, Mark 16:20)

Dixie-1:13 A bundle of myrrh is my well-beloved unto me; he shall lie all night betwixt my breasts.

Myrrh

At times in ancient history, the extract of myrrh was considered so valuable as to be equal with gold. During times of scarcity, its value rose even higher.

Different types of this substance have been used throughout the ages as perfume, incense, and medicine. Myrrh was the main ingredient in the holy anointing oil for the priests and the tabernacle. (Exodus 30:23-30) This costly substance was one of the gifts given by the Magi to the Christ child to celebrate His birth. (Matthew 2:11) Myrrh was present at the cross, Jesus' burial, and at His coronation. (Mark 15:23, John 19:39-40, Exodus 30: 22-25, Hebrews 1:8-9) Myrrh comes from a slow-flowing, aromatic resin of the pierced bark of the myrrh tree, which hardens into red drops called "tears." It is thought to represent bitter suffering, which is indeed what Christ experienced to redeem His Bride. (Hebrews 5:5-9)

In the Song of Solomon, there are seven references to myrrh. (3:6, 4:6, 14, 5:1, 5 twice,13) This rare and valued substance, fit for a king, seems to have been Solomon's signature fragrance (Song of Solomon 3:6, 5:5,13) and the Messiah's. In Psalm 45:8, it describes all the King's garments as smelling of myrrh.

Bundle of myrrh

Her perfume pendant will be a lovely reminder of her beloved Solomon throughout the day and at night. Similarly, thoughts of the Bridegroom are more pleasing to the Bride of Christ than expensive perfume. Like costly myrrh, He is unequaled and has no peers. Every sweet remembrance of Him is cherished. The Bride's increasing awareness of Christ in her daily life is reminiscent of the book by Brother Lawrence, *Practicing the Presence of God*. That is what she is learning to do.

Well-beloved

Engaged couples usually have special names to express their love or affection for each other. The Shulamite maiden calls him "well-beloved", her declaration of joy for him. After quoting a few names of God at a small dinner party during the Christmas season one year, the hostess invited the guests to give their favorite name for the Lord. First to respond, one woman answered: "Beloved," expressing in one word their relationship.

Unto me

"Whom have I in heaven but Thee? and there is none upon earth that I desire beside Thee." (Psalm 73:25) He is well-beloved and precious to her, but not to everyone. (1 Peter 2:7) There was no room in the inn for His birth. (Luke 2:7) There was no permanent place to lay His head during His earthly ministry. (Matthew 8:20) The only permanent dwelling Christ has here is in our hearts. (Ephesians 3:17, 2 Corinthians 1:22, Galatians 4:6)

He shall

Notice the word "shall." She looks forward to her wedding night and the intimacies of marriage. They are waiting with anticipation for their approaching wedding day. The couple has not been immoral in their acquaintance or courtship. They want nothing to defile their love. Without righteousness, without harmony and oneness in purpose and principle, there is no true fellowship. The Bride of Christ also wants intimacy with her Bridegroom. She looks forward to her marriage to the King of Kings and their everlasting life together in the eternal kingdom. (Revelation 19:7-8) Her eyes are only on Him; no one and nothing else will have first place in her heart and life.

Judy-1:14 My beloved is unto me as a cluster of camphire in the vineyards of Engedi.

Camphire

Camphire is an aromatic substance. It's clear this maiden is learning to love her shepherd-king as he loves her, which speaks of a greater picture beginning with God's love toward us. "We love him because he *first* loved us." "In this was manifested the love of God toward us, because that God sent his only begotten Son into the world that we might live through him," (1 John 4:19, 9 KJV). Jesus was the message of God's love and taught His disciples to love one another, as He loved them. (John 15:12)

The phrase, "my Beloved," used by the Bride of Christ shows her feelings and possessiveness; she's claimed Him for her own. He is a sweet fragrance to her. She makes no secret of her love for Him.

Dixie-1:14 My beloved is unto me as a cluster of camphire in the vineyards of Engedi.

Flowers

The Hebrew meaning of camphire is "to cover," and "a redemption price," and the primary root word means "to forgive." The life of Jesus was the required redemption price for the Bride, and it is through Him she receives forgiveness.

Engedi

Engedi (ancient name—Hazezon Tamar), about 35 miles southeast of Jerusalem, was situated on the western shore of the Dead Sea. The mountainous region around it was replete with rocks and caves, making it a most suitable and needed refuge for David and his men when they were on the run from King Saul. (1 Samuel 23:29-24:1)

Camphire is found only at Engedi, which in Hebrew means "fountain of the wild goat." The source of the fountain is hot springs issuing from the side of a mountain about

300-400 feet above the sea. The valley of Engedi, which included an oasis of fresh water and hot springs, was a very fertile area near Jericho, where the best vineyards, palm trees, and the rare opobalsam trees grew, according to the ancient historian Josephus. (2 Chronicles 20:2, Genesis 14:7)

By her picturesque description, the maiden tells her listeners how very special her beloved is. "There's no one like him," she might say in today's vernacular. The Bride looks at her Beloved Christ and feels the same. There is no one like Jesus—none who compare to Him. He paid the price for her redemption at the cost of His own life, and the reminder of His great love and sacrifice is ever before her. The giving of His precious life is like the sweetest of fragrances to her and, like Engedi to David, Christ has become her refuge.

Notice how expressive each is in their praise of the other. Solomon is a master at it; she will improve greatly the more she is around him and as the story of their love continues.

Meditation Nine: Add to your love letter for your Beloved. Express your love to Jesus. Ask the Holy Spirit to help you find the words as you meditate on Jesus. If this is difficult, overcome your soul's reluctance and let your spirit lead.

Note: A human being is a triune entity of spirit, soul, and body, made in God's image. (1 Thessalonians 5:23, Genesis 1:26) The soul is easily described and remembered as the "I think—I want—I feel" element or the logic-desires-emotions of a human being. The believer's spirit is always aligned with and attuned to doing God's will.

Judy–1:15 Behold, thou art fair, my love; behold, thou art fair; thou hast doves' eyes.

Thou art fair

It's often said eyes have a language of their own and are the window to the soul. Twice Solomon says, "Thou art fair." I believe he sees her inner beauty. She is the focus of his eye. (Deuteronomy 32:9-10, Psalm 17:8) Solomon wants his bride to see herself as he does. More than that, he wants her to look into his eyes and let him guide her.

Dixie-1:15 Behold, thou art fair, my love; behold, thou art fair; thou hast doves' eyes.

Thou art fair

Solomon is probably looking into the lovely maiden's eyes as he says this. How this young girl must have treasured his words, since they contrasted greatly with her opinion of herself!
This Song of Solomon is Christ's love letter to His Bride. His heart and love is hers forever. Notice how encouraging; His focus is totally on her, with nothing taking attention from her. In verse 8, He termed her "fairest (most beautiful) among women;" here He repeats the compliment

twice. The Bride savors Christ's words, holds them close, meditates on them, and embraces them until she truly believes them.

Dove's eyes

The dove is referenced throughout Scripture. Verses in Genesis describe the dove that Noah sent out from the ark, and in the gospel of John, the Holy Spirit descended like a dove from heaven at Jesus' baptism. (Genesis 8:8-12, John 1:32-33) The term "doves' eyes" suggests a sweet humility and peace, unlike the haughtiness of a blue jay or the aggravating aggression of a mockingbird. The Bible also speaks of the contrast to doves' eyes: an evil eye, a high look, a mocking eye, a spiritually closed eye. (Proverbs 23:6, 30:17, Psalm 101:5, Matthew 13:15)

Doves are social game birds. They congregate in flocks as they feed, roost, and fly. Doves' main abilities are meant to support their survival, like keen eyesight which helps them locate seeds easily. However, doves cannot see in the dark. They fly only in the light. The Bride also must learn to soar in the Light of her Lord. The darkness is not for her.

The bridegroom chooses to speak of her eyes first. Why? They are the pathway to the heart. When Jesus wanted to reassure the imprisoned John the Baptist, He directed the disciples of John to go back and tell him what they had seen and heard. "When the men had come to Him, they said, "John the Baptist has sent us to You, saying, 'Are You the Coming One, or do we look for another? And that very hour He cured many of infirmities, afflictions, and evil spirits; and to many blind He gave sight."

Jesus answered and said to them, "Go and tell John the things you have seen and heard: that *the* blind see, *the* lame walk, *the* lepers are cleansed, *the* deaf hear, *the* dead are raised, *the* poor have the gospel preached to them. And blessed is *he* who is not offended because of Me." (Luke 7:20-23 NKJV)

The Bride has her eyes right where they should be, focused on her Beloved. "Mine eyes are ever toward the LORD." (Psalm 25:15) When Peter stepped out of the boat and walked on the water toward Jesus, he began to sink only when his eyes left the gaze of Jesus. It is essential for those who desire to be of the Bride to keep their eyes on Him.

Judy-1:16 Behold, thou art fair, my beloved, yea, pleasant: also our bed is green.

Fair and pleasant

The maiden is responding to Solomon, trying to return the compliment, which emphasizes her desire for him. She uses two words to describe him: fair and pleasant. They signify that he is pleasing, refined, polished, cultured, just, honest, and handsome. I don't know how she can take her eyes off him.

Our bed is green
One can only picture soft, rich green growth, no rocks or weeds, pure virgin soil as in the days of the garden of Eden, lush with grass, and conditions reminiscent of Psalm 23:2: "The Lord… maketh me to lie down in green pastures…"

When the Bride of Christ says, "Our bed is green," I believe she's still looking into His eyes and understands that He promises to provide all her needs. He wants to be the shepherd of her life and lead her in paths of righteousness, and if danger comes, she won't be afraid, because He promises to be with her all the days of her life. The Bride of Christ knows for a certainty that the Lord is her Shepherd-King, and she shall not want for anything—ever.

Dixie-1:16 Behold, thou art fair, my beloved, yea, pleasant (delightful): also our bed is green.

Fair and pleasant
I think the couple is sitting in a scenic setting of a meadow with beautiful trees bending over them (verse 17) In the previous verse, Solomon described the maiden as beautiful and having doves' eyes. His pleasure in her is obvious. The Shulamite wants to offer similar praise to her bridegroom. However, consideration of her response to his compliments shows a difference. Her remarks echo his rather than being a new expression of admiration. At the same time, she isn't focused entirely on him, but on their surroundings. She speaks of the grass, the trees (verse 17), and does not respond in the same quality of praise as he.

There is nothing so special as feeling like all your Beloved's thoughts are on you. In Psalm 40:5, it states that the Lord's thoughts dwell on those He loves. "Many, O LORD my God, *are* Your wonderful works *Which* You have done; And Your thoughts toward us… *if* I would declare and speak of *them*, they are more than can be numbered," (NKJV). The Lord is more in love with His Bride than she is with Him at this point. His focus is totally on her. Nothing takes His attention from her, yet her focus is distracted by circumstances and surroundings. In this, can you see the Bride is responsive to Him, to a certain degree, but not to the same level as He? Sensitive and warm-hearted, but distracted?

We each have to ask ourselves, "Does this describe me?"
If our answer is "yes," what should our next step be? The answer is confession, asking for forgiveness, and following that with a change in behavior through listening to and obeying the Holy Spirit's promptings.

Those who desire to be part of the Bride of Christ must develop eyes which look for Him in their daily lives, keeping their minds on Him and spending time with Him. Read through the Gospels; look for Jesus. See what His actions, even His thoughts and attitudes, reveal about

Him. Immerse yourself in His Words. Develop the habit of thinking about Him and talking with Him throughout your day; this fosters adoration and admiration for Him and also brings joy and peace to you every day. (Isaiah 26:3, Romans 15:13)

Our bed is green

Green grass is a symbol of newness, and the color represents new beginnings, so, by this comment, she expects more to come. The Bride also has an outlook of anticipation of good in her future.

Judy-1:17 The beams of our house are cedar, and our rafters of fir.

Beams of cedar and fir

The beams and rafters, which support the roof and make it a safe shelter from the storms are made of cedar and fir, both strong hardwoods from trees which grow extremely tall. This verse sounds like a continuation of verse 16, describing what the Shulamite thinks will be their dwelling place. Little does she know that her future home will be a magnificent palace! It's going to be the perfect home, flawless in every way.

Christ's words to His Bride inspire confidence and reassurance that she will always be protected. In John 14:2, Jesus said He was leaving to go to prepare a place for His Bride. To her, Christ says His people "...shall dwell in a peaceable habitation and in sure dwellings and in quiet resting places." (Isaiah 32:18). "When you lie down, you will not be afraid; Yes, you will lie down and your sleep will be sweet." (Proverbs 3:24 NKJV) "…whoso hearkeneth unto me shall dwell safely, and shall be quiet from fear of evil." (Proverbs 1:33) The Bride enters into His peace and rest by believing He will keep His word.

Dixie–1:17 The beams of our house are cedar, and our rafters of fir.

Cedar and fir

Everything looks better when you're in love, even your surroundings. With all these references to nature and the outdoors, they could be sitting under a canopy of trees, even having a picnic meal. Cedar and fir, commonly thought to be cypress, are both trees associated with Lebanon, another reason for considering the Shulamite a Gentile. (2 Chronicles 2:1-18, especially verse 9)

The wood of these trees is strong and long-lasting, symbolizing their love will endure through the years. The love story of Christ and His Bride will continue throughout eternity.

Meditation Ten: Spend a few minutes contemplating the honor the Lord Jesus conveys by wanting you for His Bride. Thank Him for His love.

CHAPTER 2 (2:1-17)

Judy-2:1 I *am* the rose of Sharon, *and* the lily of the valleys.

Rose and lily

The maiden is very humble, and that's a good quality. First Peter 5:6 says, "Humble yourselves therefore under the mighty hand of God, that he may exalt you in due time." The bridegroom certainly does exalt her in the next verse. However, she doesn't see herself as he sees her, and that's true with the Bride. "For man looketh on the outward appearance, but the LORD looketh on the heart." (1 Samuel 16:7)

Dixie-2:1 I *am* the rose of Sharon, *and* the lily of the valleys.

Sharon

This coastal plain in Israel is on the Mediterranean Sea. It extends from Joppa to Caesarea, south of Mount Carmel.

I am the rose of Sharon

Some students of the Word have assumed the speaker in this verse is the bridegroom. You've probably heard the old songs that name Jesus "The Rose of Sharon" and "The Lily of the Valley," but it is incorrect to name the male as the speaker. The Shulamite maid, having described herself as darkened by the sun and neglectful of her complexion (1:6), now refers to herself as the most common of flowers, lowly insignificant ones among a multitude. Her low self-esteem is evident in this statement. How could this handsome shepherd-king love her? She feels she has nothing which would make her attractive to him.

So, too, the Bride has seen herself as nothing; this is not humility but low self-esteem, and she believes she has nothing with which to captivate her King. A woman with humility would have confidence but would not brag about herself. One with low self-esteem would believe and repeat what others have told her about herself, letting them form her opinion of who she is. The Bride of Christ is humble but does not denigrate herself or live in the past. She's a new creation, alive in the Spirit. (2 Corinthians 5:17) As the Bride of the King of kings, she must learn to see herself as He sees her, to claim her new identity in Him; this is an important principle, crucial to her development and growth.

Judy-2:2 As the lily among thorns, so *is* my love among the daughters.

Incomparable

Solomon would tell his love, "Compared to you, everyone else looks like thorns." Christ also declares the excellence of His spouse, the true Church, to be above all the thorns of man-made religions.

Dixie-2:2 As the lily among thorns, so *is* my love among the daughters.

As the lily

"Oh, no," the Shulamite's bridegroom might say, "you are not just like everyone else; you are unique and the only one who is lovely among all. You are as beautiful as the lilies, and no one else compares."

What a lovely compliment! Christ, too, views His Bride as incomparable, beautiful, and pure. "…Consider the lilies of the field, how they grow; they toil not, neither do they spin: And yet I say unto you, that even Solomon in all his glory was not arrayed like one of these." (Matthew 6:28-29) The King's lovely words reveal His character and commitment to His Bride. His heart is hers. His sweet words are love's endearments, transmitting delight in her and regard for her. One might say she has done nothing worthy of this King's esteem and lavish praise. How true, except for one thing—she has awakened to Him and is responding to His love. She is the only one whose eyes are focused on Him with hope. The declaration of the preference for Him and His love is clear to those nearby. (1:2) Her feelings for Him are not hidden at all.

Judy-2:3 As the apple tree among the trees of the wood, so is my beloved among the sons. I sat down under his shadow with great delight, and his fruit *was* sweet to my taste.

Sweet to my taste

"How sweet are thy words unto my taste! Yea, sweeter than honey to my mouth!" (Psalm 119:103) Solomon's kind and loving words have touched her to the point she wants to return the compliments. The maiden sees an apple tree covered in beautiful fruit, giving off a wonderful aroma, so she compares him to an apple tree: tall, strong, and blessed.

The Bride of Christ also knows her Beloved Jesus is incomparable, the embodiment of the Holy Spirit, displaying in His every action those qualities inherent to spiritual life: "…love, joy, peace, long-suffering, gentleness, goodness, faith, meekness, temperance…", the fulness of which is found in no other person. (Galatians 5:22)

Dixie-2:3 As the apple tree among the trees of the wood, so is my beloved among the sons. I sat down under his shadow with great delight, and his fruit *was* sweet to my taste.

Apple tree

This reference to an apple tree may have meant the citron, which doesn't lose its leaves in winter and provides deep shade in the heat of the day; its fruit is refreshing like a lemony tangerine.

Apple tree among the trees of the wood

The Shulamite tries to equal his flattering words by describing him as a fruitful apple tree among the unfruitful, barren trees of the wood.

They are the most descriptive words she can think of to describe him. In comparison to herself, whom she described as a small lily of the field (2:1), Solomon is infinitely much greater. In contrast to all his compliments, her words of praise are not lavish and not nearly as gracious as his, but she will improve, developing more adoration and esteem for him as she continues to experience and trust in his love. This maiden understands he is the only one who sees beauty in her and ardently wants her for his own.

The Book of Hebrews is written to discuss the excellence and eminence of Jesus Christ above all others, but it is more a scholarly discussion of His superiority. The Song of Solomon is quite different. It reveals the soul of Christ, how He thinks, how He feels, and what He desires. He longs for the true love of a Bride who delights in Him and doesn't falter in her commitment to Him. The Bride of Christ must spend more time falling in love with Jesus, meditating on the beauty of His character and life, and letting the Holy Spirit develop in her a greater appreciation of Him, increasingly enhancing worship and influencing her choices. (Take a few minutes, right now, to tell the Lord Jesus, your Beloved, your King, how you admire Him, and what you love about Him.)

I sat down

The Shulamite reminisces about the moment and the location of their engagement. It thrills her to be pledged to this wonderful man. He, above all others, delights her. It's also the attitude of the awakened Bride. Her choices are now made in reference to Christ. She wants to be near Him; she wants to listen to Him.

Some would tell her, "Get into the work of God," but the Lord would say, "Learn of Me first. Let My Holy Spirit teach you the Word of God." We'll never be completely effective in the *work* of God unless we are willing to saturate in the *Word*, Jesus Christ. (Matthew 11:29, John 1:14)

The young maiden is excited about their deepening feelings for each other. Here is one way to evaluate your heart. Are you learning to delight in Jesus? Is that delight increasing as you give more time and thought to your Beloved?

Under his shadow

A shadow was so important and very desirable in a hot climate, and a tree that provided shade offered a much-needed, much-appreciated refuge from the heat. This metaphor refers to the bridegroom's protection of the maiden and speaks of the closeness they enjoy. She finds great delight in Solomon's presence, and what she receives there is sweet. The phrase "under his shadow" also pictures his greatness, as compared to hers. (Song of Solomon 2:1, Psalm 91:1)

With great delight

So, too, the Bride of Christ is pleased to sit at her Beloved Jesus' feet and enjoy the fruit of His words, as did Mary of Bethany. (Luke 10:39) It is a place of protection, security, joy, and sweet contentment in His Presence. (Isaiah 25:1,4) By the way, this is a good measuring point for every believer. Is being close to the Lord a strong desire and joy, even great delight? Do you savor His words to you? Are you eager to learn more from Him? Is there more evidence of His life in you and His lordship over you?

Note: If the answer to these questions was "No," confess it, ask forgiveness, and receive it. Then, ask the Holy Spirit to change you and transform you into the person verse 3 describes. Read 2 Corinthians 3:18 and claim that promise.

Judy-2:4 He brought me to the banqueting house, and his banner over me *was* love.

His banner

Solomon is trying to increase her confidence by showing he's head-over-heels in love with her and wants everyone to know it.

Have you ever wondered where love began? Scripture says God is love, so that's where love originated, but the human race knew it was unworthy of God's love after Adam sinned. (1 John 4:16) However, no matter how unlovable mankind was, God's love for them did not change. God sent Christ to express His love to mankind, and Jesus was the message and the messenger of it. (John 1:1,14, 3:16, 1 John 4:9-10) In doing the Father's will, Christ would receive His Bride as part of the reward for completing the work of redemption He volunteered to do; it was His inheritance promised to Him in the covenant He made with His Father before the world began. (Psalm 2:7-8, Isaiah 6:8, John 20:21, 1 Peter 1:18-20)

Dixie-2:4 He brought me to the banqueting house, and his banner over me *was* love.

Celebration

A banqueting house, literally "a house of wine," was for feasting and celebration. Picture a vast room filled with special guests who are dressed in the finest garments provided by the groom's father. Imagine long, beautifully decorated tables loaded with sumptuous things to eat. The king enters with much fanfare and majesty. Perhaps on his right walks his beautiful bride-to-be, whom he seats next to him.

Accompanied by the jubilant announcement of the king's intentions to wed, this is the scene of their engagement party. King Solomon is joyfully looking forward to marrying this Shulamite maiden, for she is his love, and his desire is for her only. That is evident to her and to everyone there.

In the demeanor of this young woman, there is no evidence of arrogance. There is no attitude of "I deserve this honor and should have gotten it long ago." On the contrary, she seems very appreciative and almost unbelieving of her good fortune. So, too, the Bride, beginning to glimpse the depths of Christ's love for her, is increasingly overwhelmed with its wonder, singular honor, and immensity.

His banner

A banner provides identification to others. The Olympic Parade of Nations is an excellent example of this. Athletes representing their nation walk proudly behind their national flag or banner. The sight of it flying over them sustains them in the competitions and provides an added incentive to continue, just as the star-spangled banner of the United States has, at crucial times, given renewed hope to those engaged in battle.

To the Bride of Christ, His banner of love identifies her as His pearl of great price, chosen and cherished forever. (Matthew 13:46) It also speaks to her of the present and future joys, eternities of bliss spent with Him.

His banner over me was love

The knowledge that King Solomon wants to declare his love before the members of his house and favored friends is thrilling to her, and is another step in her transformation by his love.

Dr. Maya Angelou, the noted poet and writer, once said when she finally realized and believed the truth of the statement, "God loves me," as she emphasized each of the three words: *God* loves me, God *loves* me, God loves *me*. It completely changed her life.

Usually, one would get a small name card to indicate their seat at a dinner party; like the Shulamite, the Bride of Christ receives a banner of love over her position, a significant honor. This symbol of the King's identity, similar to a family coat-of-arms, acts as His declaration to all His kingdom. By this, Christ forever joins her identity and future to His. Like an engagement announcement, this banner gives tangible and incontrovertible evidence of His commitment to her.

Love is the foundational characteristic and motive of the Godhead. The love of Christ was shown in everything He did and demonstrated in everything He does now. Love infuses His every decision. He loves His Bride. His banner of love will always wave over her. Nothing can separate her from His love. (Romans 8:38-39) As we will see in the later chapters of Song of Solomon, she is beginning to realize that it will change her forever. Love makes the difference.

> **Meditation Eleven:** "His banner over me [is] love." (2:4 b) Repeat several times each day. Believe it; embrace it.

Judy-2:5 Stay me with flagons, comfort me with apples: for I *am* sick of love.

Faint with love

This young woman is so entranced with her beloved, and overwhelmed with her thoughts of him, she needs help and refreshment to keep from swooning. The closer they become, the more enthralled she is with him; this is part of their courtship—she's faint with love.

Dixie-2:5 Stay me with flagons, comfort me with apples: for I *am* sick of love.

Lovesick

Flagons are thought to be similar to raisin cakes. Feeling faint and lovesick, the Shulamite, utterly spent, exhausted by all she has seen and learned of Solomon, asks for something to sustain her. She expresses awe by her unsophisticated yet transparent reaction to the glory of who he is and the amazing thought that this great king loves her.

Have you ever been so in love, you felt overwhelmed with the beauty and glory of it? That's how she feels. Have you ever felt lovesick for Jesus? When the Bride of Christ really begins to understand the expanse of His love for her, not just what He showed by His death on the cross, as immense as that was, but by every loving thought and gracious action of His on her behalf, she will be "sick with love" for Him, overcome by such knowledge and understanding. Take a few minutes to meditate on His great love for you right now.

Judy-2:6 His left hand is under my head, and his right hand doth embrace me.

His hands

The hands of the bridegroom are strong and gentle. The bride of Solomon loves how he holds her. Christ's Bride feels the same way. "Hold thou me up, and I shall be safe…" (Psalm 119:117) Knowing His Bride's need for security, Jesus said, "… I give unto them eternal life; and they shall never perish, neither shall any man pluck them out of my hand. My Father, which gave them me, is greater than all; and no man is able to pluck them out of my Father's hand." (John 10:28-29)

"Who hath measured the waters in the hollow of His hand and meted out heaven with the span and comprehended the dust of the earth in a measure and weighed the mountains in scales and the hills in a balance?" (Isaiah 40:12) Jeremiah 32:17 summarizes it quite well: "Ah Lord God! Behold, thou hast made the heaven and the earth by thy great power and stretched out arm, and there is nothing too hard for thee."

Dixie-2:6 His left hand is under my head, and his right hand doth embrace me.

His hands

This must be the kiss to celebrate their engagement. She has such confidence in him, and no fear of him. You can sense she is quite pleased with his attention. She loves his embrace. The Bride of Christ must have the same confidence in her Bridegroom. She shares a sacred closeness with her Beloved, where whispers and sweet exchanges should be the norm, and where there is no unholy fear.

Judy-2:7 I charge you, O ye daughters of Jerusalem, by the roes, and by the hinds of the field, that ye stir not up, nor awake *my* love, till it please.

Let us be

The maiden might say to the daughters of Jerusalem: "Don't push us. We're enjoying getting to know each other and letting our relationship strengthen. Working together comes later."

Dixie-2:7 I charge you, O ye daughters of Jerusalem, by the roes, and by the hinds of the field, that ye stir not up, nor awake *my* love, till it please.

Nor awake love, till it please

The Shulamite lies awake to meditate upon all that has transpired. This bridegroom is not a controller or impatient, as we will see in the next passages of this chapter. Solomon desires her to choose him by her free will, from her heart's desire, and the passion and depths of her soul. He puts no pressure on her, nor does he want anyone else to do so. Christ is the same. It is important to spend time thinking about the wonder of Jesus' love for you, to let that knowledge seep into your soul and become a treasured assurance and certainty in you.

Roes

"Roes" and the "hinds of the field" refer to the male and female gazelle and deer, typically skittish creatures but free to do as they choose. So, too, is the Bride. Her love must develop in an atmosphere of trust and freedom, where coercion or manipulation is unknown.

Meditation Twelve: Jesus sees you as His love. How do *you* see you? Is that view of you coming into alignment with His? Read Psalm 139:1-18 and think of His unfailing love for you. Sing the words to the song *Jesus Loves Me* as a declaration.

Judy-2:8 The voice of my beloved! behold, he cometh leaping upon the mountains, skipping upon the hills.

Overcomer

This shepherd-king is an overcomer. So is Jesus. Jesus said in John 16:33: "These things I have spoken unto you, that in me ye might have peace. In the world ye shall have tribulation; but be of good cheer; I have overcome the world." He was victorious in all His trials and experiences. He wants us also to be overcomers. Because He was, with His help, we can be victorious, too. It is a choice. (Revelation 3:21)

Dixie-2:8 The voice of my beloved! behold, he cometh leaping upon the mountains, skipping upon the hills.

The voice of my beloved

The Shulamite girl lived in the mountains of Lebanon, which Solomon had to climb and cross in order to reach her home. *Ain't No Mountain High Enough* could have been his theme song. No obstacle could stop him from seeing his love.

She was sure he would come back to her. She hears him from a distance. Having been with Solomon so much, she recognizes his voice before she sees his countenance. To recognize our Beloved's voice, we must spend time with Him, listening, reading His Word, and looking forward to seeing Him. (John 10:3-5, Psalm 103:20, Acts 8:29, 10:19, 1 Peter 1:8, 2 Timothy 4:8, Titus 2:13)

Mountains and hills

Location can change perspective. A person can see more and farther atop the mountains and hills than in the valleys. High up is the place to soar spiritually, where faith is strong, and where the minuscule things below take their rightful proportion. (Ephesians 1:3, 2:6, Colossians 3:1-2)

At Kadesh-Barnea, when the twelve spies reported the lay of the promised land of Canaan, only Caleb and Joshua looked at the situation with an "atop-the-mountains" mentality. They saw the strength of giants and fortified cities as meaningless in comparison to the strength of their Almighty God. (Numbers 13-14)

In the Bible, mountains and hills can represent kingdoms or troubles of one magnitude or another. Christ is the overcomer of all obstacles, trials, difficulties, temptations, kingdoms, death, hell, and the grave. (Revelation 3:21) He is above all parameters of time and space. He has conquered everything that needed conquering. He is worthy to be praised and honored for His greatness. (Isaiah 37:16, 20, Revelation 4:11, 5:8-14)

Leaping and skipping

Do you remember the phrase, "Able to leap tall buildings in a single bound," said of Superman, the comic strip character later portrayed in television and movies? That phrase came to mind as I thought about Solomon's hurry, leaping and skipping to return to his lovely bride-to-be. There's a sense of great delight and pleasure in his haste. These words also suggest great stamina and energy.

The Beloved Christ is an overcomer. He learned to leap upon the mountains and skip upon the hills of life. During His time on Earth, His Father taught Him. (Psalm 18:29, 32-33) Jesus became the unparalleled conqueror of all time. Not only does He desire His Bride to be with Him, but He wants her to have many victories in her life.

Spiritual leapers and skippers are those who, by virtue of their lofty "mountaintop" position, can see the big picture of what God intends. Or, at least, praise Him for what they are sure He will do, whether or not they know what it involves. Sometimes, what the Lord wants does not make sense immediately, but what He planned makes perfect sense as circumstances play out.

This point reminds me of the story of what Judy Rusk's husband did last year. It just didn't make sense.

> Tom Rusk bought a little deluxe, pink Barbie bicycle with white training wheels, handlebar streamers, and basket for his three-year-old granddaughter's Christmas present without knowing if the parents had already purchased one. They had. It just didn't make sense when Tom told his wife, Judy, that he didn't want to stand in the return line to get his money back for the bike. He'd rather give it away. Nor did it make sense for Judy to call and ask if I knew anyone with a small child. I didn't.
>
> A dear friend just "happened" to be visiting from out of state that weekend, so I asked her. She did know a young teen, a single mother with a three-year-old daughter. They attended her church. She was willing to transport the bike from Tennessee and deliver it to the little girl. After an eight-hour drive on a Wednesday, my friend attended her church's prayer service that evening and gave the pink bicycle to the little girl's grandfather to deliver to the child. He knew she didn't have one.
>
> The bike went from one grandfather to another, so a little girl would get a beautiful present from someone who loved her. God wanted that mother, child, grandfather, and all of us to know He loved them and would go to great lengths to engineer circumstances to bless them. Knowing God, it all made perfect sense.

Because believers intimately know their Beloved, those who become leapers and skippers over the trials of life can see the big picture from a heavenly viewpoint, the perfect sense of God's work on the Earth—and they rejoice.

Judy-2:9 My beloved is like a roe or young hart: behold, he standeth behind our wall, he looketh forth at the windows, shewing himself through the lattice.

Looking forth

This verse shows how the shepherd-king, young and strong, sure-footed as a deer, is patiently waiting for his love to join him. As she looks through the lattice of the palace window, he looks through the windows of her precious soul.

Re-read Psalm 139:1-18 again. It gives a unique picture of Christ's attention to gazing at those He loves. It's unlimited and much deeper than what Solomon can see in his loved one. Christ sees His love when she sits down and stands up. He knows her thoughts afar off and is acquainted with all her ways. The Bridegroom charts the path ahead and tells her where to stop and rest! Every moment, He knows where she is. His Bride can never be lost from His Spirit. She can't even count how many times a day His thoughts turn toward her showing the faithful commitment of His love. (Psalm 40:5, 121:1-8, 139:17-18)

> On a personal note, I know the Beloved watches over me. A couple of years back, I went to the mailbox, and stood there too long, causing my knees to lock up. I couldn't take a step. I said, "Oh, Father, help." I hardly had gotten the words out of my mouth before a young man next door ran out to his mailbox, and when I called him, he came and helped me.

Dixie-2:9 My beloved is like a roe or young hart: behold, he standeth behind our wall, he looketh forth at the windows, shewing himself through the lattice.

Roe or young hart

As the Shulamite's bridegroom approaches her home, she admires the swiftness that brings him to her side. The sight and arrival of the one who has captured her heart brings joy.

Through the lattice

What is she waiting for? Why is she holding back from welcoming him? Her beloved has come to marry her, but she seems reluctant. Fear has stepped in. An example of this fear of circumstances is evident in the biblical account of the report of giants in Canaan that kept the children of Israel from entering the land and fulfilling their destiny. (Numbers 13:26-14:4)

What holds you back? What lattice are you hiding behind? Walls between you and your Lord can be fears of failure, safety, or the unknown. Fears are evidence of a lack of trust or focus, based on not knowing or not depending on the wonderful strength and character of the Lord Jesus.

Are you willing to tear down whatever wall keeps you from venturing forth with Him? Don't let anything cause you to miss the exciting, abundant life He wants you to have by His side.

> When the daughter of one of my dearest friends was attending college in Australia, she wrote me to ask prayer for her seemingly impossible financial situation, among other things. This student was fighting against fear. As I prayed for her faith to rise, the Lord brought Numbers 13-14 to mind. I heard Him say to tell her, "Spit on the giants and go on in." She did—and everything she needed was provided in wonderful, miraculous ways.

God wants us to be overcomers—of giants, fears, our past, or whatever hinders us from trusting Him. The Bride of Christ must be as He is, fearless and courageous, leaping and skipping on the mountains and hills of life's circumstances.

Judy-2:10 My beloved spoke, and said unto me, Rise up, my love, my fair one, And come away.

An invitation

Her shepherd-king again speaks words of encouragement, he wants her to "…press toward the mark for the prize of the high calling of God in Christ Jesus." (Philippians 3:14) As Paul wrote to the church at Rome, "…now it is high time to awake out of sleep: for now is our salvation nearer than when we believed." (Romans 13:11)

Dixie-2:10 My beloved spoke, and said unto me, Rise up, my love, my fair one, And come away.

Rise up, my love

Christ Jesus wants His Bride to commit herself, her well-being, and her future to Him. She may not completely understand all that entails. She may not realize this is a golden opportunity for love to grow and faith to rise, but to also honor and please Him, she must be willing to risk her comfort and convenience.

The Bridegroom has not asked her to do something He has not done. He has already overcome and knows the joy of success. (Revelation 3:21) Like the swift roe (gazelle), the Bridegroom enjoys the high places and the expansive vista it offers. (Habakkuk 3:19) He wants her to know and enjoy the same. She will—if she trusts His wisdom. Will the desire to be with Him become so strong she'll decide to come out from behind her lattice that separates them? He patiently waits for her decision.

The Bride's soul may imagine, it's too much risk. The climb will be too great, and the cost will be more than she wants to pay. She desires to stay where it's safe and comfortable, but if she listens to her soul, she will lose more than she realizes.

In contrast, her spirit says to her, "Let go! Let go of the lattice, and all it represents, all that separates you from your Beloved. Remember Who Jesus is and how wonderful He is! Grab hold of His promises, knowing He will keep His Word to you without fail. Trust Him. Trust Him. Trust Him. There's so much ahead and nothing but good. Don't be afraid." "Let not your heart be troubled;…believe in me." (John 14:1)

To the Bride, this invitation has two major problems—leaving the familiar, and the struggle of the climb. To the Beloved, the invitation has one primary focus for the overcomer: the view from the mountaintop coupled with the success it represents. He has His eyes on the finish line, the goal, the victory, while she sees only the circumstances of the ascension, the imagined difficulties and dangers of such a journey. She will have to change her thinking to become His true partner. (Hebrews 12:1-2)

Some might think the invitation to marry and join Him in His life comes too soon in their relationship, but it does not. Jesus wants her to walk beside Him in a joyous union of love. If she trusts Him, He will joyfully teach her how to overcome all obstacles, difficulties, and trials of life, as He did. Her love for Him will cause her to cast out fears. (1 John 4:18)

In a spiritual sense, this is warrior training time for the Bride. Christ wants her to learn to walk in the Spirit and *not* be ruled by soulishness. Many victories and joy can be hers if she will put faith in His judgment. She will become a conqueror, too, just like the Beloved. What an opportunity! The highest of privileges!

Judy–2:11-13 For, lo, the winter is past, the rain is over *and* gone; The flowers appear on the earth; the time of the singing *of birds* is come, and the voice of the turtle is heard in our land; The fig tree putteth forth her green figs, and the vines *with* the tender grape give a *good* smell. Arise, my love, my fair one, and come away.

Spring has come

Springtime! The winter is over. It's a change in seasons; the earth is awakening. Everything is doing what it was created to do: flowers growing, birds singing, fruit trees bringing forth their bounty. We humans go through seasons much like nature. "To every *thing there is* a season, and a time to every purpose under the heaven." (Ecclesiastes 3:1)

God created each of us for a specific purpose and His glory. (Ephesians 2:10, Isaiah 43:7) Jesus says He is the vine. His Father is the husbandman (owner and tiller of the ground), and He gathers the fruit in due season. "Every branch in me that beareth not fruit He taketh away and every *branch* that beareth fruit, He purgeth it, that it may bring forth more fruit." (John 15:1-3) So spiritually, there are times of growth, periods of being pruned or cleansed by the Word, and seasons of bringing forth fruit.

Dixie-2:11-13 For, lo, the winter is past, the rain is over *and* gone; The flowers appear on the earth; the time of the singing *of birds* is come, and the voice of the turtle is heard in our land; The fig tree putteth forth her green figs, and the vines *with* the tender grape give a *good* smell. Arise, my love, my fair one, and come away.

The winter is past

What a joy it is to realize the cold, harsh days of winter are gone. The season of rest is over; a new day has begun. It is time for something more, something different. Spring, a time for new beginnings, growth, and activity, is God's reminder in the natural of what He wants to happen in us at the spiritual level. He wants us to flower, sing, and have our voices heard in the land, calling others to join us and Him. It is meant to be a beautiful time, one of joy, pleasure, and a season of greater faith, partnered with extraordinary accomplishment.

Faith has several phases. It comes by hearing and applying the Word of God, so there needs to be a saturation in the Scriptures to provide a strong foundation of faith. (James 1:22, 25) For instance, if you need improvement in your finances, write down and study the verses about money and abundance. Daily agree with what God has said and pray for it to manifest. Also, thank Him for what He will do, which is an expression of hope, the expectation of seeing God's answer. If you have physical problems, rehearse the scriptures which concern healing and health. Read them every day. They are part of the Great Physician's prescription for restoring your health. (Proverbs 4:20-22) Believe what God has said to you in them.

Secondly, realize that growing faith sometimes requires a wait. There may be an interval between believing and receiving. Joseph waited thirteen years before seeing God's Word fulfilled, but he didn't stop believing, and God rewarded his faith. (Genesis 41:39-46) David waited more than ten years to ascend the throne of Israel, although God had anointed him king as a young man before he slew Goliath. (1 Samuel 16:1-13, 2 Samuel 5:3-4) David didn't cease believing God's promise, and the promise was fulfilled. Although the Lord Jesus knew by the age of twelve what His ministry was, He had to wait eighteen years until He was nearly thirty, before He received permission from His Father to begin His public ministry. (Luke 2:42, 49, 3:23)

Making declarations aloud about God's character and His ability to fulfill His promises is an essential activity as you tarry. While faith waits, there are at least three requirements: expectation, focus, and acts of faith.

- **Expectation:** another word for hope, a "knowing," a confidence of receiving the longed-for desire or request, or something even better. It is looking forward to the final result. (Hebrews 10:12-13)
- **Focus:** With expectation there must be a determined focus on the future. During your wait, spirits of doubt and unbelief will try to attack. As long as you focus on the Lord and the goal is maintained by steadfast faith, there will be no wavering or doubt. For instance, this focus on the future, based on the Word given through dreams to Joseph, kept him from despair when he was sold into slavery by his brothers, and later, when thrown into prison, though innocent of any wrongdoing. (Genesis 37-41) David's focus on faith is seen in his many writings in the Psalms. (Psalms 3, 4:8, 18:50, 21:1-7, 61:6) Jesus kept His focus: "...*w*ho for the joy that was set before him endured the cross..." (Hebrews 12:2, see also Isaiah 50:7) Consistent focus enables us to endure the trial, keep the faith, and eventually stand before the Lord unashamed.
- **Acts of faith:** those things, spoken and performed, which demonstrate our faith in Him in relationship to the thing for which we believe.

Green figs and tender grapes

Figs begin forming on the trees, and grapes appear on the vines. Green figs and tender grapes are immature fruit. They need time to grow and ripen in the heat of the sun. Similarly, the Beloved declares it is a time of growth for the Bride, an adventure in faith. There has already been a positive development in her, but now is the time for more and in a new area. If the Bridegroom says to His Bride, "You're ready to do something different and more challenging. I'll be with you, and together we'll conquer the mountains and hills that life presents," then she is able and empowered by His Word to accomplish what He calls her to do. The victory is hers to claim. Christ is not just involved with regeneration but also with transformation. He is the Wisdom of God, therefore, through His Spirit, He supervises and oversees His Bride's growth to maturity and fellowship to bring about an increasing intimacy and oneness with Him. (1 Corinthians 1:24)

Arise, my love, my fair one

Answering "yes" to His invitation to advance to a new level, higher than she's ever been, takes faith and courage. Yet He would not call her if she was not ready for this, and if He would not protect her along the way. Trust is what is needed, a willingness to venture out with Him. The Bride must realize and act upon the belief that His "Come away with Me" includes the power to accomplish it. The time and season are right for them to be together in a new and greater way.

At the feeding of the five thousand, the only miracle recorded in all four gospels, the Lord Jesus extended a similar invitation to His disciples. (Matthew 14:15-21, Mark 6:30-44, Luke 9:10-17, John 6:1-14) A careful analysis of the four texts reveals that Jesus gave His disciples the command, and, therefore, the power to feed the crowd assembled to hear His teachings and receive healing, if needed. Still the apostles failed to understand this call to a heightened level of faith.

"…Jesus…saw much people, and was moved with compassion toward them, because they were as sheep not having a shepherd: and he began to teach them many things. And when the day was now far spent, his disciples came unto him, and said, 'This is a desert place, and now the time *is* far passed. Send them away, that they may go into the country round about, and into the villages, and buy themselves bread: for they have nothing to eat.' He answered and said unto them, 'Give ye them to eat.' " (Mark 6:34-37) In Matthew's gospel, Jesus replied, "They need not depart; give ye them to eat." (Matthew 14:16)

John's gospel reveals that Jesus gave this directive first to Philip, who responded that they didn't have enough money. At this point, the opportunity to do a *creative* miracle faded—that is, one where something is produced from nothing, because Philip had no faith or vision for it. (John 6:5-7) Jesus then sent the apostles to find how many loaves and fishes were available for a *multiplication* miracle. (Mark 6:38) Then Jesus commanded them again to give food to the people. "They responded, '…We have no more but five loaves and two fishes.' " (Luke 9:13) Andrew added, "…what are they among so many?" (John 6:9) Jesus was looking for a mustard seed of faith in them, but sadly, did not find it. (Matthew 17:20)

So, at this point, there was no faith among them for a miracle of *multiplication*—that is, one in which a seed or starter is used. A miracle of multiplication is of a different degree of faith than a creative miracle, but still, some spiritual growth in the apostles was demonstrated by their obedience to Christ's directives. They just didn't understand it wasn't their faith in themselves that was desired, but faith in their God to do what they by themselves could not do.

Since the apostles did not step up in faith, Jesus did the miracle Himself to feed the hungry people. Jesus didn't need the loaves and fish to do the miracle, but He wanted to bless the lad who had given all he had to the Lord's service. (Matthew 14:20, 1 Kings 17:8-16) Sadly, later in Mark 8:1-9, when four thousand men, not counting the women and children, were present and hungry, not one apostle volunteered.

None of the apostles stepped forward to say, "Let me knock on heaven's door for help, knowing the compassion and power of our heavenly Father. Let me feed them this time, as I could have done with the five thousand when You gave us the opportunity."

Jesus could tell by their remarks there was no faith in them for a miracle, even though they had found seven loaves and some fish in the crowd, and had seen what God could do when the five thousand were fed. (Matthew 15:32-33) They did not understand the tremendous power available from God to a person or people of faith. So, Jesus did the miracle of multiplication without them. He didn't let the crowd lose their blessing, even though the apostles were unresponsive spiritually.

Jesus calls His Bride to move to a loftier, growing degree of faith, into a province of wonders and courageous exploits. She has seen Him leap on the mountains and skip on the hills. Now, He invites her to learn to do the same. With new perspective, His love will see things that previously looked impossible and can now be achieved. He wants her to be an overcomer, as He is. (Revelation 3:21) He knows she has the potential, but her faith in Him and His Word must be resolute.

In the passages of Revelation 2-3, Jesus calls those seven churches to become part of the Bride, but He says to do so, they must overcome the problems that are holding them back from being all they can be. Every letter has a message about overcoming. He knows their capabilities, but they must trust Him and respond as He directs.

We do not work for salvation. It is a total offering of God's grace that a person accepts or rejects. However, once a person makes a confession of Jesus as Lord and Savior, the Holy Spirit begins the preparatory work needed for that one to become part of the Bride of Christ. (Revelation 19:7-8) The Spirit of Christ shows how to get free from those attitudes and actions that weigh the believer down. (1 Peter 1:11, Romans 8:2, 5-9, 13-18, Galatians 4:6, Philippians 1:19, Ephesians 1–4) He helps the Bride move from soulishness to the Spirit-led life, from self-centeredness to Beloved-centeredness. He draws her away from the idol of self, for Christ alone must be the focus of the Bride's adoration, and love for Him her only motive.

Come away

If this were a husband in today's era, we might deem "come away" as a suggestion to her. However, when a king speaks, much attention should be given. When Christ calls us to come, it is not a suggestion. It is a life-changing opportunity and a victory in the making.

Mountains and hills could represent kingdoms and opportunities for rulership. Conquering them signifies passing the training required for a higher position. In Isaiah 2:2-3, as part of a vision given to the prophet Isaiah for Israel, there is an interesting statement alluding to this: "And it shall come to pass in the last days, *that* the mountain of the LORD'S house shall be established in the top of the mountains, and shall be exalted above the hills; and all nations shall flow unto it. And many people shall go and say, 'Come ye, and let us go up to the mountain of the LORD, to the house of the God of Jacob; and he will teach us of his ways, and we will walk in his paths.' "

Mountain climbing—the Bride thinks that's another name for "struggle." Can she do it? She doesn't think so. She will have to relinquish her supposed safety and comfort to follow Him. It will require breaking the idol of self she has made, pictured by the Pharisee of Luke 18:9-14.

The Beloved says, "With Me, you *can* do this," but at this point, she is too wrapped up in self-protection to believe Him; likewise, this is where many Christians put their fingers in their ears spiritually. They want to avoid hearing the call of the Lord or facing a challenge. They want to stay behind the lattice, not realizing that in His Presence is the safe place and there is no other.

The Shulamite maiden over-thinks the situation. It isn't necessary for her to figure out the how-to's of mountain climbing. She doesn't have to gather the equipment or plot their course. She has to trust her beloved. Solomon will take care of every detail and will tirelessly protect her. He will even enlarge the path, if necessary, so that her feet do not slip on the way to the tops of the mountains. His right hand would support her, should she falter. (Psalm 18:33, 35-36)

Similarly, the Bride of Christ has to say, "Yes!" and to respond to what her Beloved tells her, to take the first step, which He has made plain to her: "Come." Victory begins with saying "yes" to the Beloved, the King, and doing whatever He has already asked you to do.

The maiden's lack of trust is evident when she refuses Solomon's invitation. Her fears cause her to say "no." Her focus is on herself, rather than him; on her weakness, rather than his strength; on her reasoning, rather than his knowledge and wisdom; on the struggle, rather than the victorious end. Here's her chance to be an overcomer, to gain strength, to be his partner, to achieve greater things, and to be one with him. Yet she refuses Solomon's plea. Her quality of love for him is less than it should be. She loves him, but not to the degree that casts out fear. (1 John 4:18)

The Bride of Christ cannot achieve what she wants without learning this lesson. Love, willing to be perfected, must still cast out fear because fear weakens and torments, eventually disabling, paralyzing, and eroding if left unchallenged and unconquered. (1 John 4:18) Apprehension will keep her from moving forward and upward. It will retard growth.

Casting off recognized fears will be a primary step toward achieving power and greatness, enabling her to become a worthy partner of the King of kings. Not yet at that level, the Bride, by the last chapter of the Song of Solomon, will have come to trust Him completely while loving Him with all of her heart.

> **Meditation Thirteen:** Write a short poem to your Beloved—two lines or more, rhyming or not. Here's a portion of one of Judy's:
>
> *"You saw me when I was being formed*
> *And You have never lost sight of me,*
> *I love being the apple of Your eye."*

Judy-2:14 O my dove, *that art* **in the clefts of the rock, in the secret** *places* **of the stairs, let me see thy countenance, let me hear thy voice; for sweet** *is* **thy voice, and thy countenance** *is* **comely.**

O my dove

As the Shulamite's shepherd-king calls, "Come to me, I want to see you, to hear your voice," so indeed does our Shepherd-King invite us to draw near. It's a wonderful thing to have someone who wants to see your face and hear your voice and be an intimate part of your life. "For the eyes of the Lord *are* over the righteous, and his ears *are open* unto their prayers..." (1 Peter 3:12) Philippians 4:6 states that God wants us to speak our concerns to Him "...in everything by prayer and supplication with thanksgiving let your requests be made known unto God."

The Bride's response should be, "I love the LORD, because he has heard my voice and my supplications. Because He has inclined His ear unto me, therefore will I call upon Him as long as I live." (Psalm 116:1, 2 NKJV)

Dixie-2:14 O my dove, *that art* **in the clefts of the rock, in the secret** *places* **of the stairs, let me see thy countenance, let me hear thy voice; for sweet** *is* **thy voice, and thy countenance** *is* **comely.**

Cleft of the rock

Let's look at this phrasing in two ways. The cleft can represent salvation and the secret place; in other words, communion with her beloved, which is how this passage is generally taught. However, it could be the picture of her hiding from Solomon. I lean toward the latter. The maiden is hidden behind the latticed wall of her home, listening to his words. He gently pleads for her to take the risk of stepping forth, of trusting Him. He is not asking her to climb up the stairs but to come down to him.

Uncertain and unwilling to move toward a new degree of faith with her bridegroom, she has a heart for her beloved but fears this choice for her future. Consider how her attitude has changed from a confident declaration, "draw me, we will run after thee," to a faltering message of "No, you go on alone."

Even if the first interpretation of the cleft is true, many believers resting in Christ Jesus, the cleft of the Rock, and who have found the secret place of prayer and devotion, still wrestle with a personal and real-life relationship with Jesus. Their rest is based on a beginner's faith but hasn't strengthened into a warrior's faith infused with a pledge to follow Him anywhere. Their prayer is a monologue, a one-way conversation. They never stop to consider that He fervently wants to speak to them every day. (Psalm 95:7, Hebrews 3:7) The question is, "Are we listening?"

The Bride must be an adult, a warrior, valiant and strong, because Christ desires and deserves a fully matured partner for a Bride. He isn't going to marry a baby or a child. (Ephesians 4:13) Those who want to be of His Bride must allow the Holy Spirit to bring them to full maturity. (2 Corinthians 3:18)

This verse reminds me of when the disciples were on a ship in the Sea of Galilee. (Matthew 14:27-33) In the fourth watch of the night, they saw Jesus approaching, walking upon the water. When Peter realized it was Jesus, he said, "Lord, if it be thou, bid me come unto thee on the water."

Jesus replied, "Come." Notice He didn't say, "Peter, come." He opened the invitation to all in the ship. Why, then, did only Peter climb out of the boat? At Jesus' command to come to Him, every disciple in the ship could have stepped onto the water and walked to Jesus, but only Peter had faith enough to do so.

Members of the body of Christ are pictured in these disciples. Some follow the Lord as long as there is no risk involved, no threat to their supposed security, and no possibility of loss of standing or reputation in the eyes of others. There are few who, like Peter, trust Jesus and understand that His word, "come," includes the power to accomplish the command. Therefore, they accept His invitation to climb out of the boat and experience something more than they've ever known before.

Today, every disciple of Christ can be a part of the Bride, but only those empowered by His Word will trust Him enough to climb out of the boat, or to leave the security of the cleft of the rock. These disciples will then shift closer to becoming a member of that elite group of the Bride, for Christ's Bride must be of the same caliber of faith as He, strong and unafraid of what He invites her to experience. She must trust His character, love, wisdom, intentions, and motives. To each of us, the Bridegroom says, "Come with Me. Be My true partner. Let Me teach you about being victorious in life." Don't be afraid. Respond, "Yes, Lord."

Having learned Who the Beloved is, and realizing He truly desires a fellowship of love and fellowship with her, the Bride faces the next step in her development—that of self-denial: the death and burial of her soul's old ways and habits of the past, as shown in John 12:24. She is invited to join Jesus, climb with Him, learn new things, and grow in power. With Him as her beloved Companion, she will have everything needed to complete the desired transformation. What an opportunity!

In Mark 10:46-52, we can read the account of the healing of blind Bartimaeus. In verse 50, when the blind man hears that Jesus has called him to come near, Bartimaeus casts away his garment, comes to Jesus, and receives healing of his sight. The garment he threw away was a beggar's cloak, used to catch the coins people would toss his way as they passed him. When Jesus called him, Bartimaeus knew, without a shadow of a doubt, that he would never be a beggar or blind again. He knew he would receive the healing he desired.

Don't hold on to the things of the past or the old ways. Take a "risk" on Jesus—it's not one—and learn to soar with Him. That's what He is calling us to do. Trust Him and soar!

Judy-2:15 Take us the foxes, the little foxes, that spoil the vines: for our vines *have* **tender grapes.**

A warning

How the maiden needs to listen to the words of love, concern, and warning from the one who loves her deeply. When the Bride puts our Beloved first, everything else falls into place. If we don't respond to the Lord in the obedience of faith, we will lose so much. The one thing we don't ever want to hear are the words said to the church of Ephesus in Revelation 2:2-4: "I know your works, your labor, your patience, and that you cannot bear those which are evil. And you have tested those who say they are apostles and are not, and have found them liars; "and have persevered and have patience, and have labored for My name's sake and have not become weary. Nevertheless, I have *this* against you that you have left your first love." (NKJV)

Dixie-2:15 Take us the foxes, the little foxes, that spoil the vines: for our vines *have* **tender grapes.**

Little foxes

The maiden is safe behind the lattice of her home, a choice made by internal fears. She doesn't want to venture forth. She wants him, but on her terms, not his. Solomon warns his love that, if allowed, the little foxes will steal her potential harvest of mature fruit that should be nurtured and protected. She must not let that happen. She must capture and get rid of anything that would harm the coming fruit. Notice Solomon uses "us" and "our" to indicate he is with her in this effort. He will not leave her to handle it on her own. The little foxes, her fears of the future, and what consequences will happen flood her mind.

Are you trying to call the shots in your relationship with Jesus? Are you trying to lead rather than letting Him be Lord? It won't work. The Bride consists of those who have surrendered completely to *His* leadership. They do not cling to the false notion that their ideas are as good, as wise, or as important as His. Christ invites the Bride to join Him and learn to be an overcomer of the "hills and mountains" of this life. At this juncture, He gently but clearly cautions her to walk in the Spirit and not permit her soul to lead. Often, there is a conflict as to which we will allow to rule our lives, the Spirit or the soul. Too many believers live a soulish life, where logic, emotions, and self-centeredness rule supreme, and the Holy Spirit's leadership is ignored, neglected, or dismissed.

The Bride of Christ must choose to walk in faith and be led by the Spirit of God. (Romans 8:14) The Bridegroom challenges her to capture the little foxes, to get rid of anything that might spoil their deepening relationship and destroy the growth that has begun in her. (2 Corinthians 10:4-5) By saying, "our vines," He reminds her she is not alone in this. It is not something she has to do by herself. (John 15:5)

By the way, our Bridegroom isn't looking for perfection. The fact that He provides forgiveness tells us perfection is not expected from us. (1 John 1:9) He knows the Bride's character and personhood are in the process of development. Understanding it will take time for her to realize her full glory, Jesus is willing to give her that time and to wait patiently for her. Such wisdom and love He shows!

Meditation Fourteen: What little foxes have you encountered since you became a Christian? Make a note of this in your journal. It will help you monitor your progress. Read 2 Corinthians 10:3-5. We bestow glory on our Beloved when we overcome in the power of His Name and with the strength He gives us. (Hebrews 4:16, Psalms 18:32, 27:1, 84:7)

Judy-2:16 My beloved *is* mine, and I *am* his: he feeds *his flock* among the lilies.

My beloved

"Feeding among the lilies" suggests Solomon is tending to his lovely garden on his own. Though the Shulamite has refused to go with him, she does not question his love for her. She isn't afraid he will lose patience or give up on her.

The Bride knows Christ has promised never to leave her nor forsake her. (Hebrews 13:5) "For I am persuaded, that neither death, nor life, nor angels, nor principalities, nor powers, nor things present, nor things to come, nor height, nor depth, nor any other creature, shall be able to separate us from the love of God, which is in Christ Jesus our Lord." (Romans 8:38-39) It's our free will to hold tight or not, but we know He won't ever let go of us.

Dixie-2:16 My beloved *is* mine, and I *am* his: he feeds *his flock* among the lilies.

My beloved is mine, and I am his

The maiden makes a loving declaration: "My beloved is mine, and I am his." This statement by the Shulamite is very revealing, especially in how she repeats it later in 6:3 but changes its order. Here, she knows and declares she has the heart of her beloved, even though she has just turned down his invitation. With great joy, she proclaims her delight in their relationship. She does not doubt as to his love and his allegiance to her. There is no question in her mind of his faithfulness. What a wonderful feeling to know your beloved is completely devoted to you!

Love, real love, must grow and always be evolving. True love in one person calls the other to greater heights, to challenges and victories, and, if possible, to withhold nothing good from the loved one. The Bride knows Christ's commitment to her is primary, but her commitment to Him is secondary. She can count on Him, but unfortunately, the converse is not yet true. Her commitment to Him is the lesser. She is holding back. She has refused His invitation, yet tries to pretend nothing is wrong. She wants everything to go as it has previously, not realizing it cannot. Her refusal to be with Him ends their joyful communion for a time.

Do you *know* that the heart of the Lord Jesus is totally devoted and committed to you? Do you understand that nothing could tempt Him away from loving you? Jesus has already given you the greatest gift—Himself. He held nothing back, not even His life. He willingly was taken to the cross, died there, and went to hell for you. (1 Peter 3:18-20)

The good news is that hell could not hold Him. (Acts 2:24-31) He conquered death, hell, and the grave. (Hebrews 2:9, Matthew 27:62-63, 28:5-7, Luke 24:14-48, 1 Corinthians 15:25-26, 54, 57) He paid all the penalty for your sin, even though you had not yet been born. You are always in His thoughts, graced with His love and care. What a magnificent Lord and Savior!

Lilies

This term implies pure ones and loveliness of the most significant degree. "…Solomon in all his glory was not arrayed like one of these." (Matthew 6:29 NKJV) The lilies represent people with whom the Lord is working, placing them in a setting where they can bloom and which will bring out their beauty as long as they respond to the light of the Son and the water of His Word.

Among the lilies

King Solomon enjoys being among his gardens and taking care of them, and will continue to do it, whether the Shulamite joins him or not. The maiden seems to think his work among them is fine. Perhaps, for a moment, she may have thought he would change his mind and not only withdraw his invitation, but also give up any inclination of his to go forth. Her next observation is that he did not stop his work because of her choice.

Unlike Adam, who chose to follow Eve rather than God, the Beloved Christ Jesus makes no idol of His Bride but continues to do His mission, confident that her love, a product of the Holy Spirit, will eventually rule. "Among the lilies" is the place of the Lord's heart, among the people He came to claim. (Mark 9:20, Hosea 14:5-7)

Judy–2:17 Until the day break, and the shadows flee away, turn, my beloved, and be thou like a roe or a young hart upon the mountains of Bether.

Go on without me

The Shulamite admires her beloved in all his glory. I wonder if she's thinking, could she ever be so confident and courageous like him? She fails to recognize that she would be more like him if she cast out her fears, replacing them with confidence, courage, and trust in her beloved. The secret is never to give up and not let fear enter in.

The Bride of Christ must have complete confidence in Jesus Christ, the Provider, Healer, Victory Banner, Peace, and Shepherd. He is always for her and present with her. (Psalm 23:1, Ephesians 2:14, 1 Chronicles 29:11-12)

Dixie-2:17 Until the day break, and the shadows flee away, turn, my beloved, and be thou like a roe or a young hart upon the mountains of Bether.

Bether

Bether, the name of a small range of hills between Bethlehem and Jerusalem, means separation or division. The maiden calls Solomon to come back later as if getting this adventure out of his system is all he needs. She believes he should be the one to alter his plan. She doesn't understand that she is the only one who needs to change—and she must if she wants a relationship with him that will transcend all others.

She has said no to his invitation and suggests Solomon continue his work without her. Although this isn't a rejection of him, it is a rejection of his plan for their future; this is the Shulamite's refusal to accept his vision for them.

He has challenged her. She cavalierly chooses a different plan. To him, she says, "Turn, my beloved." In other words, "I'm not coming with you. You go do what you want for a little while till the day breaks. I will stay in this place of comfort and security." She tells him to return to his land and suggests he will travel more swiftly alone, even though that was never his intention. "Be…like a roe or a young hart" expresses her encouragement for him to enjoy his endeavors without her.

Several years ago, the Lord taught me a principle that applies to this situation. The Lord gives us plan A. (Jeremiah 29:11) For various reasons, we reject it and introduce our plan B, developed in our pride and disguised arrogance, and we think it is just as good, if not much better than Plan A.

That's what Cain did. The Lord gave His plan A for worship. Adam, Eve, and Abel followed it, but Cain came up with a different plan for worship—one he thought was just as good, if not better, than God's plan. He rejected the Creator's plan, instituted his own, which neither honored the blood sacrifice of the coming Redeemer nor obeyed the practice God had instituted and his father, Adam, had taught. We know the rest of the story. (Genesis 4:1-5) That is what the Shulamite has done: substituted her plan for her beloved's, thinking hers is better than his.

Why do we dismiss the Lord's plan for us, and in its place, substitute one of our own making, as if it came with a guarantee of a better outcome, as if our lack of wisdom could produce a more desirable and eternal benefit? We may pretend our plans have had the blessing of God on them, as though they were His will—but they weren't. Such foolishness!

Do you need to take a few minutes, as I did, and repent of all the Plan B's you've conjured up at different times in your life? (Make some notes in your journal about these.)

The Shulamite maiden stayed behind because the future looked too scary. She couldn't get past the dismay and fright she felt at the thought of leaving her family home. Instead of keeping her thoughts on the joy awaiting her over the mountain, she focused on the circumstances. Whether it was immaturity, pride, or fear, she stayed with her own Plan B and went against the apparent will of her beloved. She didn't stop trusting Solomon but started trusting herself more. Maybe she didn't know the principle taught in 1 John 4:18: the more I love, the less I will fear.

Her refusal to join him in his victorious life reminds me of the people described in Psalm 78:9: "The children of Ephraim, *being* armed and carrying bows, turned back in the day of battle."

Isn't that sad? Like them, the maiden also is ready for the next level of training involving victories in faith, but instead of moving forward with her beloved, she retreats, staying behind the lattice, choosing to worship at the altar of self.

He does not force her to leave with him. That is not his way. To him, her free will is sacred and not to be ignored or abused. Her trust and choice must be from her *heart*, for only then would it

be strong enough to keep her on the path to overcoming and victory. The beloved can't stay but must fulfill his duties to others, with or without her by his side. But, oh, what a loss to her!

Our Beloved calls us to join Him, come with Him, and move higher with us by His side. How unwise if we refuse! What joys we will miss if our fears hinder us from trusting His judgment! Remember 2 Timothy 1:7: "...God hath not given us the spirit of fear; but [the spirit] of power, of love, and of a sound mind." Never fear. Jesus won't give up on us. Love doesn't, even though He may have to step back for a time and let the loved one develop a yearning to be one with Him and to grow in trusting Him.

The Bride doesn't realize she is in danger. Turning from her Beloved's "come" invites troubles and attacks from the enemy, which she was never intended to have. Refusing His invitation also opens the possibility of her turning to other vineyards, trying to substitute religious activities for her following close to Him. Religious activities or works of the flesh can never win His approval and should never be a substitute for being with Him. Faith and love are what please Him. (Hebrews 11:6)

Refusal to follow Him indicates a lack of trust. What is it about the Lord that can't be trusted? His knowledge? His wisdom? He is omniscient; He is the Alpha and the Omega. He knows the solution to every problem. We don't. His wisdom is perfect, the solution to every problem or difficulty. Ours isn't. Why wouldn't we trust His will for us?

Can you—no—will you join Christ in saying, "Your will delights me, O God? I will walk with You, no matter where the pathway leads, no matter what hills and mountains are ahead." Declare it and then ask Him to make it true in your life.

Meditation Fifteen: Repeat often: "Thank You, Beloved, for freeing me from fears and leading me into Your abundant Life." (John 10:10)

CHAPTER 3 (3:1-11)

Judy-3:1 By night on my bed I sought him whom my soul loveth: I sought him, but I found him not.

Dreaming

Previously, the Shulamite had turned her beloved away when he called to her, because she lacked courage to accompany him to her new home. Now she dreams in the dark of the night about him whom her soul loves.

The Bride must not allow fear to enter or reside in her mind or forget that God has not given her "…the spirit of fear; but of power, and of love, and of a sound mind."(2 Timothy 1:7) Scripture reminds us, "Cast not away therefore your confidence, which hath great recompense of reward." (Hebrews 10:35) She should trust the One she knows loves her above all.

Dixie-3:1 By night on my bed I sought him whom my soul loveth: I sought him, but I found him not.

By night

"I call to remembrance my song in the night; I meditate within my heart, and my spirit makes diligent search." (Psalm 77:6 NKJV) "With my soul I have desired You in the night, yes, by my spirit within me I will seek You early..." (Isaiah 26:9 NKJV) "O God, You *are* my God; early will I seek You; my soul thirsts for You; my flesh longs for You in a dry and thirsty land where there is no water. So I have looked for You in the sanctuary, to see Your power and Your glory. Because Your loving kindness is better than life, my lips shall praise You. Thus I will bless You while I live; I will lift up my hands in Your name. My soul shall be satisfied…and my mouth shall praise You with joyful lips. When I remember You on my bed, I meditate on You in the night watches. Because You have been my help, therefore in the shadow of Your wings I will rejoice. My soul follows close behind You; Your right hand upholds me." (Psalm 63:1-8 NKJV)

Once the Bride has known the joy of Jesus' fellowship, she will long for it when it's missing. She knows He is the only true source of joy and satisfaction. He is her treasure—not things, not ministry or good works, but a person—her Beloved. He has done nothing to reject her. It is up to her to recognize what fear has cost and how necessary it is to be restored before the "little foxes" steal her future joy.

Our Beloved will not be found by our dreaming or meditating on what might be. The Christian life isn't a game where the outcome doesn't really matter, or a "let's pretend" situation of the imagination. In dark times, when failure has entered the picture, meditation isn't the whole solution, and the *desire* to be different is not enough.

We must go back to where we left Him, to where we refused to follow, and confess our error. Then, we must also understand that change isn't change until *we* have changed. Meditation and even confession are not enough. True repentance is manifested when transformation occurs, and the person acts differently, in a godly way, and continues in that manner.

I sought him, but I found him not

Her dream pictures her desire to be with her beloved, and she feels the frustration of not accomplishing her goal. Grieved, she is determined to seek him.

Judy-3:2 I will rise now, and go about the city in the streets, and in the broad ways I will seek him whom my soul loveth: I sought him, but I found him not.

I will seek him

Matthew 7:13 states, "Enter ye in at the [narrow] gate: for wide *is* the gate, and broad *is* the way, that leadeth to destruction, and many there be which go in thereat..." The Bridegroom is not to be found in the broad way—that's going back to law. Only on the narrow road to grace can He be found.

Dixie-3:2 I will rise now, and go about the city in the streets, and in the broad ways I will seek him whom my soul loveth: I sought him, but I found him not.

I will arise

Earlier, Solomon had wanted her to rise and come with him (2:10, 13), but she didn't agree to his first request. A friend of mine taught at a school for the mentally challenged. One of her goals was to get every child to respond quickly to teacher's first instruction or directive without procrastination. If mentally challenged children can learn to do that successfully, so can the Bride. She can admit her failure and repent of it without waiting or delay. Though not perfect soul-wise, Christ's Bride is learning the fellowship that accompanies love is a precious thing to be guarded and protected. Again, in this dream, the maiden knows her heart's desire is near, still in the city (3:4). She is willing to do whatever it takes to re-establish the closeness of her relationship with him. No doubt, this dream, like the "little foxes" (2:15), is another warning for her not to miss the opportunity to be with him.

Whom my soul loves

The Bride's feelings for Christ are deepening. Though she is apart from Him, He is still in her thoughts and heart. This separation, this interruption of fellowship between them which she has caused, spotlights the importance of being led by the Spirit, not by her soul. To respond lovingly when offered new experiences, the Bride must move from her self-centeredness to Christ-centeredness and trust in *every* area of her life.

Meditation Sixteen: Repeat several times daily: "I love You, my Beloved Jesus."

I sought him, but I found him not.

This statement in verse 2 is a repetition of verse 3:1. Desire for her beloved has become stronger. The Bride knows what is missing and wants that intimacy back, but it will only be found by looking in the right places. However, the important thing is that she doesn't quit seeking.

I'm reminded of the Syrophoenician woman of Matthew 15:21-28 and Mark 7:24-30. A careful reading of these passages shows the mother sought healing for her daughter three times before receiving it, but she didn't give up after the first or second try.
Her faith was so strong she refused to go home without the blessing of mercy and healing for which she had come. This is the attitude of the Bride.

Judy-3:3 The watchmen that go about the city found me: *to whom I said,* **"Saw ye him whom my soul loveth?"**

Seeking

Life is our classroom. The watchmen may represent Old Testament law or legalism, because "the law was our schoolmaster *to bring us* unto Christ, that we might be justified by faith." "…before faith came, we were kept under the law…" (Galatians 3:23-24) "But when the fullness of the time was come, God sent forth His Son, made of a woman, made under the law, to redeem them that were under the law, that we might receive the adoption of sons." (Galatians 4:4-5) After faith comes, through Jesus we become adopted into the family of God, and therefore we are elevated to being heirs of God. (Galatians 4:7, Romans 8:16-17)

The Bride knows her Beloved's promise that she shall find Him when she searches for Him with all her heart. He has assured, "I will be found of you…" (Jeremiah 29:14)

Dixie-3:3 The watchmen that go about the city found me: *to whom I said***, "Saw ye him whom my soul loveth?"**

Watchmen

Able to see afar off from the ramparts of their towers, watchmen guarded the palace and warned the inhabitants of the city when danger approached. Whom do these watchmen represent? Perhaps they represent the law (Old Testament). If so, the Bride of Christ is looking in the wrong place. The law can't aid in growing into a deeper love with Christ. Yes, the law is a "schoolmaster" pointing to Christ but not the means of keeping you there and deepening your relationship in Him. (Galatians 3:24-25) The law is there to warn, but it is not the answer to her problem. Romans 10:4 confirms that.

As 1 Corinthians 10:11-12 states about Old Testament writings: "Now all these things happened…for examples: and they are written for our admonition…" The law and the things of the past cannot help to re-establish her fellowship with Him, neither can becoming more religious or filling her schedule with church activities or rituals. Maybe the watchmen represent formal religion, those man-made institutions with vestiges of truth but very little light of God in them.

Could the watchmen collectively represent her conscience? In a quick study of this subject, I found conscience is a record or recorder, giving witness to our deeds, accusing or excusing us of guilt. (Romans 2:15, 9:1) It provides testimony in the consciousness of personal sins because conscience can bring conviction. (2 Corinthians 1:12, Hebrews 9:9, 10:2, John 8:9) However, conscience only helps if we listen to it and let it humble us and lead us to repentance. The Bride can have a conscience void of offense, called a good and pure conscience in 1 Timothy 1:5 and 3:9, if she responds to her Beloved with love from the depths of her spirit and soul. (Acts 24:16)

Are the watchmen guardian angels assigned to help the Bride? (Psalm 91:9-12) No, in a later dream, they strike her and take away her veil. (5:2-7) Are they evil people in her life? No, they couldn't be, for they are part of the security detail for the city. Are these observers of her life, who are disappointed with her wishy-washy behavior? Do they represent spiritual leaders and teachers of the Bride, who are to guard and guide believers, pray for them, and intercede on their behalf? Do a quick study of scripture about watchmen and decide. (2 Samuel 18:24-27, 2 Kings 9:17, Psalm 127:1, Ezekiel 3:17, 33:1-7, Jeremiah 6:17, Isaiah 21:6, 52:8-9, 56:10-11, 62:6, Hebrews 13:7, 17)

Him whom my soul loveth

The Bride realizes that none can take the place of Jesus in her heart. No one else can satisfy the longing of her soul. No fellowship, no companionship offers as sweet a joy as His.

Are you beginning to feel that way about your Bridegroom? Open your heart and thoughts to His love. Take some time to add to your love letter to Jesus.

Judy-3:4 *It was* **but a little that I passed from them, but I found him whom my soul loveth: I held him, and would not let him go, until I had brought him into my mother's house, and into the chamber of her that conceived me.**

I found him

Thankfully, in her dream, the maiden found him again. She held him this time and would not let him go. Our Beloved is the God of second chances and understands, so in patience, He waits, saying, "I love them that love me; and those that seek me early shall find me." (Proverbs 8:17)

Dixie-3:4 *It was* **but a little that I passed from them, but I found him whom my soul loveth: I held him, and would not let him go, until I had brought him into my mother's house, and into the chamber of her that conceived me.**

I passed from them

The maiden finally recognized the watchmen could not help her; this was a search she must do alone. The fervent desire to find him again brings her to the right place.

I found him

Notice the beloved was near his loved one, not in a far country, but close enough to be found, when she began seeking him. Remember, Solomon loves her deeply and is desirous of her being with him. At first, unrewarded in her dream-search, she discovers him after giving the watchmen a strong witness of her love for him. Like the maiden, the Bride of Christ is of those who diligently seek closeness with her Beloved. Jesus has never abandoned us; He never will. (Hebrews 11:6, 13:5)

Him whom my soul loveth

The fourth time in consecutive verses the maiden refers to her beloved as the one whom her soul loves. In the same way, the focus of the Bride of Christ is once more on her Beloved and not herself. Reunion with the Lord is always sweet. Although adamant in declaring her love, her behavior must match her passionate words.

I held him, and would not let him go

The Bride has realized by letting her fears mandate her refusal of His invitation (2:10,13), she has jeopardized her fellowship with Him. She reminds me of the account of Jacob wrestling with an angel, not with his puny physical strength, but with a strength of will and faith. In Genesis 32:26, Jacob says to the angel, "I will not let thee go, except thou bless me." To the Bride, Christ Jesus *is* the blessing, and she will not let go. Her passion for Him has intensified.

Brought him into my mother's house

The Shulamite has yet to come to grips with the main problem. She wants him, but still on her terms, not his. If she understood her problem, she could immediately have said to him, "O beloved, I am sorry I dismissed your gracious invitation to me. I was wrong to be afraid, wrong to send you away, wrong to want my own will. Please forgive me for not trusting you and give me another chance to go with you to conquer those mountains and hills." Believers must join in this maiden's confession when they make unwise decisions which do not reflect love or trust for the Lord.

Into the chamber of her that conceived me

The best bedroom suite in the palace would be a royal apartment for the honored guest, King Solomon. Yet the palace itself represents a safe place in the Shulamite's mind. Spiritually, this might represent the church, which should be a secure haven for the Bride to acknowledge her passion for the Lord. However, that is not where He asked her to go, and it does not announce her love for Him to the world. She isn't addressing the original problem. Isn't that familiar? When we've failed to respond rightly to the Lord, we want to be back in fellowship, but we try to ignore the problem that caused us to lose our fellowship in the beginning. It won't work.

Note that I said "loss of fellowship," not loss of salvation, because it is not about Christ as Savior, but Him as Lord of her life. The Bride will not lose her salvation by refusing to follow Him, but she can momentarily lose the closeness of their fellowship by a poor choice.

Depriving herself of joy and companionship with Him, sweet intimacy with the One Whom her soul loves, wakes her to her need of Him. Still afraid to throw off her fears of the new and unknown, the King's Bride must come to the place of trusting Him completely. Can she trust Him? Absolutely! Will she trust Him? Read on.

Judy-3:5 I charge you, O ye daughters of Jerusalem, by the roes, and by the hinds of the field, that ye stir not up, nor awake *my* love, till he please.

Waiting

Mentioning the roes and hinds of the field sounds like the Shulamite is still on ground level, not anxious to climb the mountain with her love. She tells the daughters of Jerusalem to back off, though still reluctant to give herself totally to her beloved.

I recognize her reluctance; I've gone through the same thing. The problem is trying to forget "… those things which are behind, and reaching forth…" to those better things that wait ahead. (Philippians 3:13-14) It all centers on making the right decision, not staying where we are, but going forward with Him.

Dixie-3:5 I charge you, O ye daughters of Jerusalem, by the roes, and by the hinds of the field, that ye stir not up, nor awake *my* love, till he please.

Roes and hinds

The roebuck is known for his strength and decision-making, and the hind for her grace and beauty. Both are climbers suited for the high places of the mountains. (Habakkuk 3:19) Christ and His Bride are destined for the high places, victory, and rulership.

Hinds of the field

I wonder if this phrase "hinds of the field" is an expression of the maiden's wish to stay in the flat land rather than attempting the higher reaches of the hills and mountains with Solomon? Do we want to stay in the valley when Christ our Beloved lovingly invites us to join Him on the mountaintops where victory is the norm?

Don't stir up love or awaken it

Here, the bride-to-be asks for no interference by her companions' words or plans in her unfolding relationship with her bridegroom. She wants love to develop and deepen naturally, without outside manipulation. This maiden loves him, but to a lesser degree than he does her. There is still a hesitation to trust him completely, without reservation. What will it take to make her let go of the familiar and give her the strength to answer the challenge of having an abundant life with him?

Judy-3:6 Who *is* this that cometh out of the wilderness like pillars of smoke, perfumed with myrrh and frankincense, with all powders of the merchant?

Like pillars of smoke

The coming of the king must have been quite a scene to behold. Imagine her surprise when the maiden found out it was her beloved Solomon. In the Old Testament, God usually appeared in a flame of fire. (Exodus 3:2) When a sacrifice was acceptable, God would send down fire to consume it. In Judges 13:2-24, after Manoah and his wife sought the Lord for the promise of a son, a flame consumed their offering; they fell on their faces. God had answered their prayer.

In Song of Solomon, this verse 6 and the following four verses describe the grand magnificence of King Solomon's procession and cause me to think of the song *I Can Only Imagine* composed by Bart Millard. His father had just died, and he wrote a song about what heaven would be like. He imagined seeing Jesus for the first time. Have you ever thought about when you will glimpse Jesus for the first time? What will it be like to see Him in all His glory? I often wonder how I would react, bowing while weeping for joy, or joyfully shouting my praise. Will I sing to Him or fall weak-kneed in humble adoration? Surely, in the presence of His splendor, I will shout a multitude of "Praise the Lord" and "Hallelujahs" to Him, my Redeemer, my gracious Lord and King.

Dixie-3:6 Who *is* this that cometh out of the wilderness like pillars of smoke, perfumed with myrrh and frankincense, with all powders of the merchant?

Who cometh

The scene has changed. Beginning with this verse and continuing through verse 11, Solomon comes as king in all his grandeur to marry her. Previously, she has known him as shepherd, teacher, and her beloved. Now she sees him anew with another peek at the greatness of his majesty. (2 Chronicles 9:1-28)

Wilderness

Symbolically, the wilderness sometimes represents the world, even the trials of life. This man has conquered them all. Previously, he'd come to her unassumingly; now, he comes in great glory.

Having enjoyed his wonderful company in a more casual way, she now must develop a respect and esteem for his authority and position of rulership.

Fulfilling prophecy, after the cross, Jesus Christ came forth from the tomb to enter heaven and be crowned victorious King by His Father. (Psalm 2:6-8, Hebrews 1, Isaiah 6:1-5) Christ has been given all power in heaven and in Earth. (Matthew 28:18) His Bride loves Him and respects His great position of authority. He is her Beloved, a Man of exquisite refinement, but He is sovereign King, too. His Bride should never take His love for granted or treat their relationship casually. She must always give honor and worship to Him. Her knee should be the first to bow to Him. Certainly her reverence and love for Him will influence others to do the same.

Judy-3:7-8 Behold his bed, which *is* Solomon's; threescore valiant men *are* about it, of the valiant of Israel. They all hold swords, *being* expert in war: every man *hath* his sword upon his thigh because of fear in the night.

The valiant

These sixty guards, surrounding their king, armed with swords, are the bravest and most heroic of Israel. They act in the same manner as the United States Secret Service would in protecting our president.

Dixie-3:7-8 Behold his bed, which *is* Solomon's; threescore valiant men *are* about it, of the valiant of Israel. They all hold swords, *being* expert in war: every man *hath* his sword upon his thigh because of fear in the night.

Bed

Here, we are told of a special, covered travel compartment specifically designed by Solomon. Camels carried smaller compartments. This one was larger and transported by a chariot, as verse 9 describes.

The valiant

Warriors of the highest caliber accompany it. They act as guardians of their king, reminiscent of the guardian angels of Psalm 91. "Because thou hast made the LORD, *which is* my refuge, *even* the most High, thy habitation; There shall no evil befall thee, neither shall any plague come nigh thy dwelling. For he shall give his angels charge over thee, to keep thee in all thy ways." (Psalm 91:9-11)

Threescore valiant men

These sixty elite warriors, properly equipped and trained, are ready to fight if necessary. Their swords are near, not stored away, not rusty with disuse. These strong men serve Solomon and are prepared to give their lives for his protection. His bride will be proffered that same kind of loyal and dedicated service.

In 2 Samuel 23:8-39, there is a description and list of the mighty men who followed Solomon's father, David, the second king of Israel. These trusted, stalwart men were the best of their peers. The first three, Adino, Eleazar, and Shammah, differed from the more than thirty others listed as mighty men, because they were not only strong, valiant men, but they had a heart for David their king, shown by the jeopardy and danger they risked to fulfill a wish of David's. (2 Samuel 23:13-17) The Bride of Christ must be the most valiant of all. She must have a heart for her King and be willing to risk all for Him.

Christ's Bride enjoys even greater protection than King Solomon's. Jesus promised that no one could take her from Him. "...I give unto them eternal life; and they shall never perish, neither shall any man pluck them out of my hand. My Father, which gave them me, is greater than all; and no *man* is able to pluck them out of my Father's hand." (John 10:28-29)

The Bride can say, "I will both lay me down in peace, and sleep: for thou, LORD, only makest me dwell in safety." (Psalm 4:8) She will replace worry with trust.

Expert in war

Spiritually, these warriors may represent angels and certain men and women appointed to leadership, mentorship, or as spiritual parents. God calls leaders to protect the church with prayer, the sword of the Word, and sacrificial love. (Titus 1:5, 2 Thessalonians 2:15, 2 Timothy 1:13, 4:2-5) A leader and defender of the faith must be strong, "holding fast the faithful word as he hath been taught, that he may be able by sound doctrine both to exhort and to convince the gainsayers. For there are many unruly and vain talkers and deceivers...whose mouths must be stopped, who subvert whole houses, teaching things which they ought not, for filthy [money's] sake." (Titus 1:9-11)

Fear in the night

This word "fear" means "a sudden alarm". These bodyguards were not afraid of the dark but were alert, even at night, ever mindful of any possibility of danger. The army of King Jesus can fight the powers of darkness and win. So, too, can His Bride. She will learn to be unafraid in the night or day, and alert to any danger. (Ephesians 6:12-13, 2 Corinthians 10:3-5, Luke 10:19, Matthew 12:28-29)

Meditation Seventeen: Pray to be a beautiful warrior Bride for your Beloved. Listen and cooperate with the Holy Spirit as He trains you each day. Memorize 2 Corinthians 3:18, then study Ephesians 4:13, 6:10-18.

Judy-3:9-10 King Solomon made himself a chariot of the wood of Lebanon. He made the pillars thereof *of* silver, the bottom thereof *of* gold, the covering of it *of* purple, the midst thereof being paved *with* love, for the daughters of Jerusalem.

Paved with love

King Solomon designed this conveyance for his bride and commanded it built to certain specifications; this would be their transport to Jerusalem after the wedding.

Every part of the chariot was significant. The pillars of silver represented redemption, the gold pictured his great love, and the canopy and draperies of purple signified royalty. How sumptuous and lavish the carriage prepared by her beloved! He wanted it perfect for her, so he spared no expense.

Christ is making preparations for His Bride, too. He said, "…I go to prepare a place for you…I will come again and receive you unto myself; that where I am, *there* ye may be also." (John 14:2-3) What Christ makes for His Bride will supersede anything Solomon had ever done by design and glory.

Dixie-3:9-10 King Solomon made himself a chariot of the wood of Lebanon. He made the pillars thereof *of* silver, the bottom thereof *of* gold, the covering of it *of* purple, the midst thereof being paved *with* love, for the daughters of Jerusalem.

Paved with love

Solomon was an architect and builder. (Ecclesiastes 2:4) He ordered this chariot built to his design, and named what materials were to be used, including wood from his bride's country, Lebanon, to honor her. Gold, silver, royal purple coverings—nothing was too expensive or too valuable to be utilized in the fabrication of this chariot planned for his bride's comfort in traveling from her home in Lebanon to Israel at the culmination of their wedding festivities.

The Shulamite must have felt very special when she and others saw such an extravagant display of Solomon's regard for her.

If a mortal man spared no expense for his bride, how much more would the Lord Jesus do for His Bride? He gave His life for us. How could we ever doubt His love and willingness to shower us with His grace? (Hebrews 4:16) Jesus has paved your journey with His love—perfect love, everlasting love, all-encompassing love, unfailing love. (Ephesians 3:17-19, Romans 8:35-39) This love brings His Presence, and protection, and much more. (Hebrews 13:5, Matthew 28:20, John 10:28-29)

Judy-3:11 Go forth, O ye daughters of Zion, and behold king Solomon with the crown wherewith his mother crowned him in the day of his espousals, and in the day of the gladness of his heart.

A day of gladness
"Sing praises to the LORD, which dwelleth in Zion: declare among the people his doings." (Psalm 9:11) King Solomon's mother, Bathsheba, gave him a crown when he got engaged to be married to his beloved. Now it's time for his wedding, a day of great rejoicing.

Go forth
The encouraging words are go forward. Don't turn back! Don't look back. "Go forth" is a commandment, which sounds like a new beginning.

Dixie-3:11 Go forth, O ye daughters of Zion, and behold king Solomon with the crown wherewith his mother crowned him in the day of his espousals, and in the day of the gladness of his heart.

Go forth, O ye daughters of Zion, and behold king Solomon
The time has come for the wedding, and with joy and eagerness, Solomon approaches her home in all his glory to show her honor and to make her his queen. His thoughts have dwelt on this auspicious day. He has planned and prepared, and now, finally, the long-awaited day has come. The bride is so excited when she realizes the King of Israel is in sight. She wants her companions to see her beloved in all his grandeur.

Are you looking forward to Jesus' return for you? If not, ask the Holy Spirit to change your attitude. I had to do this very thing many years ago. (Titus 2:13-14, 2 Timothy 4:8, 1 Peter 1:7)

Daughters of Zion
Why does she switch from "daughters of Jerusalem" to "daughters of Zion" in this verse? Jerusalem speaks to a natural or human reference; Zion refers to the spiritual and heavenly connection. (Hebrews 12:22-24)

Psalm 125:1 explains her hope and prayer for these companions: "They that trust in the LORD *shall be* as mount Zion, *which* cannot be removed, *but* abideth for ever." Her prayer is answered in later chapters.

The Bride will be one to show the Jewish people the truth of Jesus of Nazareth as Messiah through her intimate and powerful relationship with Him. (Romans 11:11) "O that they were wise, *that* they understood this, *that* they would consider their latter end!" (Deuteronomy 32:29) In a future time of great tribulation, a faithful-to-God Jewish remnant who live through that terrible time will acknowledge Jesus as Messiah and King.

They will accept the opportunity to enter into a new covenant with Him. (Ezekiel 20:33-44, Hebrews 8:7-12, 9:1-15) They will in truth become the daughters of Zion!

At His birth, wise men came to Jerusalem asking, "Where is he that is born King of the Jews?" (Matthew 2:2) Pilate acknowledged Jesus as King of the Jews at Calvary. (Matthew 27:37) His Father made Him King of heaven and Earth, which makes Him King of kings (men) and Lord of lords (angels). (Psalm 2:6, Matthew 28:18, 1 Timothy 6:15)

Why is seeing Him as King so important? If people claim Him as Savior, they may feel thankful, but will feel little impetus to serve Him as Lord. They stay soulish, as the Corinthian church did for a time. When believers not only acknowledge Him as Lord and King, but embrace His sovereignty over them, they bow their knee and obey Him as faithful subjects from a heart of love for Him. (Philippians 2:9-16) This is another example of the comparison between the body of Christ and His Bride.

Behold

The definition of this word implies an earnest intent, serious contemplation, careful observation with a desire to learn lessons of faith. The Bible gives four very important commands regarding this word:

- **Behold the Lamb** through His death. He is your Savior; receive Him. (John 1:29, 36, Revelation 13:8, 1 Peter 1:18-19)
- **Behold the Man** through His life. He is your example; follow Him. (John 19:5, Psalm 63:8, John 10:27, 1 Peter 2:21)
- **Behold the Bridegroom** through His love. Give yourself to Him completely; be one with Him. (Matthew 25:6, 2 Timothy 4:8)
- **Behold the King** through His magnificence. Crown Jesus Christ as the Ruler in your life; bow down, love, worship, and serve Him. (Matthew 21:5, John 19:14) Our Beloved King is worthy. Meditate on Him. (Psalm 2:6-8, 45:1-17) His beauty is matchless, His speech gracious. He is mighty, glorious, and majestic...think on Him in His splendor. Truth, meekness, and righteousness are part of His character. Reflect on Him as King of

kings, for He is exalted above all. (Psalm 45:6-7) Behold Him: your Lamb, your example, your Bridegroom, your King. He is indescribably wonderful and powerful, and He loves you and wants you for His Bride…praise Him!

Meditation Eighteen: Spend a few minutes each day meditating on a different one of these four characteristics: Lamb of God, Man of God, Bridegroom, and King

CHAPTER 4 (4: 1-16)

Judy-4:1 Behold, thou *art* fair, my love; behold, thou *art* fair; thou *hast* doves' eyes within thy locks: thy hair *is* as a flock of goats, that appear from mount Gilead.

Thou art fair

On their wedding night, before their union is consummated, he woos her with loving words. The words, *behold thou art fair*, are repeated twice. It's a declaration. Solomon wants her to take a good look at herself, as if to say, "Catch a glimpse of the loveliness I see."

Doves' eyes

The dove is the symbol of the Holy Spirit and represents peace. Eyes also symbolize spiritual discernment. Solomon describes her as having "doves' eyes"; they are the window to her soul. He loves them because of what they tell him about her.

Thy hair

To him, her hair is like a flock of goats moving down the slopes of Mount Gilead. Spiritually, shining tresses suggest beauty of thoughts and conduct of a godly person, even "…a meek and quiet spirit, which is in the sight of God is of great price." (1 Peter 3:4)

Dixie-4:1 Behold, thou *art* fair, my love; behold, thou *art* fair; thou *hast* doves' eyes within thy locks: thy hair *is* as a flock of goats, that appear from mount Gilead.

Cherished

Ephesians 5:25-29 states that the Lord loves, nourishes, and cherishes His Bride. Nourish is to sustain with substances necessary to life and growth. Cherish means to hold dear. In chapter 4 of the Song of Solomon, verses 1-7, the reader gets a broader understanding of the Beloved's extraordinary love and His passion for His Bride.

Verse 1 begins a passage outlining seven spiritual graces of Christ's Bride, pictured by seven physical aspects of the Shulamite bride. They are her eyes, hair, teeth, lips, temples, neck, and breasts, each one an essential and vital part of that which makes up the Bride of Christ. Each represents a spiritual attribute which pleases the Beloved.

Behold, thou art fair, my love

This part of the Song of Solomon commences with the king's expression of her beauty to him. Instead of recriminations for her previous lack of trust, Solomon speaks from his heart of love. Rather than berating her for past behavior, he gently encourages her with sweet words. She is his and is to be treated with respect and honor, paving the way for love to effect the change he desires in her. He doesn't pressure her and is willing to be patient in the continued courtship of his bride.

Solomon focuses on what will build confidence in her and their relationship. His judgment is according to truth; these sweet words are not empty flattery, but how he truly sees her. His gracious words become food for her soul. He knows her potential. At times, she still views herself as unlovely (1:6), so she needs to hear his appreciation for her, and he is lavish in his praise.

To Christ, His Bride, even with weaknesses, is still beautiful. Knowing praise is an important part of courtship, He tells her how lovely she is and attributes to her the beauty of holiness.

Doves' eyes

This verse speaks of the Bride's single-mindedness toward her Beloved, a focus on Him. She isn't fickle, looking at others as if there might be a better choice around the corner. Her eyes are toward the Lord. (Psalm 25:15) She looks at Him as if there is no other, and there isn't for her. He is the best she could have ever found. Keeping her focus on Him brings her joy and peace, and her loyalty delights Him.(Philippians 3:7-8, Romans 15:13, Isaiah 26:3)

Doves' eyes within thy locks

This may imply her spiritual sight is veiled somewhat, as the following two verses state: For now "we see through a glass, darkly; but then face to face: now I know in part; but then shall I know even as also I am known." "Beloved, now are we the sons of God, and it doth not yet appear what we shall be: but we know that, when he shall appear, we shall be like him; for we shall see him as he is." (1 Corinthians 13:12, 1 John 3:2*)*

Our increase in faith, responsiveness, and obedience all hinge to some extent on our spiritual eyes. Being able to see clearly in the Spirit—to picture things from heaven's point of view— is very important. The more we see, the more we will rest, rely, and trust Him. We will begin to work *from* victory rather than *for* victory.

Seeing starts with the written Word of God, as well as listening to the Holy Spirit. "Open thou mine eyes, that I may behold wondrous things out of thy law [Word]." (Psalm 119:18) Part of the Messiah's commission was to open blind eyes, not only for salvation, but also in the process of growing in faith after the profession of salvation. (Isaiah 42:7) Remember the two disciples walking with the resurrected Jesus on the road to Emmaus? He opened their understanding concerning Himself through the Old Testament Scriptures. (Luke 24:27, 44-45) The apostle Paul was later sent with the same commission in Acts 26:18.

Judy-4:2 Thy teeth *are* like a flock *of sheep that are even* shorn, which came up from the washing; whereof every one bear twins, and none *is* barren among them.

Teeth

Her teeth are beautiful, and none are missing. She is mature and strong enough to take in the Word of God as spiritual food and allow it to guide her and change her life. Scripture tells us, "… man doth not live by bread only, but by every *word* that proceedeth out of the mouth of the LORD…" (Deuteronomy 8:3) The Word of God is the bread of life, and we must eat it daily. We are to bite off a portion and chew it to the point of understanding and being nourished by it. We start with the milk; next comes the bread of the Word, and then we progress to the meat—the more challenging topics. Paul wrote to the Corinthians, "I gave you milk, not solid food, for you were not yet ready for it." (1 Corinthians 3:2 NIV)

The writer of Hebrews penned,"In fact, though by this time you ought to be teachers, you need someone to teach you the elementary truths of God's word all over again. You need milk, not solid food!" " But solid food is for the mature, who by constant use have trained themselves to distinguish good from evil." (Hebrews 5:12,14 NIV**)**

Dixie-4:2 Thy teeth *are* like a flock *of sheep that are even* shorn, which came up from the washing; whereof every one bear twins, and none *is* barren among them.

Thy teeth

Bad teeth might indicate poor care, digestion problems, infections, etc. In that culture and ours, healthy teeth are very crucial. Solomon makes many comments on the beauty and excellent condition of his bride's teeth.

Spiritually, the ability to chew and digest the Word of God is crucial. Seemingly, an increasing number of Christians had poor teeth, a metaphor used in Hebrews 5:11-14 to describe those who neglected their spiritual growth.

As a flock of sheep

Has anyone ever been scared of the teeth of a sheep? Probably not. Sheep don't awaken fear in people, but the same cannot be said of those who serve the devil by persecuting the innocent, or of false prophets who act like wolves in sheep's clothing seeking to devour God's people. (Psalm 7:1-2, Matthew 7:15) The teeth of the enemy are alluded to in 1 Peter 5:8-9: "Be sober, be vigilant; because your adversary the devil, as a roaring lion, walketh about, seeking whom he may devour."

Up from washing

Solomon notes how she's changed, and for the better, in contrast to her statements in chapter 1 about self-neglect and development. Being loved by him and being with him have made a difference.

The Bride is settled; her eyes are on her Beloved. Her discernment comes from the ability to digest the Word. These have given her confidence. She has studied to show herself "…approved unto God, a workman that needeth not to be ashamed, rightly dividing the word of truth." (2 Timothy 2:15) Her concentration on His words, and her focus on Him are two of the many things that make her beautiful in His eyes.

Judy-4:3 Thy lips *are* like a thread of scarlet, and thy speech *is* comely: thy temples *are* like a piece of a pomegranate within thy locks.

Lips

The Shulamite's lips are thin and red. What makes them beautiful are the words that come out of her mouth. She's careful to guard her words because they are the meditation of her heart. (Psalm 19:14) The temples enclose the mind, and it's the thoughts from her heart that her lips reveal. Scripture tells us that people speak out of the treasure of their hearts. (Luke 6:45) "Set a watch, O LORD, before my mouth; keep the door of my lips." (Psalm 141:3 See also Proverbs 21:23, 23:7)

Dixie-4:3 Thy lips *are* like a thread of scarlet, and thy speech *is* comely: thy temples *are* like a piece of a pomegranate within thy locks.

Lips

The maiden's loveliness is matched by the beauty of her heart. Solomon loves the gracious way she speaks to others. It reminds me of the description of a "perfect" or spiritually mature person in the book of James, where one with superior control of their words, not using them for cursing but for blessing and sweetness, applies wisdom from heaven. (James 3:17-18)

A thread of scarlet

Historically, this scarlet thread provided a way of escape for two Hebrew soldiers sent by their commander, Joshua, to spy out the Jericho area. (Joshua 2) The red cord was supplied by a Canaanite woman, Rahab, who saved the lives of the scouts. In return, the men gave her the means of saving her family from ruin by telling her to display that same scarlet rope in the window of her dwelling. The scarlet cord became her and her family's shield of protection from the destruction soon to come upon the city of Jericho. (Joshua 2:15, 18, 21, 6:17, 25)

Rahab's actions were based on her knowledge of what people had told her about the power of the God of the Hebrews, shown forty years before at the Red Sea and thereafter. (Joshua 2:9-13) In the passage of time, she had not forgotten it. Rahab believed the word which had come to her.

Have you ever met someone who talked incessantly about unimportant things as if every detail was crucial? The Shulamite was the complete opposite of that in character and judgment. Solomon describes his love as having restraint in her conversation, not needing to be in the spotlight at all times. He admires her humility and discretion.

The Bride of Christ will speak in the same way as Jesus, referenced in John 8:26: "...I speak to the world those things which I have heard [from the one who sent me]." (BRG) This is the thread of scarlet: words of life, salvation, protection, healing, comfort, grace, mercy, and more. When we speak or write to others about Jesus and the plan of redemption, we provide a scarlet cord, a way of escape, to those who are headed for destruction. (Matthew 7:13-14, John 14:6) Like Rahab, if they believe the Word of God, they can be saved by the "scarlet thread" of His holy blood in receiving the good news of Jesus Christ and the salvation and eternal life offered through Him.

Thy speech is comely

This maiden has learned the lesson of guarding her speech. Her words have delighted Solomon. His bride censors her speech by wisdom, as the psalmist wrote in Psalm 39:1, "I said, I will take heed to my ways, that I sin not with my tongue: I will keep my mouth with a bridle..." She is a pleasure to hear. Her words are lovely, kind, and generous. What a contrast to the speech of the ungodly, as described in Psalm 140:3 as a dangerous serpent's poison! The Shulamite has learned to guard her tongue and be wise in her speech.

If the Lord Jesus were describing you, would "lovely speech" be a characteristic for which He could commend you?

Thy temples

Like the maiden, the Bride's temples house her thoughts. Naturally, these would be precious to Jesus. His praise reveals He knows her heart. His compliment also shows He is a good listener and one who has enjoyed their conversations. In knowing your thoughts and conversations, could the Beloved praise you?

The Bride also pursues the habit of listening carefully to her Beloved. Her response: "I will hear what God the LORD will speak..." (Psalm 85:8) I will hear with understanding. I know... "faith *cometh* by hearing, and hearing by the word of God." (Romans 10:17) "...and those who hear will live." (John 5:25 ESV)
Those who are of God hear God's words. (John 8:47) The Beloved is delighted and blessed when we listen carefully to Him, trusting His every Word.

A piece of pomegranate

A *piece* of pomegranate suggests the fruit has been cut open. This phrase alludes to the Bride's candidness and open communication with the Lord Jesus. He likes that quality in her. She has shared her thoughts with her Beloved and doesn't try to hide them from Him. Intuitively, she knows this is an integral part in their relationship's growth. (Psalm 3:1-5)

A pomegranate is a fruit that contains hundreds of edible seeds, hence a reference to her many good thoughts. Philippians 4:8 has long been a Christian's guideline for thoughts—things that are truth, honesty, justice, purity, loveliness, excellence, worthiness, and blessing. Before we speak, we must get in the habit of evaluating our thoughts by quickly measuring them against Philippians 4:8. It's one way of taking thoughts captive and controlling their possible consequences. (2 Corinthians 10:5)

Judy-4:4 Thy neck *is* like the tower of David [built] for an armoury, whereon there hang a thousand bucklers, all shields of mighty men.

Tower of David

King David's tower housed a thousand shields of his mighty warriors. With this thought, Solomon is struck by his bride's increasing strength of character and purpose.

The Bride of Christ is to have wisdom and discernment and not let either slip, because they give life to her soul and grace to her neck. (Proverbs 3:21-22) They increase her spiritual beauty and, in turn, bring glory to God. The apostle Paul had wisdom and discernment, too, and served the Lord Jesus with humility of mind. He was a tower of strength to whomever he witnessed. Paul endeavored to live his life with joy and testify of the gospel of God as long as he had breath. (1 Thessalonians 2:2)

The opposite of being a strong tower is being stiff-necked. (Exodus 32:9) An example of this is the generation that came out of Egypt with the opportunity to enter the Promised Land. Due to their rebellion and unbelief, they died in the desert and lost the reward that faith would have brought them. (Hebrews 3:8-19) The older ones missed out on all that God had prepared for them. (Numbers 13-14:38) Instead, the younger generation was allowed to go into the Promised Land, where grapes were so heavy it took two men to carry one bunch. (Numbers 13:27) The Bride must be careful not to become stiff-necked in her relationship with her Beloved.

Dixie-4:4 Thy neck *is* like the tower of David [built] for an armoury, whereon there hang a thousand bucklers, all shields of mighty men.

Thy neck

What an amazing description for Solomon to make! We would not have described the Shulamite that way. We would have dwelt on her failures, weaknesses, and how her trust didn't measure up. Her beloved sees her strengths and successes, knowing improvement will eventually come.

Christ views His Bride, not in her failures and weaknesses, although He is well aware of them, but sees her with eyes of love, dwelling on her positives and loveliness, as she learns to trust Him.

The Lord recently taught me a lesson about this. Several times, I heard different people question, "Is the glass half full or half empty?" Eventually, I asked the Lord how I should look at things in this world, with the eyes of realism or with a more optimistic view. He showed me that half full viewpoint springs from an attitude of thankfulness for what you have enjoyed and still have. It is also one of hope that what you have left will be enough for your need until the expectation of more is fulfilled. The half empty view does not promote thankfulness and will disintegrate into complaining, murmuring, moroseness, and hopelessness, given time. (Exodus 16:1-2, 7, Numbers 14:26-27, Philippians 2:14-16)

Our Beloved Jesus is so excellent in that He sees our potential. He knows time will bring about our maturity, and patiently encourages us in that endeavor with His words.

Built for an armoury

An armory is a storehouse for weapons and military equipment. If Solomon had described the armory as empty, we would know in a manner of speaking, his bride was unprepared and lacking in what it took to win victories in the battles of life. Still, there is no drooping head bowed down in defeat, no discouragement or beaten demeanor in his description of her. He says she is well-equipped to handle any attack of the enemy and has been victorious already! He compares the quality of her fortitude to those who had fought battles and won, applying such terms as tower, armory, shields, and mighty, to speak of her strength of purpose and will. Perhaps you don't see that in her. Maybe she doesn't either, but Solomon does.

Christ gives a similar commendation, earned by His Bride's pursuit to re-establish their fellowship and closeness. She chases after Him, unwilling to continue without Him. She knows what she needs—Him above all others. She's won the battle over her fears and lack of trust. Now her will is steadfast like a tower, immovable under the banner of *Thy will be done,* no matter what that entails.

Judy-4:5 Thy two breasts *are* like two young roes that are twins, which feed among the lilies.

Thy breasts

Breasts represent the capacity to feed and nourish others. Solomon sees his lovely maiden as able to help his people, including the daughters of Jerusalem, with those things which will strengthen them.

The Bride of Christ has learned the Word of God and continues to add to her knowledge. She will increase in wisdom, gain inner strength, and reach a mature point of being able to cheer others with words of faith and encouragement. (1 Timothy 4:6)

Dixie–4:5 Thy two breasts *are* like two young roes that are twins, which feed among the lilies.

Two

The use of the female breast is two-fold: for the couple's pleasure, and to nourish the offspring produced from their pleasure. The nourishment provided is to supply little ones who cannot feed themselves. Spiritually, Christ views His Bride as one who will teach spiritual truths to those new in the faith. (2 Timothy 2:1-3, Hebrews 5:12)

In this verse we find a powerful emphasis on the words "two" and "twins." This then leads to the question applicable to the spiritual realm: what "two" would the Bride have to nourish and feed others? Indeed, we might suggest the Word of God, given in two sections, the Old and New Testaments. It is so important for believers to know and study all of the Word so they can provide the life-sustaining spiritual milk from on high to those who desire to grow in the Lord or those who are malnourished, not even knowing what they need. Those who neglect the study of the Old Testament forget that *all* Scripture is given for our instruction. (2 Timothy 3:16) "…whatsoever things were written aforetime were written for our learning, that we through patience and comfort of the scriptures might have hope." (Romans 15:4)

Knowledge stimulates expectation. Hope in the hearts of the Hebrew people of Old Testament times was fostered by the Scriptures and teachings they had received concerning the character, advent, and future events of the coming Messiah of Israel and the world. (Luke 1:70, John 1:41, 45, Romans 1:1-6, John 5:39, Luke 24:25-27, 44-45) Another reason we have the Old Testament is to give us wisdom: "Now all these things happened unto them for ensamples: and they are written for our admonition, upon whom the ends of the world are come." (1 Corinthians 10:11)

Another possibility to consider is the phrase "two breasts" may represent the graces of faith and love, without which the Bride cannot be a true partner of her Bridegroom. These graces work together, as seen in the following verses. "…in Jesus Christ neither circumcision nor uncircumcision avails anything, but faith working through love." (Galatians 5:6 NKJV) "Now the purpose of the commandment is love from a pure heart, *from* a good conscience, and *from* sincere faith…" (1 Timothy 1:5 NKJV)

The apostle Paul wrote: "I thank my God, making mention of thee always in my prayers, hearing of thy love and faith, which thou hast toward the Lord Jesus, and toward all saints." (Philemon 4-5) "Wherefore I also, after I heard of your faith in the Lord Jesus, and love unto all the saints, cease not to give thanks for you, making mention of you in my prayers…" (Ephesians 1:15-16)

It's also possible for the two breasts to represent grace and truth, the same qualities Jesus brought to mankind. (John 1:17) No matter if this explanation is correct, or some combination of others previously mentioned, the Bride has plenty to give and is thoroughly equipped to join Christ in His tending of the lilies, those people who need His gentle care.

Judy-4:6 Until the day break, and the shadows flee away, I will get me to the mountain of myrrh, and to the hill of frankincense.

Until the day break

The loving couple is finally married: "…for this cause shall a man leave father and mother, and shall cleave to his wife: and they twain shall be one flesh…" "…wherefore they are no more twain, but one flesh. What, therefore, God hath joined together, let not man put asunder." (Matthew 19:5-6, Genesis 2:24)) The bridegroom doesn't want anything or anyone to come between them on their wedding night, so he might say, "Leave us undisturbed until the morning."

Jesus says the same thing to us. He wants to be first in our lives. "If any *man* come to me, and hate not his father, and mother, and wife, and children, and brethren, and sisters, yea, and his own life also, he cannot be my disciple." (Luke 14:26) Like any loving and devoted husband who cherishes his wife, the Beloved would say, "…I am jealous over you with godly jealousy…" (2 Corinthians 11:2) He doesn't want anything to come between Him and us. His Bride's mutual love responds, "Cause me to hear thy lovingkindness in the morning; for in thee do I trust: cause me to know the way wherein I should walk; for I lift up my soul unto thee." (Psalm 143:8)

Dixie-4:6 Until the day break, and the shadows flee away, I will get me to the mountain of myrrh, and to the hill of frankincense.

Until the day break

These phrases suggest the king eagerly looks forward to their wedding night and the consummation of their union. To be one with her is his desire. He has expressed kindness in his gracious words to her. With some ups and downs in their relationship, he hasn't given up on her. Love doesn't falter; love holds on. Love never fails. (1 Corinthians 13:8)

What a beautiful picture of Christ's passionate desire to have an ardent relationship with His own, to be one with His Bride! His love for us has never changed but has been ever constant as He waited for our love for Him to thrive and mature.

Mount of myrrh...hill of frankincense

Myrrh is a bitter substance; frankincense gives off a sweet fragrance. What did Solomon mean by putting the bitter and the sweet together? He understands that his love for his bride is at a greater level than hers, but he has the expectation that love will continue to grow. In the past, fears have blocked the full expression of her love, but he has not been discouraged. He is willing to give her more time to develop a deeper love for him. His love does not wane; his faithfulness to her is without exception; his patience extraordinary! Does this love Solomon has for his bride speak to you of the vast and unfailing love of Jesus?

In your spirit, do you feel the Lord's gentle arms around you? Do you hear His voice, whispering His sweet comfort to you? He wants you to sense His tenderness toward you. Do you realize that all the goodness in your whole life, all the kindness, and all the genuine expressions of love from other people were sent to you from Jesus? It was always Him, loving you. You are truly, passionately, eternally loved, and beautiful in His eyes.

You've had His attention from before the beginning of time. When the Word of God offered Himself to do His Father's will before the world began, He knew you would be the prize for His obedience. (John 1:1, Hebrews 12:2, Psalm 2:8, Isaiah 53:10) Even then, He loved you and eagerly awaited your coming to Him. (Revelation 1:5, 3:9) He rejoices in you and your growing relationship with Him. What pleasure it gives Him when you believe!

Judy-4:7 Thou *art* all fair, my love; *there is* no spot in thee.

All fair

In the previous verses, the bridegroom talked about how beautiful the maiden was and how he looked forward to their becoming one. Now, their day has arrived; the moment is upon them, and his joy is evident as he views her glory. Heaven sets the standard for marriage. God told Adam it was not good for man to live alone, so He made woman—a helpmate so the couple could enjoy life and work together. (Genesis 2:18) ç says: "*Whoso* findeth a wife findeth a good *thing,* and obtaineth favor of the LORD." In Ecclesiastes 4:9-11, Solomon wrote: "Two *are* better than one; because they have a good reward for their labor. For if they fall, the one will lift up his fellow: but woe to him *that is* alone when he falleth; for *he hath* not another to help him up. Again, if two they lie together, then they have heat: but how can one be warm *alone*?"

There's strength in being united, but the greatest sense of oneness is found in unity with God. "…If anyone loves Me, he will keep My word; and My Father will love him, and We will come to him and make Our home with him." (John 14:23 NKJV)

As on any wedding day, there's great anticipation of the groom seeing the bride in her wedding dress. The Bride of Christ is no exception, as Isaiah 61:10 expresses. "I will greatly rejoice in the LORD, my soul shall be joyful in my God; for he hath clothed me with the garments of salvation, he hath covered me with the robe of righteousness, as a bridegroom decketh *himself* with ornaments, and as a bride adorneth *herself* with her jewels."

Dixie-4:7 Thou *art* all fair, my love; *there is* no spot in thee.

No spot

Christ speaks so sweetly to His Bride. How lovely He is in His behavior toward her, and His patience is amazing. "…Christ…loved the church, and gave himself for it; that he might sanctify and cleanse it with the washing of water by the word, that he might present it to himself a glorious church, not having spot, or wrinkle, or any such thing; but that it should be holy and without blemish." (Ephesians 5:25-27) "…You…now hath he reconciled In the body of his flesh through death, to present you holy and unblameable and unreproveable in his sight." (Colossians 1:21-22) How do a blemish, spot, and wrinkle differ? A blemish comes from within the person; a spot occurs with a close brush from the world or environment around you; a wrinkle is from carelessness.

Christ's loving and lovely words are a picture of His character. He isn't waiting to pounce on us, nor is He eager to criticize. We do Him a terrible disservice when we assign a condemnatory attitude to Him. At this point in our development, He doesn't expect flawlessness. He is pleased with what progress has occurred. He understands the power of encouragement and how it can motivate. The Lord Jesus enjoys telling us how much He loves us. A friend from church related how she had heard the Lord sing to her several times a few lines of the song, *Have I Told You Lately That I Love You?*

Meditation Nineteen: Have you ever sung a song specifically to the Lord Jesus? Think of your Beloved; ask the Holy Spirit to bring a song for Jesus to your mind. Sing it to Him.

Judy-4:8 Come with me from Lebanon, *my* spouse, with me from Lebanon: look from the top of Amana, from the top of Shenir and Hermon, from the lions' dens, from the mountains of the leopards.

A repeated invitation

Solomon invites the maiden again to the heights of the mountains and to cross over them to his home in Israel. (2:10) This time, she says, "Yes." She trusts him more now and is confident that he has her best interest at heart.

Not long ago, my husband invited me to ride to the top of Lookout Mountain, just across the Tennessee southern border from Chattanooga. It wasn't as lofty as the mountains mentioned in this verse, but it was wonderful! High enough to feel the change, the air was light, breezy, and pollution-free. We were far enough away from the house not to be concerned about housework or the gardening awaiting us. Suddenly, the only thing that really mattered was enjoying our time together. That's how it is when we turn our eyes upon Jesus and look fully into His wonderful face, putting our trust completely in Him. Our priorities take new order, and problems take their rightful place.

Meditation Twenty: Whatever trial or difficulty you have right now, look down on each as if you are in heaven and viewing it from that perspective. What is the bigger picture the Lord wants you to see? In your notes, write what the Holy Spirit shows you. (Romans 8:28, Ephesians 2:6-7, Colossians 3:2)

Dixie-4:8 Come with me from Lebanon, *my* spouse, with me from Lebanon: look from the top of Amana, from the top of Shenir and Hermon, from the lions' dens, from the mountains of the leopards.

From Lebanon

Solomon was quite familiar with Lebanon. He had good relations with Hiram, the king of Tyre, who supplied the cedar for Solomon's building program in exchange for wheat and oil. (1 Kings 5:1-11, 10:17, 21) The Shulamite maiden may have been King Hiram's granddaughter. (Song of Solomon 7:1)

Amana...Shenir and Hermon

These are mountains in the range which borders Israel and Lebanon. Amana overlooks Damascus, Syria; Shenir and Hermon seem to be two peaks on the same mountain. (Deuteronomy 3:9) Although lions have disappeared, leopards are still known to roam the area today. In Scripture, Mount Hermon is equated with a place of unity and blessing. (Psalm 133)

Judy-4:9-12 Thou hast ravished my heart, my sister, *my* spouse; thou hast ravished my heart with one of thine eyes, with one chain of thy neck. How fair is thy love, my sister, *my* spouse! how much better is thy love than wine! and the smell of thine ointments than all spices! Thy lips, O *my* spouse, drop *as* the honeycomb: honey and milk *are* under thy tongue; and the smell *of* thy garments *is* like the smell of Lebanon. A garden inclosed *is* my sister, *my* spouse; a spring shut up, a fountain sealed.

Thou hast ravished my heart

Twice, Solomon says she has ravished his heart. He's filled with joy at her loveliness as he gazes into her eyes, and even looking at one link in the chain around her neck stirs his heart. He's still telling her of her beauty and longs for them to be even closer. What she doesn't understand is that with him she can be much more than she is without him.

How much better is thy love than wine

1 Corinthians 13:4-7 (NKJV) describes true love. "Love suffers long *and* is kind; love does not envy; love does not parade itself, is not puffed up; does not behave rudely, does not seek its own, is not provoked, thinks no evil; does not rejoice in iniquity, but rejoices in the truth…" Solomon is saying that her love is better than wine, sweeter than the smell of spices and like milk and honey. What could be sweeter or more comforting to his heart than her love?

Thy lips drop as the honeycomb

"Let the words of my mouth, and the meditation of my heart, be acceptable in thy sight, O LORD, my strength and my redeemer." (Psalm 19:14) How important it is to follow the Holy Spirit's leading so the Word goes out for its intended purpose and doesn't return void. Proverbs 25:25 says, "As cold waters to a thirsty soul, so *is* good news from a far country." God's Word is always refreshment to a hurting soul.

A spring shut up

Solomon describes his bride as a spring shut up and a fountain sealed. A closed spring or a fountain sealed doesn't provide refreshment to anyone. The water would eventually become stagnant.

With Christ, the Bride will be as if she is a fountain full of living water, a steadily flowing stream from the Holy Spirit. "He that believeth on me, as the Scripture hath said, out of his belly shall flow rivers of living water." (John 7:38, see also Psalm 78:16) Presently ministering to only a few, she, exemplifying a sweet spirit of Christ, will become a blessing to all those with whom she comes in contact. (2 Corinthians 2:15)

Dixie-4:9 Thou hast ravished my heart, my sister, *my* spouse; thou hast ravished my heart with one of thine eyes, with one chain of thy neck.

Thou hast ravished my heart

The maiden's agreement to cross the mountains and go with Solomon to his home brings delight beyond measure. She has put away her fears and replaced them with trust. A full and unreserved commitment of her heart and life to Solomon brings forth a joyful, exuberant response, seen in this verse and those to follow. The decision to take her place at his side, fully his partner, elicits a passionate response of words from him as to how pleased he is. Can you imagine the joy of the Lord when we give ourselves wholly to Him without any reservation?

The Hebrew word for "ravished" means "to be enclosed." Solomon feels wrapped in her love, which the next verse conveys. The twice-spoken "thou hast ravished my heart" pictures the king's joy in her transformation. Sweet words from one who truly loves have more power to effect change than harsh, condemning speech. (Proverbs 16:24, Psalm 119:103) Like Solomon, Christ uses passionate words to express how constant, deep, and abiding His love is for His Bride. He is so expressive in His love for her. She has His heart. She is His peculiar treasure, valued and cherished. What joy we should have, what confidence this knowledge should instill in us!

"He also brought me out into a broad place…He delighted in me." (Psalm 18:19 NKJV) Sometimes we have difficulty understanding and believing that the Lord Jesus is delighted with us. He is entranced with His Bride, her acceptance of His love, and her trust. It is good for her to understand how much her trust pleases Him. Trust is one of the greatest expressions of our love for the Lord Jesus.

with thine eye…one chain of thy neck

"Eye" refers to spiritual vision, and "neck" speaks of the will. Solomon longs to be as close to her as that chain; Solomon revels in his bride's increased wisdom, for she now sees as he sees and desires what he wants. She is aligned with his vision and plan for their future. In one accord and singular purpose, she has one principal goal—to be with him. She has changed considerably in maturity. Christ, too, is much pleased with the one who looks to Him alone and has eyes for no other. (Matthew 6:22) Jesus longs for intimate oneness with His Bride. The heart of Christ is filled with joy when this happens.

My sister, my spouse

Christian couples can have the same type of relationship. In spirit, the wife is a sister-in-Christ to her believer husband; physically, she is his spouse. Dual titles are given to the Bride: sister, in the fact that she has been adopted into the family of God, and spouse, in that she is pledged to Him as His Bride. "For whosoever shall do the will of my Father which is in heaven, the same is my brother, and sister, and mother." (Matthew 12:50)

Men and women who passionately love the Lord Jesus, put Him on the throne of their daily lives and first in their considerations, are a part of this Bride of Christ who has ravished His heart with their trust and adoration.

Dixie-4:10 How fair is thy love, my sister, *my* spouse! how much better is thy love than wine! and the smell of thine ointments than all spices!

My sister, my spouse

Here Solomon repeats "my sister, my spouse." By this, he commends her doubly for loving the same things he loves.

By doing the will of her Beloved Christ, while seeking to develop their relationship of love, the Bride displays new choices. What joy for both of them! How wondrous when two people are one in love and principle, one also in purpose. Together, they can accomplish great things. "Verily, verily, I say unto you, He that believeth on me, the works that I do shall he do also; and greater works than these shall he do…" (John 14:12)

Much better is thy love than wine

In chapter 1 verse 2 of Song of Solomon, she says his love is better than wine; here Solomon returns the compliment. The comparisons he uses in this verse speak of his wholehearted devotion. Her love is better than the life-sustaining drink of the desert and the commemorative drink of celebration. Even her distinctive perfume is better than all others. Solomon's lavish compliments are evidence of his forgiveness for her prior shortcomings and the restoration of their fellowship. He has not failed to encourage, bless, cherish, and love her. There have been no railings, no browbeating, and no accusations from him. He refers to her as his spouse, even though the consummation of the marriage has not yet taken place. She is his true love forever, and he greatly desires her. Apply Solomon's words and delight in his bride to Jesus. See in Him everything you could desire for your future.

Christ desires our love more than any service we could render. Some Christians think the opposite, but 1 Corinthians 13:3 (NKJV) says differently: "…though I bestow all my goods to feed *the poor*, and though I give my body to be burned, but have not love, it profits me nothing."

Dixie-4:11 Thy lips, O *my* spouse, drop *as* the honeycomb: honey and milk *are* under thy tongue; and the smell of thy garments *is* like the smell of Lebanon.

Honey and milk

These two substances are sweet and nourishing to the partaker. "…desire the sincere milk of the word, that ye may grow thereby." (1 Peter 2:2) The maiden's lips give forth gracious words which edify and nourish: "Pleasant words *are as* an honeycomb, sweet to the soul, and health to the bones." (Proverbs 16:24)

The smell of thy garments

His garments are fragrant, and so are hers, from perfume singular and particular to no one else. (Psalm 45:8) Her freshness reminds him of the essence of the cedars of Lebanon, a place he had probably visited several times.

Dixie-4:12 A garden inclosed *is* my sister, *my* spouse; a spring shut up, a fountain sealed.

A fountain sealed

How beautiful yet poignant his language on his wedding night! His words are lovely, and a reminder that our Beloved also speaks to His Bride with such sensitivity. Indeed, Christ is a man of exquisite refinement, so we would not expect anything less in His speech.

Garden and spring

An enclosed garden was a small, secret place of delights accessible only to the owner, who alone had the key to unlock its gate. This virgin maiden, depicted as a garden with splendid flowers and scents, delicious fruits, and bowers of rest, is a depository of beginnings: investment, growth, and harvest. She has so much within her that has been hidden; he knows she has so much to offer. To the beloved's eyes, his bride is full of delights, and the thoughts of her purity bring joy to his heart. He calls her a "spring shut up," for she is a virgin, and a "pearl of great price," for whom he would give his life. (Matthew 13:46) She has kept herself pure for him. In doing so, she might have thought, *I loved you before I knew you, for I kept myself pure for you alone. You had my loyalty from the beginning. I have been faithful to you, and this is the way I chose to honor you. I have desired no other but you. This purity is evidence of my love, my wedding gift to you.*

The Bride of Christ has similar intense feelings for her Bridegroom. Her love for Him determines her faithfulness. Christ's Bride is loyal and keeps herself pure for Him, even though at this point, she has not seen Him face to face. She may also say when they do meet one day, "I love You, for I kept myself for You alone. I have desired none but You." (Matthew 22:37, Psalm 18:1, 1 Peter 1:8, 1 John 4:19)

Notice the description of a giving person in Isaiah 58:10-11. "If you extend your soul to the hungry And satisfy the afflicted soul, Then your light shall dawn in the darkness, And your darkness shall *be* as the noonday. The Lord will guide you continually, And satisfy your soul in drought, And strengthen your bones; You shall be like a watered garden, And like a spring of water, whose waters do not fail." Betrothed to the Lord, the Bride has been turned into the garden of God, set apart for Him, holy unto the Lord, called "…the planting of the LORD, that he might be glorified." (Isaiah 61:3, 51:3)

Fountain

"A fountain sealed" is Solomon's bride, but so may be Christ's Bride, needing to extend herself to bless others. Her prayer might be similar to Jabez's, which is recorded in 1 Chronicles 4:10 (NIV): "…Oh, that you would bless me and enlarge my territory!" In other words, change me from a sequestered spring to a free-flowing river, reaching out to the needy of spirit, soul, and body. The Beloved understands her condition and knows oneness with Him is the remedy. The river of life and the flow of the Holy Spirit will produce growth, flowering, and fruit-bearing. Every part of her will respond to the Word of God and the voice of the Holy Spirit. By them, she will be transformed into the wonderful partner and companion Christ the Beloved deserves and desires. (2 Corinthians 3:17-18)

Meditation Twenty-One: Remind yourself of the wonder of the Lord Jesus and His love for you. (Review the titles given to Jesus listed in the analysis of 1:3) Begin your day saying: "Beloved, how extraordinary You are." Repeat this often.

Judy-4:13-15 Thy plants *are* an orchard of pomegranates, with pleasant fruits; camphire, with spikenard, spikenard and saffron; calamus and cinnamon, with all trees of frankincense; myrrh and aloes, with all the chief spices: a fountain of gardens, a well of living waters, and streams from Lebanon.

Orchard of pomegranates

The bridegroom first described the bride as a lily among thorns (2:2), but now she is an orchard of pomegranates. That's how much she has changed and matured. She lacks nothing. In her are all the valued qualities he seeks—everything that is pleasing to him. She's like a fountain, a well of living waters, and cool streams, refreshing all who come to her.

We sometimes read over good statements without thinking, but consider what she had done to overcome her past and to become who she is now. The Bride of Christ is learning to put God's ways first, following His precepts: "Love the Lord your God with all your heart and with all your soul and with all your mind," and "…love your neighbor as yourself."

(Matthew 22:37, 39 NIV) Then, the commandment found in Luke 6:31, often referred to as the Golden Rule, will become part of who you are.

In Matthew 5:44, Jesus said, "…Love your enemies, bless them that curse you, do good to them that hate you, and pray for them which despitefully use you and persecute you." That would be a big one for the Shulamite to overcome, remembering how her family put her out to tend the flocks and how her skin turned dark being in the sun all day. She has continued to mature in love, forgiveness, understanding, and courage. That's what the Bride is to do in reaching Christ's level of love.

Dixie-4:13-14 Thy plants *are* an orchard of pomegranates, with pleasant fruits; camphire, with spikenard, spikenard and saffron; calamus and cinnamon, with all trees of frankincense; myrrh and aloes, with all the chief spices…

Delights

Planted by God, the Bride is full of precious treasures like valuable spices, which are choice, prized, suitable for healing, soothing comfort, and flavor. (Psalm 1:3, see also 45:13) Christ the Bridegroom sees her as a delightful garden filled with pleasant fruits, not weeds or thistles. Do you see yourself as He sees you, or do you tend to concentrate on the unlovely parts that still need changing? Focus on your potential as He does, and ask the Holy Spirit to continue His marvelous work to transform you. (Romans 12:1-2, 2 Corinthians 3:18)

Orchard of pomegranates

If you have ever cut open a pomegranate, you know it contains many seeds. Researchers have found pomegranates which has as many as 1,400 seeds. One of the high priest's garments had pomegranates embroidered on its hem. This fruit is thought to represent the fruit of the Spirit. (Exodus 28:33-34, Galatians 5:22-23) It's possible the many seeds in this fruit also represent the gifts of the Holy Spirit. (1 Corinthians 12:4-31)

Christ speaks of His Bride as an orchard of pomegranates, assuring her of the great potential for spiritual fruitfulness and for a magnificent hundred-fold harvest from the innumerable possibilities represented by those seeds. (Matthew 13:23)

Spices

"…As the bridegroom rejoiceth over the bride, so shall thy God rejoice over thee." (Isaiah 62:5) The Beloved compares the loveliness of His Bride with fragrant substances, suggesting that He is overwhelmed and delighted with her and her progress. He is willing to be patient in His love. He knows what she is now will not compare with what she will become as she learns to trust Him more.

Dixie-4:15 ...a fountain of gardens, a well of living waters, and streams from Lebanon.

Fountain, well

Described as a garden full of herbs for healing, balms for comfort, spices that enhance flavor, perfumes that fill the air with fragrance, and pure, refreshing water that quenches thirst, the Bride of Christ has it all. To Him, she is a "fountain of gardens," a source of help to others. Her life has such potential to refresh and sustain. The LORD names Himself as "the fountain of living waters" in Jeremiah 2:13. Isn't it interesting that He would describe her similarly? She is "a well of living waters." Within her is the life of the Spirit, which fills her and satisfies her. "...Whoever drinks of this water that I shall give him will never thirst. But the water that I shall give him will become in him a fountain of water springing up into everlasting life." (John 4:14 NKJV) Words "...of a [person's] mouth *are* as deep waters, *and* the wellspring of wisdom *as* a flowing brook." (Proverbs 18:4)

Streams from Lebanon

These living waters produced by the Holy Spirit within provides wisdom as the Bride ministers. In contrast to the Bride being called "a well of living waters," the ungodly are called "wells without water" (2 Peter 2:17). They have nothing in themselves to help anyone live and grow spiritually.

Judy-4:16 Awake, O north wind; and come, thou south; blow upon my garden, *that* the spices thereof may flow out. Let my beloved come into his garden, and eat his pleasant fruits.

Come

The moment finally comes when the two become one. This is what they have waited for. They've looked forward to sharing their love, laughter, and lives. Now they will help to further each other's dreams and be a great joy each to the other.

It's precisely the same with the Bride of Christ. When Jesus left Earth, He said, "...I will come again, and receive you unto myself..." (John 14:3) This begins a time of advancement, even acceleration, and anticipation of being forever united with our coming King.

Love

In the meantime, work is going on in heaven and on earth. In heaven, Christ is preparing a place for His love. He said, "In my Father's house are many mansions:...I go to prepare a place for you." (John 14:2) On Earth, He gave a commandment that, until He comes back, we are to love one another in the same way He loved us. (John 15:12) Are you wondering how we do that? Love is revealed in everything we do whether it's smiling at our neighbor, setting the table, writing a note, or answering the phone. Do it all as unto the Lord. (Colossians 3:23)

Most of the time, our love for others is regulated by their appearance or how they treat us. Not so with God. He's the One Who teaches us to love unconditionally. I have a friend who helped take care of her brain-injured grandson for more than seventeen years. She completely put her life aside and devoted time and strength to him, until the Lord called him home. That's sacrificial love.

Then there's a supernatural type of love. My pastor and his wife usually do a mission trip during the summer. His wife often ministered to people with AIDS and leprosy. A ministry like that would have to be God-inspired and with God also working through the person.

We also have love letters in God's Word to read daily to be encouraged. Jesus said, "In the world ye shall have tribulation: but be of good cheer; I have overcome the world." (John 16:33) He's calling back to us, warning there will be tough times, but because He overcame, so can we.

The key to overcoming is following Jesus' example of keeping His eyes on the Father. Before His arrest and trials, Jesus said the hour was coming when everyone would go to his own home, and He would be left alone. Because the Father was with Him, He was not alone. (John 16:32) Jesus through the Holy Spirit, said to us: "I will never leave thee, nor forsake thee," and He can't lie. (Hebrews 13:5, Titus 1:2)

So, we are to walk in wisdom among those that are outside the faith, conserving the time until our Beloved returns. (Colossians 4:5) When He comes to receive His Bride, she will have nothing to be ashamed of, and will be dressed in white linen, a virgin ready to be received by her Bridegroom. Christ and His Bride will be joined and go forward, acting as one, in agreement, sharing their passions, and blessing each other.

> I can relate to all this. In 1969, Tom, my husband-to-be, was seeking to emigrate from Liverpool, England to the United States so we could be married. It took him one and a half years to complete government paperwork to enter legally. At one point, I learned that, if he had a job to come to, it would speed up the process. I also managed to get the endorsement of Tennessee's U.S. Congressman, Bill Brock. However, after months of separation, naturally I got anxious, wondering how much longer it would take before Tom would arrive. Our love letters to each other kept us encouraged as we waited. Then, one day at work, I was summoned to the phone. Tom was calling from New York! Everything had happened so fast in England that he arrived before his letter! What a good lesson for Christians as well. We don't know when the Lord will come. We are just told to be ready.

Dixie-4:16 Awake, O north wind; and come, thou south; blow upon my garden, that the spices thereof may flow out. Let my beloved come into his garden, and eat his pleasant fruits.

Come

The long-awaited wedding night has come. The beloved has spoken sweet, tender words to his bride, making her feel beautiful. She lovingly invites him to make them one. On Earth, the Bride of Christ eagerly awaits her Beloved's appearance and His gathering her to be forever with Him. The Holy Spirit and the Bride together say to the Bridegroom, "Come." (Revelation 22:17)

Wind

Invisible to the eye, wind exhibits power, movement, and brings change to what it touches. In the Bible, it is used as a metaphor for the Holy Spirit (John 3:8), as are oil (Isaiah 61:1-3), water (John 7:37-39), breath (Ezekiel 37:9-10, 13-14), and fire. (Acts 2:3) God the Holy Spirit moves like the wind with power to change and transform those who yield themselves to Him. (2 Corinthians 3:18) Give yourself anew to the Holy Spirit. Give Him full reign to transform you. (Romans 12:2, Philippians 1:6)

North wind...south wind

Job 37:21-22 states that fair weather comes out of the north, resulting from the wind passing over the land and cleansing it of clouds and shadows. Like the Shulamite, the Bride of Christ calls for the Holy Spirit to sweep away all hindrances to His work in her, to cleanse her of the polluted thinking of the past. She wants everything gone that is contrary to her Bridegroom.

The south wind brings warmth and rain to nurture the growth and full perfection of the garden fruits, flowers, and herbs. After cleansing, the Bride expresses her desire to be one with the Beloved, so she can become all she can be through the Holy Spirit's unhindered work in her life. She asks Him to bring her fruit to perfection, so she will be a greater delight and blessing to Christ, and that all she is and does will be worthy of her Beloved.

I think it's interesting that Solomon's bride, in chapters 1 and 2, had seen herself as a common flower, little and unexceptional, but now regards herself as a lovely garden of spices and pleasant fruits. She believes what her bridegroom has said and wants to see the truth of his words portrayed in her life.

In chapter 2, the maiden was reluctant to accept Solomon's invitation to his kingdom; here, she is the one who invites him to come to their marriage bed. The bridegroom has spoken beautiful and loving words to his bride in chapter 4, verses 1-15.

No one could fail to feel cherished. The answer to her beloved's sweet words of commendation includes her invitation to complete intimacy as a married couple. She holds nothing back. She is his, without reservation.

The following poem expresses this passage about the Bride of Christ beautifully.

A garden enclosed,
    a fountain sealed,
        I was a life
            still seeking,
                searching for
                    unquenchable,
                        unfailing,
                            glorious,
                                eternal
                                  Love.
                                  I found it in Jesus,
                                      and trusted Him with all of me.
                                          (Dixie D. McClintock)

> **Meditation Twenty-Two**: In a quiet time of your day, close your eyes, clear your mind, relax, and ask the Lord how He sees you. You will get a vision (usually like a snapshot picture). When I asked, I saw a necklace, a string of pearls perhaps sixteen inches long. Inquiring further about where God was in the vision, He indicated the Holy Spirit was the thread that held the pearls together, and Jesus was the clasp to give it purpose and function. The Father was behind me as if He would wear it when finished. When one friend did this same spiritual exercise, she saw a bridge, and that's what she has been in her ministries to others. Another friend, participating in this adventure of faith, saw herself as a puppy, easy to be with, one who listens to what's troubling without judgmental response, and who gives sweet comfort in that moment.

CHAPTER 5 (5: 1)

Judy–5:1 I am come into my garden, my sister, *my* **spouse: I have gathered my myrrh with my spice; I have eaten my honeycomb with my honey; I have drunk my wine with my milk: eat, O friends; drink, yea, drink abundantly, O beloved.**

Marriage feast

The king and his new bride are at the wedding feast, and he calls for all to eat and drink and join in the marriage celebration. We, as Christians, are to rejoice with those who have reason to be joyful and weep with those who sorrow. There is to be no division in the body, but the members should care for each other. (Romans 12:15, 1 Corinthians 12:25) Even heaven joins in, for we are encircled with a great cloud of witnesses. (Hebrews 12:1)

Dixie–5:1 I am come into my garden, my sister, *my* **spouse: I have gathered my myrrh with my spice; I have eaten my honeycomb with my honey; I have drunk my wine with my milk: eat, O friends; drink, yea, drink abundantly, O beloved.**

Celebration

Her invitation of 4:16, "Let my beloved come into his garden," has been answered by his, "I am come." The king is very pleased with the gift of herself to him. He describes it as if he has attended a banquet of great delights. With words like "milk" and "wine," Solomon alludes to the purity of his bride and the intoxicating aspects of their union.

When Christ's Bride gives herself totally and without reservation to her Beloved, she gives the greatest gift she could bestow—her complete trust. Blessings from her life go to Him first, then others receive blessings in their rejoicing with the couple. Observers of her life benefit from her newfound trust and confidence in Him. Her light will illumine them; her knowledge will call to them; her joy will draw them to her Beloved. "A city that is set on [a] hill cannot be hid." (Matthew 5:14)

Friends; drink, yea, drink abundantly, O beloved

During the wedding festivities in the week of celebration, the bridegroom speaks first, then his bride invites their friends and guests to join them for the wedding supper. The bride instructs the wedding guests to enjoy their meal; to her beloved, she encourages him to drink abundantly, subtly reminding him that she is his fountain unsealed and a spring no longer closed. (4:12) The intimacy with him that she has experienced makes her long for more.

The Bride of Christ, having tasted of and enjoyed the oneness of His love, cannot wait for more. There is an eternity of joy and happiness ahead of her.

Judy–5:2 I sleep, but my heart waketh: *it is* **the voice of my beloved that knocketh,** *saying***, Open to me, my sister, my love, my dove, my undefiled: for my head is filled with dew,** *and* **my locks with the drops of the night.**

I sleep, but my heart waketh

The wedding and celebration is over. Time has elapsed, and her beloved has gone out to work while his bride is still in bed. This girl probably thinks her job is done. She's married, and she can do what she wants now that she's a queen. She hasn't learned to discipline herself, develop her life as a wife, and be helpmate to her husband. Her life is out of balance. Many people accept Jesus Christ as their Lord and Savior and stop there. They don't go on to study God's Word and apply it to their life or develop a closer relationship with Him. What takes precedence in your life?

When Elizabeth II became queen of the United Kingdom of Great Britain and Northern Ireland from 1952 to 2022, she set her priorities in the right order. At the end of her first Christmas message broadcast to millions of people on December 25, 1952, she said, "I want to ask you all, whatever your religion may be, to pray for me—to pray that God may give me wisdom and strength to carry out the solemn promise I shall be making, and that I may faithfully serve Him and you, all the days of my life."*

*(royal.uk/queens-first-Christmas-broadcast-1952)

Dixie–5:2 I sleep, but my heart waketh: *it is* **the voice of my beloved that knocketh,** *saying***, Open to me, my sister, my love, my dove, my undefiled: for my head is filled with dew,** *and* **my locks with the drops of the night.**

I sleep, but my heart waketh

This new bride of King Solomon drifts into sleep and is given a dream of her beloved. She hears her beloved seeking her company and intimacy, but she is very slow to respond. The dream reveals an unrealized attitude that needs to be examined and changed. It exposes soulish thinking and warns again of the little foxes that may rob her of joy, if she's not careful. (Song of Solomon 2:15)

As in many dreams, things are revealed that might not be seen or acknowledged in waking hours. A dream may be a specific word of God to a person, and some who receive dreams treat it as such. Others, ignorant of the Scriptures, dismiss all dreams as insignificant, thereby losing their special message from God. "For God may speak in one way, or in another, Yet *man* does not perceive it. In a dream, in a vision of the night, when deep sleep falls upon men, while slumbering on their beds, Then He opens the ears of men, and seals their instruction."

In order to turn man *from his* deed, and conceal pride from man, He keeps back his soul from the Pit, And his life from perishing by the sword." (Job 33:14-18 NKJV) In Jeremiah 23:28 (NKJV), the Lord connects a dream with His Word: "The prophet who has a dream, let him tell a dream; And he who has My word, let him speak My word faithfully…"

"I sleep, but my heart waketh." Unfortunately, this parallels too closely the condition of the church. In Song of Solomon 3:1, she was upon the bed; in 5:2, she is asleep. Sleep is defined as resting with a suspension of consciousness. Doesn't that describe the body of Christ? Didn't the Lord warn about this through Paul's writings to the Roman church, "…knowing the time…is nearer than when we *first* believed. The night is far spent, the day is at hand. Therefore let us cast off the works of darkness, and let us put on the armor of light. Let us walk properly, as in the day, not in revelry and drunkenness, not in lewdness and lust, not in strife and envy. But put on the Lord Jesus Christ, and make no provision for the flesh, to *fulfill* its lusts." (Romans 13:11-14 NKJV)

Paul warned the Corinthian church: "Awake to righteousness, and do not sin; for some do not have the knowledge of God. I speak *this* to your shame." (1 Corinthians 15:34 NKJV) To the Ephesian church, Paul wrote, "Awake, you who sleep, Arise from the dead, And Christ will give you light. See then that you walk circumspectly, not as fools but as wise, redeeming the time, because the days are evil. Therefore, do not be unwise, but understand what the will of the Lord *is*. (Ephesians 5:14-17 NKJV) To the Thessalonian church, he exhorted: "Therefore let us not sleep, as *do* others; but let us watch and be sober. For they that sleep, sleep in the night; and they that be drunken are drunken in the night. But let us, who are of the day, be sober, putting on the breastplate of faith and love: and for [a] helmet, the hope of salvation." (1 Thessalonians 5:6-8) Was it not the Lord Jesus who warned His disciples that, "…while men slept, his enemy came and sowed tares among the wheat…"? (Matthew 13:25) In the parable of the ten virgins, (who portray Israel, not the Bride), the sleep and lack of preparation of the five foolish virgins result in robbing them of the joy of attending the wedding celebration of the returning bridegroom. (Matthew 25:1-30)

The Shulamite has retired to bed and fallen asleep while her beloved has been working in the night and early morning, evidenced by his head being wet with dew. She was not alert, watching for him with a heart prepared to welcome him.

The spiritually mature do not retire from spirit work. I am retired from public school teaching, but not from the work the Lord has ordained for me. (Ephesians 2:10) In Joshua 14:6-15, we read of Caleb, who at eighty-five years old had not quit serving the Lord. Instead, trusting the word given him by the Lord, he took on giants, dispossessed them of the land given to him by God, and secured an inheritance for his descendants. His testimony was "…I wholly followed the LORD my God." (Joshua 14:8) Caleb's strength in the physical realm was founded on his faith in the spiritual realm. So is the Bride's. Her faith, based on the Word of God and the direction of the Holy Spirit, enables her to face the giants in her life and conquer them.

My head is filled with dew, and my locks with the drops of the night

Here, locks of Solomon's hair drip with the dew of the night, evidence of his work for his bride and his kingdom. He is busy; she is not.

In His sufferings, the Lord Jesus' head was crowned with thorns, which pierced His skin and caused precious drops of His holy blood to fall to earth. They were part of the evidence of His great sacrifice and unflinching service to His Father, to His Bride, and to the world.

Notice the leaping on the mountains in chapter 2 follows the shepherd-king's work in the valleys. Heart-wise, our thoughts need to stay at the highest elevations, but our work is not there. The people of the Bride must follow Christ's example and go where He is working and join Him there. (Ephesians 2:6, 3:8-11, Colossians 3:1-2)

The Lord is working in every person's life on this planet to draw them to Himself. He allows us to help in this endeavor. It is a privilege to be with Him and to serve beside Him. What He gives us to do is varied. No one has the same assignment. Our assignment is given specifically with our gifts, talents, character traits, strengths, and weaknesses in mind. Primarily, what God desires is for each of us to delight in Him and to be willing to join Him, wherever He leads, in the same way Jesus delighted to do His Father's will. (Psalm 40:8)

My heart waketh; it is the voice of my beloved

The Spirit of Christ, her Beloved, is at work in her soul. His Presence and voice are unmistakable. His Bride hears His endearments and instruction.

Open to me, my sister

This title acknowledges their spiritual connection first. We all serve in the same family of God. "For this cause, I bow my knees unto the Father of our Lord Jesus Christ, Of whom the whole family in heaven and earth is named. That he would grant you, according to the riches of his glory, to be strengthened with might by his Spirit in the inner man…" (Ephesians 3:14-16)

My love

The Shulamite said, "He is mine," and the Holy Spirit made that fact plain in Romans 8:35,37-39: "Who shall separate us from the love of Christ? *shall* tribulation, or distress, or persecution, or famine, or nakedness, or peril, or sword? Nay…For I am persuaded, that neither death, nor life, nor angels, nor principalities, nor powers, nor things present, nor things to come, Nor height, nor depth, nor any other creature, shall be able to separate us from the love of God, which is in Christ Jesus our Lord."

My dove

Christ knows His Bride's devotion to Him. He treasures her gentleness and faithfulness.

My undefiled

The Lord Jesus knows there has been no promiscuity, that is, idolatry in her life. She has no interest in pursuing the gods of this world and the idols of deception. He takes pleasure in her loyalty to Him. What a gift!

Open to me

In chapter 2, Solomon invited her to accompany him, and the Shulamite refused. Now, he only instructs her to open the locked door to him, and, as we see in the next verse, she says no. Do you see how much easier it is for her to refuse him again, because she has done it previously? How careful, how on guard, how wise the Bride of Christ must be to have "yes" in her heart and on her lips whenever Jesus comes to invite her to fellowship with Him, or to join Him in His endeavors of grace and mercy.

Do the words, "open to me," remind you of the scripture in Revelation 3:20, written to the churches, (not the heathen)? "Behold, I stand at the door, and knock: if any man hear my voice, and open the door, I will come in to him, and will sup with him, and he with me." Through Jesus, the Way, the heavenly Father opened His door to us; therefore, the door to our hearts should never be closed to Him.

Judy-5:3 I have put off my coat; how shall I put it on? I have washed my feet; how shall I defile them?

Apathy

She's removed her coat or robe and washed her feet, and doesn't feel like getting up and letting him in. This new bride has forgotten that Solomon is not only her husband, but the king, and she is privileged to be his queen. After all, she's reminded later (6:8) there are threescore queens, fourscore concubines, and virgins without number, yet he has chosen her. In that culture, marriage really was the highest calling for a woman. The Shulamite was honored to be chosen as his wife, to keep his home, and to be the mother of his children. Given such positions of favor and esteem "…the heart of her husband doth safely trust in her… she will do him good…all the days of her life." (Proverbs 31:11-12)

The Shulamite's apathy portrays Christians who accept Christ as their Savior, but then don't glorify Him by putting Him first in every part of their lives. "Charm *is* deceitful and beauty *is* passing, But a woman who fears the Lord, she shall be praised," another distinguishing characteristic of the Bride. (Proverbs 31:30 NKJV) She respects and honors her King.

Dixie-5:3 I have put off my coat; how shall I put it on? I have washed my feet; how shall I defile them?

Complacency

Complacency is worse than the fears that stopped the maiden from joining Solomon in chapter 2. Later, as she came to understand his greatness, she realized his invitation to come to a higher level of intimacy and understanding would have been matched by his protection and care for her. He would let nothing harm her.

However, here we see something different: complacency in a heart takes its blessings for granted and becomes ungrateful. Likewise, the Bride of Christ revels in the bliss of being His, pleased with the accompanying comforts and graces. Smugness is a dangerous condition. Bordering on indifference and apathy, precursors of coldness in a relationship, it is centered on self and is a form of spiritual laziness. Her Beloved should come first with her, not second to her self-satisfaction.

> In a Sunday School class I attended, the teacher used an illustration of a highway in the western United States with lush, green vegetation and forest on one side and barren, arid desert on the other. One student hesitantly commented that it seemed God was unfair by not blessing the desert side with rainfall. I understood her view, but the comment bothered me so much that I asked the Lord what the problem was with her remark.

> He responded with the word, "entitlement," and then began to teach me about a spirit of entitlement. I realized all the land should have been desert, and it was only through God's mercy and grace that rain came to bless one side. (Exodus 33:19) It later occurred to me that, after all, if God were really "fair," we'd all be in hell, with no exceptions. Like Adam and Eve, sometimes we fail to recognize and appreciate God's grace.

Illustrated in this verse, the Shulamite believes in entitlement, rights and privileges owed her, based on her own achievements.

Although bestowed with unearned and undeserved grace, the Bride of Christ may feel no need for a quick reaction to the Lord's call or prompting. The temptation to delay a response is there, pointing to a conflict between her spirit, which always wants to say "yes" to Him, and her soul, which at times chooses self above His will. This is followed by a loss of humility, a neglect of thankfulness, and a failure to give God His rightful glory as Creator and sovereign ruler of all. (Romans 1:21-22)

This mindset of unwise entitlement, if left to fester, will eventually generate an attitude of resentment and a "why me?" view of crises, which might invite additional spirits of depression and defeat to enter the picture. We need to take every thought captive and examine each to determine if it is truth or a lie that needs to be cast out. (2 Corinthians 10:4-5) It's crucial to develop and maintain a thankful heart.

One day, Judy described a conversation, in which a woman said she had good days and bad days. Judy responded, "You can't look at it like that. 'Every day with Jesus is sweeter than the day before.'" When I heard that, I realized her words were what the Bride should be declaring all the time.

How shall I…?

The Shulamite doesn't give an outright "no." She disguises her rejection by asking, "How shall I?" rather than "I don't intend to stir myself for you." He calls to her, and she makes excuses. It's inconvenient. Her refusal is worse in some ways than the refusal of Felix, the Roman Governor of Judea, who said to Paul, "Go away for now; when I have a convenient time, I will call for you," after Paul had testified of his faith in Christ. (Acts 24:25) Felix had no prior knowledge of or relationship with Jesus. The Bride can't say that. She knows the Beloved and has given herself to Him, yet in essence, she acts the same as Felix. When we look at our spiritual health, or lack thereof, we should remember we are as close to Him as we have chosen to be. He is always willing to be with us. Are we willing to make time for Him?

In temptation or trial, there is a choice—to follow your spirit, which is always aligned with the will of God, directed by Him, perfect in Christ, and walks in the fruit of the Spirit, *or* to follow the soul, which is led by the mind, will, emotions, (I think-I want-I feel). Note "I" is the focus of the soul. The Christian life is about choosing to walk in the Spirit, not in soulishness.

I have put off my coat…washed my feet; how shall I defile them?

Was there no expectation of his coming? What happened to anticipation? Her desire should have matched Solomon's desire to be with her. She has prepared, but for what? She is willing to trade his fellowship and intimacy for clean feet! What good are clean feet if they don't take you where you need to go? Why does she think her comfort is more important than being with him? What frivolous excuses she offers in her dream!

Her rationalizations are ridiculous, considering who he is and the fact that he wants to be with her. Her justification for the lack of welcome reveals a slight remainder of shallowness in her love for him.

The Shulamite should run to open the door; her eyes should light up with gladness to know he is near. But because of her apathy, she misses a lovely opportunity to be with him. Her soulishness is blatant here. There is always this conflict in the believer as to whether to allow the spirit or the soul to rule. The spirit is aligned with the Spirit of God and His will; the soul, which is still in a transformation process, is in agreement with self and its indulgences at times. If she chooses to let soul rule, it will show that although she may love him to a degree, she loves herself and her comfort more. "But they all with one *accord* began to make excuses…" (Luke 14:18) Sadly, the most trivial of circumstances can become more important to us, when it should be time to listen to the Lord and take advantage of the opportunity He gives us.

> A young missionary couple, traveling with their four little children, had been invited to speak about their work to our small church congregation. During their presentation, one of the men in the assembly, as he told his wife later, was prompted by the Holy Spirit to give the couple an extra love offering apart from what the church would provide. It was over one hundred dollars, a lot of money back then. He talked himself out of doing it. His thoughts mirrored the Shulamite's attitude. Being soulish and disobedient resulted in missing a blessing. The Lord knew the man would reject His leading and the opportunity to give. The Holy Spirit impressed another member of the congregation to give the couple one hundred and twenty dollars. That person obeyed and later found out the couple used the gift to replace the bald tires on their van.

Like the Shulamite, when the believer fails to respond immediately to the voice of the Lord, even though he may eventually rethink his action and repent, nevertheless, he has missed the blessing that comes with correct first responses. His conscience will chasten him, even after his repentance, with the knowledge and the regret of the missed chances of sensing the Lord's presence, having the pleasure of His company, and hearing His words of love.

The Bride must understand she deprives herself of the best in life when she makes selfish or soul-focused decisions. Transformation will occur when the Bride finally realizes what she loses every time she permits her soul to rule. Never will the Bride of Christ become defiled by doing whatever it takes to welcome Him.

No sacrifice is too great for her to make for His fellowship. (Luke 21:1-4) Also, to earn the right to a great position in the kingdom to come, the Bride needs to make the choices now that serve to train her for rulership.

First, by learning to rule her body and soul, she can be trusted to rule over others in the kingdom of heaven on earth. (1 Corinthians 9:24-27, 1 Timothy 6:11) Secondly, by consistently letting the Holy Spirit rule in her, she will be like her Beloved and a true partner to Him. Lastly, her free will and soul must align with her spirit; only then will she choose the eternal over the temporal, and unity over division.

Meditation Twenty-Three: What problem did the Bride have in chapter 1? Chapter 2? What does she overcome in chapter 4? What problem reveals itself in 5:2-3? Ask the Lord to reveal a habit, an incorrect belief, a grudge, or an attitude that you should address. Let Him cleanse your soul and more closely align it with your spirit and His. (James 4:7, 10, 1 John 1:9, 4:18, 2 Timothy 4:18)

Judy-5:4 My beloved put in his hand by the hole *of the door*, **and my bowels were moved for him.**

Moved for him

In her dream, the Shulamite saw Solomon reach in to open the door. The fragrance of his cologne remained on the wood. His bride caught the scent of his nearness and inwardly she longed for him. The fragrance reminded her of how much she loved him, but by the time she got up, he was gone. She regretted not answering his call.

Dixie-5:4 My beloved put in his hand by the hole *of the door*, **and my bowels were moved for him.**

His hand

In Bible times, an inner door had a wooden bolt-latch system, which acted as a locking mechanism to a hole carved in the door. That's why she was able to see his hand.

Moved for him

The sight of his hand brought her to her senses. Once on a Sunday when two followers of Jesus met the resurrected Christ on the road to Emmaus, and invited Him to dinner, it was the sight of Jesus' hands, probably His horrendous scars, that helped open their eyes. The marks of the holy covenant He had made with His Father were revealed as He reached out to offer bread to them. That's how the two men knew the Lord Jesus had risen indeed, as they later announced to the other disciples in Jerusalem. (Luke 24:13-35) When Christ appeared at that gathering in the upper room, He encouraged the disciples to behold His hands. (John 20:27)

Those wrists held the dreadful evidence of His crucifixion and revealed His undeniable identity. (Acts 17:31) When you sense in your soul an attitude of I'm-too-comfortable-to-want-any-more, picture your Beloved Christ's hands. Remember He sacrificed His life for you. Think what those hands suffered for you. Meditate on them until it moves you to gratitude and a desire to be in His Presence again.

Judy-5:5 I rose up to open to my beloved; and my hands dropped *with* myrrh, and my fingers *with* sweet smelling myrrh, upon the handles of the lock.
Another missed opportunity! It was too late to say, "I wish…" or "If only…" Life is short, and time is precious. We need to love Him enough to respond to His first call in an eager, fervent way.

Dixie-5:5 I rose up to open to my beloved; and my hands dropped *with* myrrh, and my fingers *with* sweet smelling myrrh, upon the handles of the lock.

I rose up

To overcome certain negatives in our lives requires us to get up, to get out of our comfort zone, and welcome the Lord into our hidden places of stubbornness or rebellion. No part of us, past, present, or future, should be closed to Jesus. Instead, we must open the door of our hearts and surrender all: mind, will, and emotions.

Why is the door locked against Solomon? Why was this new bride's response to him so slow? What clouded her thinking, produced such indolence, and caused this negligence? What happened to the excited, lovesick maiden of chapter 1, who couldn't think of anything better or more wonderful than being with her beloved?

When things are going well, we can get complacent in our relationship with the Beloved Jesus. This scene serves as a warning to believers and gives us a reason to be on guard. The Shulamite's reluctance to arise, her slowness to respond to him, and her disregard of their relationship shows us the danger of weakening sensitivity. (Hebrews 5:11-12) In the believer's life, when intimacy with Jesus is ignored or neglected, dullness of spiritual ears and eyes creeps in, and, if left uncorrected, it may result in deafness and blindness to the things of God.

Myrrh upon the handles

His distinctive signature fragrance would give thoughts of him. In chapter 1, the Shulamite described him as a "bundle of myrrh" (1:13), and in 3:6, he came to her "perfumed with myrrh." When she touched the handle, she felt and smelled the alluring scent of her beloved.

French philosopher, Maurice Blondel, once said, "If you would really want to understand a man, don't just listen to what he says, but watch what he does." quotefancy.com   When denied access to his own, the bridegroom Solomon does not yell or pound the door in anger, nor does he call her names or force his way in. Instead, he leaves a lovely perfumed remembrance and goes back to work in the gardens. (6:2) How gracious he is! It is amazing that she hears no rebuke from him but receives a token of his love.

Christ always reminds His Bride of His love, even when she is tardy in her response to Him. True love includes loyalty and patience. Jesus shows these traits repeatedly to us. This extraordinary quality of love is something the Bride of Christ must continue to learn.

Judy–5:6 I opened to my beloved; but my beloved had withdrawn himself, *and* was gone: my soul failed when he spake: I sought him, but I could not find him; I called him, but he gave me no answer.

Where is he

In this dream, the young bride finally decides to get up and unlock the door, but she's too late. Her husband-king had left. She looked for him but to no avail. Her beloved is patient and gentle, giving her time to realize her mistake. She holds such a high honor to be chosen as his bride, but her slow response doesn't reflect her gratitude.

Dixie-5:6 I opened to my beloved; but my beloved had withdrawn himself, *and* was gone: my soul failed when he spake: I sought him, but I could not find him; I called him, but he gave me no answer.

Missed opportunity

Solomon wants a passionate, fiery love; he gets a banked pile of coals with flickering embers. Ultimately, his love makes the right move, but at the wrong time. His bride misses the blessedness and bliss of fellowship with her beloved by being slow to respond. Her tardiness to open the door to her beloved results in lost intimacy with her new bridegroom. What treasures he might have given her, what joys she might have experienced with him, but her lethargy and delay robbed her of all potential rewards of his company.

In studying Luke 18:9-14, the parable of a publican and a Pharisee going to the temple to pray, the Lord said to me the Pharisee had made an "idol of self." The Bride must be on guard, and if she has made or is making an idol of self, she must allow the Lord to reveal it. The Beloved needs to be first with her, and she must be responsive to Him. How easy it is to miss an opportunity to be with the Lord!

> A Bible teacher in my church, actively pursuing intimacy with God, told the following story. He was strolling on a sidewalk along the beautiful Gulf of Mexico when the Lord turned his attention to a young man across the street. "Tell that

young man, 'God really loves you.' " The teacher resisted the instruction for a few steps, but then turned to obey. The young man was gone.

The Christian had failed to respond quickly to his Beloved. He was sorry for his disobedience, which had caused him to lose the chance to serve his Lord and plant a seed of God's love in that young man's life.

My beloved had withdrawn himself, and was gone
Keep sight of your Beloved. Don't take Him for granted. Choosing the natural over the spiritual or the temporal over the eternal might cause you to miss the experience of the astounding grace of His presence, whenever and however He comes to you.

My soul failed when he spake
Like the Shulamite, has your soul failed to respond to His call? Do you thrill at His Words and His fellowship? Be honest with yourself and with Him.

I sought him, but I could not find him; I called him, but he gave me no answer
Realizing her error, Solomon's bride sets out to restore their fellowship. Notice how quickly this turn-around occurred. A situation like this is evidence of spiritual growth in a person's life. Wasting no time, recognizing the wrong done, repenting of the error, and desiring forgiveness are all indicators that one is maturing in wisdom. At this point, the Shulamite's priorities are straight; her heart is renewed. She will not quit until their intimacy is re-established.

Meditation Twenty-Four: Make a concerted effort to center your thoughts on your Beloved Jesus by repeating this during your day: "Jesus, I love You and trust You."

Judy-5:7 The watchmen that went about the city found me, they smote me, they wounded me; the keepers of the walls took away my veil from me.

Watchmen
It has not been long since this bride said her marriage vows to her beloved. However, since the Shulamite has made the mistake of ignoring her beloved's voice more than once, guilt is setting in. Her conscience bears witness to the error of her ways, but she has the chance to change.

Conversations with the Holy Spirit are invaluable because He is our teacher who brings knowledge of Christ's words to our remembrance. (John 14:26) The Bride of Christ is warned not to extinguish the Holy Spirit. When she hears His voice, she is not to harden her heart. (1 Thessalonians 5:19, Hebrews 3:7)

Dixie-5:7 The watchmen that went about the city found me, they smote me, they wounded me; the keepers of the walls took away my veil from me.

Search continues

I think part of verse 6 goes with verse 7. In this dream, the recognizing that her willful disregard for her husband has hurt her relationship with her beloved causes the frantic search for him in all the wrong places. She probably searched within their home, calling his name, and outside the premises. When others learn of her problem, they reproach her. The watchmen know she is a married woman, so they wonder why she is out by herself at night. They remove her veil, representative of honor saying, "If you don't want to be with your husband, then dress like a harlot." They have seen her folly and are unsympathetic. They look with censure on one who is inconsistent, and rightly so. They recognize a disconnect between what is professed and what is lived. They are trying to shake her up so she will admit the truth to herself. Remember, this is the second time she has refused him.

When the Bride of Christ disregards her Beloved's desires, and refuses to respond to His Words, her conscience will beset her. The fruit of self-control and joy has indeed been eaten by the little foxes just as the warning had stated. (2:15)

Judy-5:8 I charge you, O daughters of Jerusalem, if ye find my beloved, that ye tell him, that I *am* sick of love.

Tell him for me

The Shulamite tells the daughters of Jerusalem that she is lovesick and wants her beloved back. Confessing the sin of ignoring his voice, she asks for a second chance. A needlework piece I made some years ago reads: "Please be patient with me, God isn't finished with me yet." We have a wonderful heavenly Father Who doesn't set a limit on the number of mistakes we can make. He's always ready to forgive us as we continue to mature spiritually. (1 John 1:9)

Dixie-5:8 I charge you, O daughters of Jerusalem, if ye find my beloved, that ye tell him, that I *am* sick of love.

Tell him I love him

His absence and her actions have made her miserable. This young bride confesses her sorrowful state to others. From despair and desperation, she has moved through remorse, sorrow for sin, repentance, and a longing for restoration. How this weary soul desires a renewal of the sweet fellowship she once had with her beloved.

"You, God, are my God, earnestly I seek you; I thirst for you, my whole being longs for you, in a dry and parched land where there is no water. I have seen you in the sanctuary and beheld your power and your glory. Because your love is better than life, my lips will glorify you. I will praise you as long as I live, and in your name I will lift up my hands. I will be fully satisfied as with the richest of foods; with singing lips my mouth will praise you. On my bed I remember you; I think of you through the watches of the night. Because you are my help, I sing in the shadow of your wings." (Psalm 63:1-8 NIV) "By day the Lord directs his love, at night his song is with me—a prayer to the God of my life." (Psalm 42:8 NIV) I can never thank You enough, Beloved, for the joy You bring me!

In studying the accounts of the Roman centurion who sought healing for his servant, and the Syrophoenician woman who sought healing for her daughter, we find several common threads in the gospels which should also be true of the Bride of Christ. Both were described by Jesus as having great faith. (Matthew 8:10, 15:28, Mark 7:26) In fact, out of all the multitudes healed by Jesus, these two Gentiles were the only ones designated this way. Christ's Bride must have great faith like these two.

What distinguished them from all the others? Though the centurion was highly regarded by both Rome and the Jews, in contrast to the woman, who was considered an unimportant female foreigner, neither had attitudes of offense or pride which would have kept them from asking for help. Neither had been reared in the study of the law as the Jews had, and they weren't focused on Jewish prejudices, which would have deemed them unworthy of receiving a miracle and attention from a Jewish rabbi.

The Syrophoenician and the Roman had recognized Jesus' spiritual credentials. They knew God had sent Him. Both had eyes only for Jesus, already convinced of His character and compassion, not just His power. Their total focus was upon Him; they knew Jesus' word was all they needed. They didn't require His personal presence or His touch to know their requests had been honored. Both knew that *with His Word* came the power to accomplish whatever had been spoken. As a result of their faith, both received healing for their loved ones. These qualities describe the Bride of Christ faith and her desire to stay close with her Beloved and remain in unity with Him.

Judy-5:9 What *is* thy beloved more than *another* beloved, O thou fairest among women? what *is* thy beloved more than *another* beloved, that thou dost so charge us?

Your beloved

Acknowledging the Shulamite is the fairest among women, the daughters of Jerusalem ask what makes the beloved Solomon more special than any other man, so much so that she wants them to help her look for him. I have a friend from Brazil who is a Christian. She has many foreign friends who worship other gods. They asked her the same question, "Tell me about your Jesus…why is He special?"

How would you answer if asked this same question? Here's what I might say:

- **My Jesus is above all gods.** "For the LORD *is* a great God, and a great King above all gods." (Psalm 95:3)
- **My Jesus is not carved from stone or wood.** Being then "…the offspring of God, we ought not to think that the Godhead is like unto gold, or silver, or stone…" (Acts 17:29)
- **My Jesus is strong.** "Ah Lord GOD! behold, thou hast made the heaven and the earth by thy great power and stretched out arm, and there is nothing too hard for thee." (Jeremiah 32:17)
- **My Jesus heals the broken-hearted, binding up their wounds.** I am healed because His wounds paid for my healing. (Psalm 147:3, Isaiah 53:5)
- **My Jesus died, arose from the grave, and is now alive in heaven.** "He was wounded for the wrong things we did. He was crushed for the evil things we did. My punishment…was given to Him." (Isaiah 53:5,6 ICB-International Children's Bible)
- **My Jesus prays to the Father for me.** (Hebrews 7:25) There is nothing or no one to compare to my Jesus. His love is so amazing! "… For he hath made him to be sin for us…" (2 Corinthians 5:21), God "…both raised up the Lord and will also raise up us by His own power" (1 Corinthians 6:14 NKJV). God "…worked in Christ when He raised Him from the dead and seated *Him* at His right hand in the heavenly places." (Ephesians 1:20 NKJV)

Dixie-5:9 What *is* thy beloved more than *another* beloved, O thou fairest among women? what *is* thy beloved more than *another* beloved, that thou dost so charge us?

Tell us about your beloved

They are so astounded by her passion to find him again they ask her the question twice, and what a loaded question! Here is her opportunity for the "spring shut up" to begin to flow in the Spirit, to provide life-giving refreshment to the needy.

Let me add to the beautiful things Judy said about our Beloved Jesus:
- **My Jesus took my place.** Because of Him, I don't have to die for my sins. He bore the brunt of my punishment for me. Jesus was the *last* Man Who ever had to die to pay sin's penalty. (1 Corinthians 15:45) People do not now have to die for their sins *if* they accept the payment Jesus Christ made for them and claim Him Lord of their lives. He loved us so much that He became the Way for us to receive eternal life, not eternal death. How astonishing His grace!
- **My Jesus would never lie to me.** He can't lie. He speaks the truth because He is the Truth. (John 14:6, Titus 1:2, 1 John 2:27)
- **My Jesus is faithful to me.** He would never betray me or forsake me. (Hebrews 13:5) I am not alone in this world.

- **Jesus, nothing and no one satisfies as He does.** "…whosoever drinketh of the water that I shall give him shall never thirst…" (John 4:14)
- **Jesus is personally sweet to me.** A close friend of mine recently had a dream and, since it involved me, called to relate it. In the dream, she was visiting me and knew I had acquired something and had changed my mind about it. As she was leaving my home, the Lord said, "Go back and tell Dixie not to make a hasty decision. Weigh it out with love." There the dream ended.

When she told me about the dream, I didn't get any connection, but since my brother has the gift of dream interpretation, I called him. He said it involved another person and a choice I either had made or would make. The Lord was not condemning or commanding my decision, but was counseling me to reconsider, mixing it with more love for the person and less logic. By the end of our short conversation, I knew what it meant. I had already made the decision in question and knew who and what it concerned. Recently I had received some money as a reimbursement and wanted to use it to bless a certain person. I talked myself out of that idea for several legitimate reasons, the primary one being I thought the person would be embarrassed. I re-considered my position, this time "weighing it out with love." I immediately sent the gift with a note containing the words the Lord had given me. The person accepted it with joy.

The thought that the Lord would help me correct a decision I had made astounded me. The loving kindness of my Beloved overwhelmed me. The more I contemplate His beauty of character, the more I fall in love with Him.

The Shulamite describes her beloved as how she has seen him and how he has revealed his character. If someone asks you to explain your faith in Jesus Christ, remember they haven't asked about your denomination's platform, your particular church, or religious traditions. Focus on the Person of Christ Jesus and how wonderful He is. When Christ is truly your Beloved, the relationship cannot and will not be hidden.

If this seems difficult to you, spend some time meditating on Jesus. In the worship of Him, speak aloud your response to why your Beloved is more than any other. There is much evidence of His sweetness and kisses. Truly the most eloquent words cannot adequately express the beauty of His character and personality, and the depth of His love for us. All our collective praise is less than a speck of sand on the seashore compared to His magnificence and how much He deserves to be exalted and adored. Yet what we have, and what we are, we offer and ask the Holy Spirit to transform it into a gift worthy of our Beloved.

Judy-5:10 My beloved *is* white and ruddy, the chiefest among ten thousand.

Greatest to me

Solomon's bride focuses on him, a standard bearer of perfection and an example to be followed. We can say that about our Jesus, because He did no sin, and there was no deceit in Him. He was reviled and threatened, but He refused to respond in kind. He suffered but threatened not. (1 Peter 2:21-23) He is pure and holy. (1 John 3:3) His wisdom from heaven is "…peaceable, gentle, *and* easy to be entreated, full of mercy and good fruits, without partiality, and without hypocrisy." (James 3:17) His words are genuine words "…as silver tried in a furnace of earth, purified seven times." (Psalm 12:6) The Shulamite can boast that her beloved is the chiefest among ten thousand, but the Bride knows Jesus Christ is truly the one Man that is perfect in heaven above and in the earth.

Dixie-5:10 My beloved *is* white and ruddy, the chiefest among ten thousand.

Outstanding

To the question of the daughters of Jerusalem, "What is your beloved more than another beloved?", this new bride answers with a description of Solomon's outward appearance, for everything about him recommends her trust, esteem, and love. Solomon's bride wants them to understand his loveliness. No doubt, Solomon was very handsome, as the offspring of an attractive father, David, and a most beautiful mother, Bathsheba. (1 Samuel 16:12, 2 Samuel 11:2)

White and ruddy

The Shulamite comments on Solomon's complexion as ruddy, or rosy, perhaps indicative not only of his parents' coloring but also good health and youthful energy. (1 Samuel 16:12) She also describes him as white, but the Hebrew word means "dazzling." What a wonderful visual of our Beloved Jesus! He indeed is dazzling in every way, and the more time we spend with Him, the more dazzled we become. The Bride adores her Bridegroom.

Chiefest among ten thousand

She immediately puts him at the top of the list of all men she has met or heard of, assigning, I suppose, the highest number she could think of.

Meditation Twenty-Five: Develop the habit of saying, "I adore you, Beloved."

Judy-5:11 His head *is as* the most fine gold, his locks *are* bushy, *and* black as a raven.

He's wonderful

Her beloved Solomon is wealthy and influential; after all, he is the king. To her, he seems confident and at peace. His father, David, had such peace. He said, "I foresaw the Lord always before my face, for he is on my right hand that I should not be moved: Therefore did my heart rejoice, and my tongue was glad; moreover also my flesh shall rest in hope;" (Acts 2:25-26) God gives the same promise of keeping in peace the person who focuses on Him, trusting in Him. (Isaiah 26:3)

Picturing Solomon in her mind, she begins to describe him. His hair symbolizes his submissiveness to God. (1 Kings 3:3, 5-15) Jesus is the perfect example of this principle, "... the head of every man is Christ... and the head of Christ *is* God." (1 Corinthians 11:3)

Can you imagine facing the cross yet making time to heal someone's ear, or hanging on the cross and comforting the repentant man next to you and accepting that man into your kingdom? Or, in your agony, remembering to make provision for your mother? Amazing! Jesus kept His mind on the Father. That is the only way He could have endured His suffering and the cross. He never failed to serve His Father, doing His will, down to His last minutes on earth.

Dixie - 5:11 His head *is as* the most fine gold, his locks *are* bushy, *and* black as a raven.

His head as the most fine gold

To the Bride, Christ's knowledge and wisdom are more outstanding than any other's. His thoughts demonstrate the beauty of the holiness within Him. Speaking of the purity of His mind, the Bride of Christ would describe it as "most fine gold," no dross, no corruption, and free from any harmful element. Jesus Christ was of a holiness and purity that has had no match before or since.

Look at a few of the many verses that support this most important quality of Jesus' holiness: "He was taken from prison and from judgment: and who shall declare his generation? for He was cut off out of the land of the living: for the transgression of my people was he stricken. And he made his grave with the wicked, and with the rich in his death; because *he* had done no violence, neither *was any* deceit in his mouth." (Isaiah 53:8-9) God "...hath made him *to be* sin for us, who knew no sin; that we might be made the righteousness of God in him." (2 Corinthians 5:21) As you read Scriptures, get into the habit of making note of verses that testify of Jesus' purity of mind and actions like Malachi 4:2. (See also Hebrews 7:25, 9:14, 1 Peter 1:18-20, 3:18, 1 John 3:5)

His locks are bushy, and black as a raven

As was said previously, spiritually this feature represents the person's submission to higher authority. Before the world began, the Word of God surrendered every part of Himself and His future to His Father volunteering to become the kinsman-redeemer of mankind. (Isaiah 6:8) Christ trusted the Father's promises made to Him. (Psalm 2:7-9, 40:7, 9, Hebrews 1:5-13, 10:12-13)

On Earth, Jesus again submitted Himself to the authority of His Father, demonstrating humility and His desire to do the Father's will. (John 12:49-50, 8:28-29) Only one who trusts completely would do that. (1 Peter 4:19)

In Matthew 11:29, Jesus designated two qualities on which believers were to concentrate: meekness and humility, both of which are learned and demonstrated in trials. Meekness is a picture of an intercessor's heart. (Numbers 11:2, 12:1-14, 21:5-9, Deuteronomy 9:20, 22-29, Matthew 5:43-48) Humility is a quality of a servant's heart. (Philippians 2:5-8, Matthew 18:4, Mark 10:42-45, 1 Peter 2:23) This emphasis shows how vitally important they are in the Christian life and how needful that we focus on letting the Holy Spirit develop them in us.

When our thoughts and will are submitted to the Lord, for example when we can call the trial we're in a blessing more precious than gold, we'll know it has drawn us closer to the Lord. In gratitude, we can offer abundant thanks to Him for another opportunity to be an overcomer. We then have reached the mountaintop and achieved victory—for Christ, and with Christ by our side. He alone will have helped us every step of the way. (1 Peter 1:7, Ephesians 5:20, Hebrews 13:15, James 1:2-4, Romans 8:28)

Meditation Twenty-Six: Take some time to thank the Lord Jesus for His wonderful attributes mentioned in 5:9-11. Add some thoughts to your first meditation's love letter. He deserves your lavish praise.

Judy-5:12 His eyes *are* as *the eyes* of doves by the rivers of waters, washed with milk, *and* fitly set.

His eyes

Her beloved's eyes are like doves' eyes, peaceful and calm, like still waters. They are clear, bright, and seem to be bathed in cream and set just right. Looking into his eyes, this new bride gains reassurance that he is everything she needs in a husband who provides for her needs: love, protection, and encouragement. Most of all, she knows she will always have favor with him.

Looking into Jesus' eyes reassures us. He is the great I AM, the One Who is everything we need and more. (John 8:58) He will provide whatever is essential to our well-being. When we look at Jesus, into His wonderful face, the things of earth fade in importance.

The sweet and comforting chorus of the song *Turn Your Eyes Upon Jesus* is a gentle reminder of keeping our eyes on Him.

Turn your eyes upon Jesus
Look full in his wonderful face
And the things of earth will grow strangely dim
In the light of his glory and grace.
~Helen H. Lemmel (Public Domain)

Dixie-5:12 His eyes *are* as *the eyes* of doves by the rivers of waters, washed with milk, *and* fitly set.

His eyes

When you look into someone's eyes, you can see their soul's response to you. No doubt, Solomon's eyes brightened every time his bride approached him. She could see in his softened look the depth of his appreciation and desire. When this newly married woman thought of her husband's eyes, she remembered his gentleness and love.

The Bride of Christ knows the eyes of her Beloved look upon her with a gentleness produced from His heart of love. "…Christ also loved the church, and gave himself for it…" (Ephesians 5:25) Jesus taught "…as I have loved you,…love one another." (John 13:34) "Behold, I will make…the synagogue of Satan…come and worship before thy feet, and to know that I have loved thee." (Revelation 3:9)

Judy-5:13 His cheeks *are* as a bed of spices, *as* sweet flowers: his lips *like* lilies, dropping sweet smelling myrrh.

Sweet

Solomon's face is so bright. He loves the Lord, and the Lord loves the righteous. His countenance is reflected in the face of the upright. (Psalm 11:7)

This verse also reminds me of Jesus. Imagine how sweet his words are to us. Why wouldn't they be? He's our perfect example. No guile, insincerity, dishonesty, or inaccuracy was ever found in Jesus' mouth. He knew that in guarding His words, He kept His life. (Proverbs 13:3) "Death and life *are* in the power of the tongue: and they that love it shall eat the fruit thereof." "Whoso keepeth his mouth and his tongue keepeth his soul from troubles." (Proverbs 18:21, 21:23) His words are "…always be with grace, seasoned with salt…" of truth. (Colossians 4:6, John 1:17)

Dixie-5:13 His cheeks *are* as a bed of spices, *as* sweet flowers: his lips *like* lilies, dropping sweet smelling myrrh.

His cheeks, his lips

Accompanying Solomon's gentle looks are smiles for her. Have you ever pictured Jesus smiling at you? He does. You give Him great pleasure, especially when you are enjoying being with Him and leaning on Him. During worship one Sunday morning, I turned my head and knew Jesus was standing to the right of the teens' section in the sanctuary of my church. Then, for a moment, I was inside Him, looking through His eyes, and I could feel His great delight at being with so many people who loved Him. He was so joyful!

Solomon's lips always dropped sweet words of encouragement and comfort, even praise for his bride. Do you hear the Lord's voice in this Song of Solomon, whispering sweet comfort to you? He wants you to sense His tenderness toward you. All the kind, loving words and good deeds that have and will come into your life emanate from Jesus.

You've had His attention from before the beginning of time. He loved you and eagerly awaited your coming to Him. It has always been Him, blessing, cherishing. You are loved, greatly loved, and are truly special to Him. He rejoices in you, so beautiful in your potential. He rejoices in you and your growing relationship with Him. What pleasure it gives Him! What pleasure *you* give Him. Believe His love; revel in it.

Judy-5:14 His hands *are as* gold rings set with the beryl: his belly *is as* bright ivory overlaid *with* sapphires.

His hands

This shepherd-king's hands are strong yet soft. Overseeing his lovely gardens I imagine he enjoys getting his hands in the soil. He also uses his hands to bless his family and others, never to hurt them, and so his hands are beautiful to the Shulamite. Now, think about the greatness of Jesus' hands. God says He has inscribed us upon His palms. (Isaiah 49:16) Jesus says He has given us life, and we shall never perish because we are in His hands and His Father's hands. (John 10:28, 30)

Have you ever noticed that in all the instances of Jesus using His hands, it was always with a gentle touch? Parents brought their little children to Him so He could put His hands on them and bless them. (Mark 10:13-16) In John 13:4-5, after supper, Jesus poured water into a basin, and began to wash the disciples' feet, afterward gently wiping them with a towel. At another time, Jesus healed Peter's mother-in-law by touching His hand to hers. Fever gone, she arose and served them. (Matthew 8:14-15, Luke 4:38-39) When Jesus walked on water, He invited Peter to come to Him. The wind became more boisterous, and the spirit of fear attacked Peter's mind. But Peter cried out for help, and immediately Jesus stretched forth His hand and lifted him up. (Matthew 14:29-31) These verses are reassuring that no situation can occur that our Jesus can't handle.

> We are so blessed to feel that loving, gentle, compassionate touch of our Beloved today. One day, I was on the phone with a friend, and her husband who was out of town phoned her. She answered, learned his car had broken down on the side of the road, and then immediately called me back. We prayed. Within about five minutes, a state trooper stopped to see if her husband needed assistance and said he would stay until help arrived. Road service came, and her husband was back on the road in 30 or 40 minutes. We saw the hand of the Lord move in quick response to our prayer. After I pray and get an immediate answer, to me, that is the sweetest touch.

Dixie-5:14 His hands *are as* gold rings set with the beryl: his belly *is as* bright ivory overlaid *with* sapphires.

His hands, gold rings set with beryl

I love beautiful rings, so this description caught my interest. Two forms of beryl are aquamarine and emerald; however, here this word is thought to refer to topaz. My dear friend, Sybol, upon occasion, wore a very large emerald-cut, golden topaz ring, a gift from her husband. I picture its beautiful color when imagining how the king's hands appeared to his bride.

It is wonderful to think about the beauty of the hands of the Lord. Have you ever meditated on His hands? His pierced hands reached out to include the whole world in His embrace from the cross. (John 3:16) He said, "Come unto me…and I will give you rest." (Matthew 11:28) His hands reach down to rescue and lift up sinners, out of a horrible pit. (Psalm 40:2)

Like a father putting his hand on the head of his child and speaking a blessing over him, it is also the pleasure of the Lord to bestow a multitude of blessings on His children in the natural and eternal realms. Through His death and resurrection, He established the way for His followers to enjoy all that pertains to life and godliness, as well as providing all spiritual blessings in Him. (2 Peter 1:3, Ephesians 1:3)

The Hands of Jesus

The hands of Jesus are hands that heal,
Touching you with loving care.
The hands of Jesus lift you up,
Gently holding you close to His heart.

The hands of Jesus comfort you,
Encouraging you to lean on Him.
The hands of Jesus bless you,
Giving perfect-for-you gifts.

The hand of Jesus holds yours
As He walks beside you.
There is no better place to be
Than in the hands of Jesus.

There's not a more excellent place
for you at this time. Rest in the hands of Jesus.

~Dixie. D. McClintock

His belly...ivory and sapphires

Ivory and sapphires suggest the finest of substances. This new wife chooses the most opulent words to characterize her beloved. She sees the best in him. The Bride of Christ should do the same by letting her speech be free from complaints and wholly given to speaking of the wonder of her Beloved. Jesus is Life. (John 14:6) From His very center flow rivers of living water to all who will hear Him. This living water represents the Holy Spirit Who was given to Jesus without measure. (John 7:37-39, 3:34) Naturally, all that comes from Him is living and life-giving. (John 1:4, 5:26, 10:10, Romans 6:4, 1 John 5:11)

Judy-5:15 His legs *are as* pillars of marble, set upon sockets of fine gold: his countenance *is* as Lebanon, excellent as the cedars.

Strength

Her beloved's legs appeared long and solid. The strength she sees results from Solomon's activities, including mountain climbing. He has done what it took to develop his great strength.

In contrast to the emphasis that mankind puts on the physical, God does not value the strength of a man. (Psalm 147:10-11) He delights in the heart of a person devoted to Him, who is humble and gives honor to Him. True strength is developed through reading and applying the Word of God. One must learn "…by every *word* that proceeds from the mouth of the LORD" (Deuteronomy 8:3 NKJV). The Word of God is living and active, and sharper than any double-edged sword, "…piercing even to the dividing asunder of soul and spirit, and of the joints and marrow, and *is* a discerner of the thoughts and intents of the heart." (Hebrews 4:12)

Dixie-5:15 His legs *are as* pillars of marble, set upon sockets of fine gold: his countenance *is* as Lebanon, excellent as the cedars.

His legs

Solomon's strength impressed his bride. The power of our Beloved Jesus is stronger than any other. We needn't hesitate to trust Him or to cast all our burdens on Him. He is so mighty that those things that seem heavy weights to us are lighter than the weight of a feather to Him. (Luke 9:43, 24:19, Matthew 28:18)

Sockets of gold

Gold figures prominently in the description of her beloved: his head, hands, and now his legs. To me, gold symbolizes the finest and most significant degree of love. At the same time, sockets are associated with the movement or actions of love. The Bride of Christ sees her Beloved as One Whose character and soundness are mixed with and supported by love, which governs all He does.

His countenance is as Lebanon

Reminded of the stunning beauty of her homeland, the young bride can think of no better comparison for her wonderful husband. She remembers no frowns or judgment from him, no condemnation, just overwhelming love and kindness. Pleasure in her and their growing relationship is what she sees in his smiling face, too. These qualities are what the Bride recognizes in her Beloved.

Judy-5:16 His mouth *is* most sweet: yea, he *is* altogether lovely. This *is* my beloved, and this *is* my friend, O daughters of Jerusalem.

Altogether lovely

The Shulamite is so proud to call him her beloved. She's no longer just a friend but now his beloved, and he is hers. She longs for his sweet kisses.

Jesus said the person that has His commandments and keeps them, loves Him "…and he that loveth me shall be loved of my Father and I will love him, and will manifest myself to him." (John 14:21) So we enjoy being part of the family of God, (Ephesians 3:15) The Bride of Christ knows that in His presence is full joy and pleasures forevermore. (Psalm 16:11) This is a promise.

Dixie-5:16 His mouth *is* most sweet: yea, he *is* altogether lovely. This *is* my beloved, and this *is* my friend, O daughters of Jerusalem.

His mouth

In the writings of her husband-king, much was said about speech. In the book of Ecclesiastes, Solomon wrote, "The words of a wise man's mouth are gracious…" (Ecclesiastes 10:12) In his book of Proverbs, he penned: "The mouth of a righteous man *is* a well of life…" (Proverbs 10:11) "The lips of the wise disperse knowledge…"(Proverbs15:7) and "...the lips of knowledge *are* a precious jewel." (Proverbs 20:15)

Under the continued direction of the Holy Spirit, Solomon wrote: "…the words of the pure are pleasant..." (Proverbs 15:26) and "pleasant words *are* as [a] honeycomb, sweet to the soul, and health to the bones." (Proverbs 16:24) The king had also discovered "The heart of the wise teacheth his mouth, and addeth learning to his lips." (Proverbs 16:23) In discussions, the righteous person carefully considers his answer, knowing "…a soft answer turneth away wrath." (Proverbs 15:1) "A man hath joy by the answer of his mouth: and a word *spoken* in due season, how good *is it!*" (Proverbs 15:23) Solomon understood the power and importance of wise words.

The Bride could speak even more eloquently of Christ, Who is the personification of wisdom (1 Corinthians 1:30): "Hear; for I will speak of excellent things, And the opening of my lips shall *be* right things. For my mouth shall speak truth; and wickedness *is* an abomination to my lips. All the words of my mouth *are* with righteousness; *there is* nothing froward or perverse is in them. (Proverbs 8:6-8) "For wisdom is better than rubies, And all the things one may desire cannot be compared with her." (Proverbs 8:11) In the gospel of Luke: "So all bore witness to Him, and marveled at the gracious words which proceeded out of His mouth." (Luke 4:22 NKJV, 1 Corinthians 1:24)

The king's kisses and the words the Shulamite heard from her beloved were the sweetest to her. She had been the sole recipient of his gracious words, undergirded by his loving actions and patience. How could a woman not be in love with a man who cherished her this way? How could we not fall in love with Jesus and His overwhelming grace, love, patience, and encouragement?

Altogether lovely

The Shulamite has tried to do her beloved justice by beginning with "he's dazzling" and concluding with "he's altogether lovely." They are meager words for such as he—beautiful words, yet so inadequate. However, her summary expressed her heart. Her praise for him, compared to her compliments in chapter 1, has intensified and zeroed in on his magnificence.

She has learned to praise her beloved and tell others how wonderful he is. The Bride of the Lord Jesus should be able to do this easily. Praise expressed to God is evidence of the freedom that has begun and will continue to develop in a believer's life. It signifies a move from self-centeredness and soulishness to a Spirit-filled life.

Praising the Lord is simply bragging about Him, expressing adoration and admiration. Two aspects of it are: praise for Who He is, in other words, His wonderful person and character, and praise for His works, what He has done, is doing, and will do. An awe-inspiring and helpful search for the names of God (God of grace, God of hope, the Lord my Shepherd, etc.) can enhance your time of praise, using a different name every day. A compelling four-page list of the names of God was sent to me by a friend. Reading through it, I could not help but be overwhelmed and filled with exaltation of the Lord.

Blessing the Lord is our privilege and can be done throughout our day, in our worship, daily activities, repose (before we sleep), and in the throes of spiritual warfare. (Psalm 149) Esteem for the Lord Jesus is also expressed in our obedience, faithfulness, and desire for excellence in all we do, and it can draw others to praise the Lord, too. (Psalm 8:2, Matthew 21:16, 5:16) If you're a mechanic, nurse, business person, student, or if you're working outside or inside the home, et cetera, you can praise the Lord by exhibiting exceptional or quality service in whatever the Lord has appointed you to do.

Praise gives voice—whether in work, thoughts, song, speech, art, or anointed, worshipful movement in dance or music—to that which honors and praises the Lord and doesn't detract from Him. It is what should be His from every person living on this planet and from every part of creation. (Revelation 5:12-14, Psalm 149:3, 150:4) We join with the great host of heaven when we praise the Lord. (Psalm 148:1-13) I believe that when we, be it one person in the quietness of a home or on a hillside, or even many people in a church congregation, sing with heart and voice to the Lord, some choir of heaven joins us to lend even more power and joy to that moment, creating a magnification and, at the same time, a sweet oneness in our worship.

My beloved, my friend

"Friend" is more than a word to describe a casual relationship. It signifies covenant status and an elevation in a relationship. "And the scripture was fulfilled which saith, Abraham believed God, and it was imputed unto him for righteousness: and he was called the Friend of God." (James 2:23) In John 15:15-17, Jesus told His disciples He no longer called them servants, but friends, and with that designation came the assignment of election, ordination, mission, and the power of attorney in prayer.

"My beloved, and…my friend" is a phrase easily overlooked as to its significance. The Bride has passed from a level of "believing" to a much higher level of "knowing." (2 Timothy 1:12) Jesus has truly become her Beloved. Without a doubt, this wording is evidence of a magnificent transformation. Their covenant relationship has blossomed into an actual wedding of her soul with His.

> **Meditation Twenty-Seven:** Memorize Song of Solomon 5:16, "His mouth is most sweet: yea, he is altogether lovely. This is my beloved, and this is my friend…"(omitting "O daughters of Jerusalem"), and say it aloud to Him every day for a week. Write it in your journal.

CHAPTER 6 (6:1-13)

Judy-6:1 Whither is thy beloved gone, O thou fairest among women? whither is thy beloved turned aside? that we may seek him with thee.

Fairest among women

The daughters of Jerusalem are talking to the bride, and again refer to her as "fairest among women." (5:9) She's different; she stands out among the rest. With a new standard of living and supported by distinct motives, she now lives to please her beloved. This attitude parallels the Bride of Christ's. She, too, is to be set apart from the world, because she's sanctified in Christ and has a different model to live by than the rest of the world. She operates with love in every move she makes.

Whither is thy beloved

What is a wife without the husband and vice versa? My husband Tom and I were invited to an anniversary party, and I couldn't attend. I suggested Tom attend for us. At the end of the evening, the hosts took a group picture. All the guests were with their spouses, but Tom was alone. Incomplete. The daughters of Jerusalem want to know the location of her beloved. They want to see the two together, which completes the picture.

Dixie-6:1 Where is thy beloved gone, O thou fairest among women? where is thy beloved turned aside? that we may seek him with thee.

Fairest

Solomon called her fairest among women in 1:8. Having observed her for some time, the daughters of Jerusalem agree. Becoming one with him has so transformed her that others can see her inner beauty. Her statement: "I am lovesick," coupled with her description of his attributes in the previous chapter, has made them even more curious. (1:2-4, 5:9-16) His kindness and patience, heard and seen previously, stir her attendants and they are desirous to know more about him.

Like the daughters of Jerusalem, and other witnesses in the palace, today's observers of the Bride of Christ may have similar important questions to ask of her: "What is your Beloved more than any other?" (5:9) and "Where has your Beloved gone?" (6:1) They need to know who He is and how to find Him, and His Bride must have the answers.

Our knowledge of the beauty of Christ and our witness should attract others to Him. Strong in love for Him and operating in their spiritual gifts, the Bride may be part of the group who will draw Israel to desire Christ the Messiah for their own. (Romans 11:11,13-14, Deuteronomy 32:21) Our lives and testimony could bring a multitude to the Beloved One.

Jesus Himself said, "And I, if I be lifted up from the earth, will draw all *men* unto me." (John 12:32) He related this in the context of John 12:33, revealing crucifixion would be the manner of His death. However, the underlying principle of lifting Him up—that is, exalting Christ, rather than exalting self—is also true and is the way to lead others to Him.

Like the daughters of Jerusalem, at one time I desired a spiritual tutor to guide me in my quest for the King. Wanting to learn to hear God more clearly, I asked the Lord to send someone to teach me how to do that. The Lord always knows what we need and graciously provides it.

Soon after, my mother, who was in a wheelchair, and I attended a Bible study at a church where we were not members. The room was full of big round tables and chairs. Alice, a lady sitting at the back, quickly began rearranging chairs at her table so there would be enough space for Mother and the wheelchair. She motioned us forward, introduced herself, and indicated a chair for me next to where she had been sitting. During our few minutes before the study commenced, Alice began to talk about what the Lord had said to her that morning. My ears perked up. She mentioned how she had learned to hear from God, and how she and the Lord were having conversations. I knew she was the answer to my prayer and sent from God to help me. In the years since then, Alice has taught me much about hearing God and helped me come closer to Him.

Judy-6:2 My beloved is gone down into his garden, to the beds of spices, to feed in the gardens, and to gather lilies.

Sweet spices
Sweet spices like stacte, onycha, and galbanum, were highly prized in Solomon's time. The spices were mixed with pure, costly frankincense. The people often used spices to make a perfume tempered with salt. After the art of the apothecary, Moses beat other spices into tiny pieces and put them before the ark of testimony in the tabernacle of the congregation, where God would meet with the people. The people were not to copy this particular perfume for themselves; it was holy for the Lord (Exodus 30:34-38). Spices were also used in anointing for healing and in preparing a body for burial.

His garden
Her beloved has gone into the garden to check his beds of spices. He had planted seeds, and they are growing, so his job now is to tend the garden and to keep it. Then when Solomon is ready to leave, he gathers the lilies, taking them home for the pleasure of their sweet fragrance. These are similar duties and rewards to the directions God gave Adam regarding the care of the garden of Eden. (Genesis 2:15)

This Scripture reminds me of Christ and His loving care for His sheep. They are precious and of great value to Him. He is our Shepherd, and "...*we are*...the sheep of his pasture." (Psalm 100:3) He goes before us, and we follow because we know His voice. (John 10:4) At the end of our lives, we "...will dwell in the house of the LORD for ever," as He promised. (Psalm 23:6)

Dixie-6:2 My beloved is gone down into his garden, to the beds of spices, to feed in the gardens, and to gather lilies.

In his garden

The daughters of Jerusalem asked two questions of their queen: where is your beloved, and where do his interests lie? (6:1) Answering their questions with an outline of his work, Solomon's bride replies: he is near, specifically in his garden checking the beds of spices, feeding his garden, and gathering lilies. The words "to feed" in the Hebrew language is translated "to tend" as one may care for a flock. He is where one of his primary interests lies, overseeing the work of beautiful gardens where he finds pleasure. Lilies must be his favorite flower. He knows he has gathered the most beautiful lily by marrying her. (Song of Solomon 2:2)

Oh, what joy it must be for Him to come into His garden and see those who will operate in His anointing, join Him in intercessory work, and lead others into His presence through worship and Holy Spirit-directed ministry. (Hebrews 7:24-25, Psalm 100:4) I believe He finds especially pleasing the beauty of those who are doing what He created them to do. (Hosea 14:5) "...Thou hast created all things, and for thy pleasure they are and were created." (Revelation 4:11) Like lovely lilies, His people bloom where He has planted them with great purpose in mind. Too, they live to bring Him pleasure, glory, and honor. (1 Peter 1:7)

Judy-6:3 I *am* my beloved's and my beloved *is* mine: he feedeth among the lilies.

My beloved is mine

The Bride rests securely in who she is and knows beyond a shadow of a doubt, she is His one and only love. Knowing Christ's word is truth, she's confident that His love is sincere. The question is, do you really know who you are in Christ? Believe God's truth about who you are, so you will mature spiritually. Ask God to cement these truths in your heart.

In Christ: you are a new creation. (Romans 6:4, 7:6) You are dearly beloved...completely forgiven and freed forever from condemnation. (Jeremiah 31:3, John 15:12, 3:16, 1 John 4:19) You have been adopted and are a child of God. (Ephesians 1:5-6, Romans 8:15-16, 8:14, 1 John 3:1-2), and you have been given every spiritual blessing and direct access to the Father. (2 Peter 1:3, Romans 5:1-2) You are now invited to come into His presence at any time. (Hebrews 4:16) And the list of truths could go on.

Dixie-6:3 I am *my* beloved's, and my beloved *is* mine: he feedeth among the lilies.

I am my beloved's

In this declaration of the Solomon's bride, she shows she has advanced; love motivates her every thought and action.

In John 14:21, the Lord Jesus said the person who obeys His word loves Him. The obedient one demonstrates a quality of love for the Lord, but it may be duty-oriented, deferring out of a sense of correctness. It's the right thing to do. This submission shows a degree of love, but not of the highest caliber. Two verses later, in John 14:23, Jesus reversed the order and said whosoever loves Him will keep His word. This verse speaks of someone who loves Him so much that they naturally want to follow the Lord Jesus. Love for Him is the motivating factor, not duty, and shows a higher quality and level of love for Him.

When this same sentiment was spoken by the Shulamite in 2:16, notice the order of what was written first: "My beloved is mine, and I am his," which indicated she had more confidence in his love and allegiance to her than hers to him, and rightly so. In contrast, in 6:3, "I am my beloved's..." comes first. The significance could be missed if not read carefully. Something has changed. There is no holding back, no reservation in her. She is his, first and foremost. She is his, no matter what the invitation or command. She is his, with no concern as to the situation or location. He may invite her to climb the highest peak or call her to go with him to a far-off country; it matters not. Mountaintops don't scare her; apathy is gone forever. She is his, with no worry of danger or difficulty. She is his, with no place for doubt to creep into her thoughts. She has surrendered every part of herself and her future to him. There is no taint of apprehension in her posture as she declares to all listeners her complete and total trust in her beloved. Her reliance upon him is seen in the sure conviction of her words, such a change from her previous statements and actions. Like the Shulamite, the Bride of Christ's adoration of her Beloved will reflect an expanded heart of love. The Bride declares her love, without any reservation. This is the position of all who would be a part of the Bride of Christ. Total surrender to His will and complete confidence in Him are their characteristics. "Yes" is their response to His every invitation and instruction. They move eagerly with trust, not apathetically. I would think the angels sing and heaven shouts for joy when they hear us declare: "We are His, and He is ours."

1 John 4:19 states, "We love him because he first loved us." The Bride's love for her beloved Jesus is a direct result of His love for her. He made the first move of giving Himself for her and to her. His love is unquestioned.

> **Meditation Twenty-Eight:** Start each day of the next week with "Beloved, I am Yours, and You are mine." Repeat it often during the day.

Judy-6:4 Thou *art* beautiful, O my love, as Tirzah, comely as Jerusalem, terrible as *an army* with banners.

Thou art beautiful, O my love

Returning from his gardens, Solomon tells her how lovely she is and compliments her in a new way. She's strong, disciplined, unafraid, and ready for whatever comes. The same goes for the Bride of Christ. Jesus always says to her, ""Be strong and of good courage; do not be afraid, nor be dismayed, for the Lord your God is with you wherever you go."" (Joshua 1:9 NKJV)

With banners

Centuries ago, when the Scottish forces marched into battle, their bagpipers would go first, and the terrifying noise of the bagpipes would be so intimidating their enemies would scatter. Similarly, the Bride of Christ's banners would strike fear in the heart of any enemy. Representing her fearlessness, fortitude, and complete confidence, with Him by her side, she can handle anything that comes along.

The Bride says the same to her Beloved, as David said to the Lord in Psalm 60:4: "Thou has given a banner to them that fear thee, that it may be displayed because of the truth." "We will rejoice in thy salvation, and in the name of our God we will set up *our* banners…" (Psalm 20:5) The victory banner also says we are already winners in any battle. We are guaranteed victory because we belong to Christ. "He *is* a shield unto them that put their trust in him." (Proverbs 30:5) Too, the Bride of Christ knows that the Lord is the strength of her life and, therefore, she has nothing to fear. (Psalm 27:1) We don't even have to fear evil tidings, because our heart is fixed, trusting in the Lord. (Psalm 112:7) "Now thanks *be* unto God, which always causeth us to triumph in Christ…" (2 Corinthians 2:14)

Dixie-6:4 Thou *art* beautiful, O my love, as Tirzah, comely as Jerusalem, terrible as *an army* with banners.

Beautiful as Tirzah

Long ago, the children of Israel were waiting for the signal to enter Canaan, the land the Lord had sworn to give them. Conquering heathen kingdoms and settling those areas were duties still ahead. Tirzah's deceased father had sired no sons to inherit his eventual allotted portion in the promised land, so, according to the law, his estate would be given to other males in his tribe.

Tirzah and her four sisters were women of faith, believing what God had promised long before. They sought an audience with Moses, Eleazar, the high priest, and the other leaders of the tribes. The women asked to be named heirs of their father's future allotment of land. After seeking the Lord's wisdom and will in prayer, Moses agreed to their request.

Tirzah and her sisters' strength and resolve, based on their immovable faith in the Word of God and His promises, brought them a great inheritance. (Numbers 27:1-11) They were extraordinary women of faith, and the Lord rewarded them for it. The name Tirzah means delightful. King Solomon eloquently expresses pleasure in the changes in his bride's beauty. Her strength is shown in her new courage. What amazing and meaningful compliments he gives her in this statement!

What transformed the Shulamite? She chose to become a different woman. Solomon's bride confronted her need and desire for changes by concentrating on her beloved, his beauty of character, the wealth of his love, and their fellowship. In being honest, she admitted that her failure to respond to his love reciprocally had caused their recent problem. Now his bride trusts her wonderful husband completely, and he rejoices in her new-found tenacity.

Terrible as an army

Too, the Bride of Christ will become a warrior, a terror to the enemy. As David had written in Psalm 18, she would gladly declare her new skills learned from her Beloved. "He makes my *feet* like the feet of deer, and sets me on my high places. He teaches my hands to make war, so that my arms can bend a bow of bronze. You have also given me the shield of Your salvation; Your right hand has held me up, Your gentleness has made me great. You enlarged my path under me, So my feet did not slip." (Psalm 18:33-36 NKJV) She has matured in wisdom and power, quite noticeable and joyfully welcomed by Christ.

He is so proud of her. His Bride is developing a strength that makes her beautiful. He is not looking for perfection, but excellence in progress. He perceives it in her. The lessons she has learned include right thinking. Thoughts of victory, picturing the goal, and keeping her soul in accord with her spirit are all a part of becoming a victorious warrior. (1 John 5:4) She has cultivated a mindset of success, not centered on self, but from believing her Beloved's words. She has discovered the truths that David had written in Psalm 121, The LORD will help her; and He will keep and preserve her from all darkness.

With banners

A confident army always marched with banners proudly raised, declaring its allegiance and identity to all, and expecting victory. The new bride has been successful in these lessons as evidenced by this mention of banners.

After her description and testimony of him in 5:10-16, Solomon knows his bride is ready to stand with him, has dedicated her faithfulness to him against all foes, and will not be guilty of putting him second anymore. He is her only love and has her wholehearted trust and loyalty.

The Bride of Christ, too, will be a warrior bride. A victorious army returning from the battlefield would fly its flags high, proud to proclaim its triumph. By the changes that have occurred, she is returning victoriously—a battle that has not been for her spirit, but for her soul. She has broken the idol of self. She has won the victory over her will, realizing nothing is better for her than being one with her Beloved.

To refer to His Bride as "an army with banners" would not just be a fanciful title on Christ's part, but a commendation for her new resolve. Prepared and ready for whatever comes, she can now meet any foe and win the victory. How thrilled He must be to see this! What delight it must bring Him!

Christ knows she is no longer afraid of what's ahead, even if incurring some battle scars is a possibility. She knows they will be evidence of her faithful service to Him and, in a sense, the scars represent her covenant with Him, not as monumental as His, of course, but still a true fellowship of His sufferings. (Colossians 1:24, Philippians 3:10)

Do you think Jesus would love her less because of those scars? No, a thousand times no! Those blows taken in His name make her more beautiful than ever, clearly testifying of her tremendous love for Him. She is truly His queen.

Judy-6:5 Turn away thine eyes from me, for they have overcome me: thy hair *is* as a flock of goats that appear from Gilead.

Overcome

Her beloved Solomon says, "Turn your eyes from me," yet still his bride's eyes are fixed on him, trusting, listening to his every word. Beholding his countenance brings her peace and confidence. She has learned well.

The Bride of Christ becomes a beautiful creation, too, as she keeps her eyes on the Lord. Like Solomon, Christ says His Bride's beauty overwhelms Him. She follows Him and has learned by watching. This brings to mind Jesus' words, "…the Son can do nothing of Himself, but what He see His Father do… (John 5:19)

Thy hair

The Shulamite's hair is her glory. It probably shimmers and sways as she walks, glistening in the light. The Bride is being renewed in her thinking and is a new person created in righteousness and holiness. (Ephesians 4:23-24) She genuinely becomes a light in her corner of a dark world. As the Bride transitions from an old soulish nature to the new Spirit-led creation God wants her to be, she takes on a brighter countenance.

> In July 2009, I lost the little diamond from my engagement ring. When I discovered it missing, I was distraught. Immediately God comforted me by giving me a word of knowledge: I would find the diamond and know it when I saw it. I didn't quite understand that last part but accepted it.
>
> About ten days later, I was praying my life would sparkle for God like my diamond. That very evening while sitting on the porch about dusk, for some reason I turned, and my eye caught a flash of light. There was my diamond! Before I could reach out to get it where it lay between two bricks, the Lord spoke very quickly, saying, "You shine in your corner of the world." What a mighty God, so loving, comforting, and gracious to care about all the things that concern me. (Psalm 138:8) He was sweetly reassuring me He's not finished with me yet, but I know I'm on the right track.

Dixie-6:5 Turn away thine eyes from me, for they have overcome me: thy hair *is* as a flock of goats that appear from Gilead.

Gilead

Gilead is a mountainous area east of the Jordan River, extending about sixty miles from the Sea of Galilee's most southern point to the northern end of the Dead Sea.

Eyes...hair

From the eyes of the Shulamite shine the love and passion of her heart, so much that Solomon is overwhelmed. His bride's tresses, wavy, abundant and shining with health, catch Solomon's attention (4:1), and remind him of the natural beauty seen in the glistening hair of goats which, at a distance, looked like human hair. Hair in the Bible often denotes strength and submission to authority. Remember Samson? (Judges 16:17)

The Beloved also brings attention to the new and higher degree of power and authority the Bride has gained during her transformation. He has made a dramatic difference in her life. Love for Jesus, which encompasses surrender and submission, complete trust, and devotion, is the key to victory in every area of her life. More importantly, it returns to Him the love and passion that has been so constant from Him to His Bride.

Judy-6:6 Thy teeth *are* as a flock of sheep which go up from the washing, whereof every one beareth twins, and *there is* not one barren among them.

Teeth

Solomon compliments his bride's teeth, but I feel he's thinking more about how she composes her conversations. In the same loving way, the Bride of Christ carefully considers her words, choosing grace seasoned with salt. (Colossians 4:6)

Salt is used in different ways. We know it mainly as flavoring for our foods, but it also can be a healing substance and a preservative. Appropriate words can bring comfort and healing to a person who is distressed. A message of assurance could be given to a person who might need some confidence. Surely blessings are added to each conversation. In every case, the Bride, depending on the Holy Spirit, would never lack the right words but would always bring forth fruit in her ministry.

Dixie-6:6 Thy teeth *are* as a flock of sheep which go up from the washing, whereof every one bears twins, and *there is* not one barren among them.

Teeth

The teeth of Solomon's lovely wife are unstained and well-cared for; there are no gaps, no missing teeth, and no decay. Spiritually, this means the Bride of Christ is growing, nourished by the meat and milk of the Word, able to digest and assimilate the things the Holy Spirit is teaching her. She is actively engaged in doing the things that will enhance her, spirit, soul, and body, and bless her Beloved. He cherishes His Bride in every way. He is pleased with her, and He tells her so. If we listen to the voice of the Bridegroom, we will also hear loving words of affirmation and encouragement.

Usually, teeth aren't seen unless the person smiles or laughs. The Shulamite bride often smiles with love for her husband. His presence and closeness bring her so much joy, and the pleasure of his company shows on her face. Does the thought of Jesus bring a smile to your heart and light to your countenance?

Judy-6:7 As a piece of a pomegranate *are* thy temples within thy locks.

Thy temples

Here the beloved reflects on her temples, which represents to him not only the beauty of her mind but the transformation of her thinking. At the beginning of their romance, she felt inferior and undeserving of him and his love, but now sees herself differently. She's learned to think on a higher level, the level of love.

The Bride of Christ has her thoughts elevated, too, because Christ says, "...for all things that I have heard of my Father I have made known unto you." (John 15:15) She chooses to see good rather than evil and contemplates things that are true, just, lovely, outstanding, and laudable. (Philippians 4:8) Not becoming anxious when problems appear, the Bride has learned to take them immediately to her King. (Philippians 4:6-7) Her heart and mind stay free from care, kept in perfect peace. (Isaiah 26:3) Her confidence is in Jesus.

Dixie-6:7 As a piece of a pomegranate *are* thy temples within thy locks.

Pomegranate

Following the exodus from Egypt and after the leaders of the Hebrews spied out the land of Canaan for forty days, they returned, bringing pomegranates and other samples of the fruitfulness of the land to show to their people. (Numbers 13:23, 25) Forty years later, recorded in Deuteronomy 8:7-10, Moses included pomegranates among the list of the seven plentiful foods growing in the land of Canaan, which God had promised to His people.

The image of the pomegranate appeared on ancient Jewish coins. Solomon used it as a motif in the décor of the temple he built. (1 Kings 7:18) Much earlier than that, God chose and designated pomegranates, along with gold bells, to decorate the hem of the robe of the high priest. (Exodus 28:34) The bells symbolized life and God's mercy when their sound was heard after the ceremony of atonement was completed. (Psalm 89:15)

A fruit usually the size of an apple, the pomegranate has a very tough outer shell. Inside it has hundreds of gelled, edible seeds. Therefore, to the Jews, it is understandable that a pomegranate represented fertility and fruitfulness. Spiritually the pomegranates represented the abundant life in Christ and God's grace, characterized by the multitude of seeds. In the pomegranate, we see the theme of unity and fruitfulness, oneness and the 100-fold harvest. (Matthew 13:23)

Temples

In describing his charming spouse, the beloved Solomon notes the change in her thinking. In her declarations to the daughters of Jerusalem, he has seen her thoughts directed toward him, his desires, his will. She has unequivocally stated her wholehearted and outspoken devotion. She is his with no reservation. (verse 3)

On a personal note, I want the Lord to be pleased with my thoughts, which are indicators of the condition of my heart. I can't stop every thought entering my mind, but I can decide which stays and finds a home.

By bringing and measuring every thought to the standard of the obedience of Christ and casting out every notion that is against God, I want to entertain only those views which honor Him, and edify or strengthen me. (2 Corinthians 10:4-5) I want every part of me to be a delight to my Beloved Jesus. Don't you?

> **Meditation Twenty-Nine**: Memorize Philippians 4:8 to help guide your thoughts. Repeat it each day.

Judy-6:8-9 There are threescore queens, and fourscore concubines, and virgins without number. My dove, my undefiled is *but* one; she *is* the *only* one of her mother, she *is* the choice *one* of her that bare her. The daughters saw her, and blessed her; *yea*, the queens and the concubines, and they praised her.

Choice one

Her beloved Solomon proudly declares to her, "Of all the women, whether they be queens or virgins or concubines, none compare to you." Then he turns and speaks to those around him and essentially says, "My wife outshines them all."

Consider the high regard Christ has for His Bride. She has allowed the Spirit of Light to change her from the inside out. Her Beloved sees that radiating from her, and He is so pleased to call her His. Being with Him has transformed her. As it is written in 2 Corinthians 3:18: "…we all, with open face beholding as in a glass the glory of the Lord, are changed… from glory to glory, *even* as by the Spirit of the Lord."

Solomon comments she's the only daughter, therefore, a favorite of her mother, displaying such beauty that the daughters, queens, and concubines of the palace all stand in awe. They bless her, meaning they invoke divine favor for her, and their praise expresses approval. Her beloved is proud to present her to the world. No one seems to find any fault in her now.

As Jesus came up out of the baptismal water, recorded in Luke 3:22, He heard His Father say to Him, "…Thou art my beloved Son; in thee I am well pleased." When Jesus comes for us, we desire to hear a similar sentiment: "You are My beloved Bride, in whom I'm well pleased." Jude 24 mentions the immense delight Jesus will have when He will present her "…faultless before the presence of his glory with exceeding joy."

Dixie-6:8-9 There are threescore queens, and fourscore concubines, and virgins without number. My dove, my undefiled is *but* one; she *is* the *only* one of her mother, she *is* the choice *one* of her that bare her. The daughters saw her, and blessed her; *yea*, the queens and the concubines, and they praised her.

Queens and concubines

What is the difference between a queen and a concubine? A queen is the wife of a king. By virtue of her marriage covenant, she has a high position and more authority than any other woman in the kingdom. In Solomon's time these queens had probably been princesses given to King David, Solomon's father, as part of political alliances, as was customary in that culture. (1 King 3:1, 11:1-3) Solomon, after he came to the throne, was required to house and provide for his father's harem as they aged, but they were not *his* queens. The law of the Lord excluded his having sexual relations with them. (2 Samuel 5:13, Leviticus 18:8-9, 1 Chronicles 5:1) In contrast, a concubine was either a woman who cohabited with a man without the benefit of legal marriage, a captive who became a servant, or, in certain polygamous societies, a secondary wife of lower legal status and socially inferior to the first wife. Generally, concubines had more rights than slaves but fewer than wives.

The reference to "virgins" and "daughters" in verses 8 and 9 makes me think they are Solomon's sisters by his father David's sixty queens and eighty concubines. If not, "virgins" would represent young maidens given to either David or Solomon as part of treaty agreements with surrounding nations.

The daughters saw her, and blessed her

Solomon states there is no conflict between the Shulamite and any other of his female family and household. Amazing! Why would they react with blessing toward this woman who might be viewed as an interloper or an intruder?

Why would they praise someone exalted over them? It would be natural to show resentment, jealousy, and even malice toward her. Surprisingly, there was no friction between them and the Shulamite; in contrast, they expressed their approval and admiration for her. Solomon himself wrote that when people's ways please the LORD, He will even cause their enemies to be at peace with them. (Proverbs 16:7)

What did these young women see? They obviously saw beauty, but I'm not sure they would be impressed, because all the women in a king's palace were chosen for their loveliness. Her speech would not have swayed them. What they saw, and that for which they blessed her was the strength of her love for Solomon—complete enthrallment with him and the resulting transformation in her. Not only does he have her heart, but he has become her heart. None of the other women have the degree of love that she has for him.

They recognized the truth of her surrender when she declared to them, "I am my beloved's." They praise her willingness to be his without her caring about anything or anyone else but him. How the Shulamite's love for Solomon has deepened! The way she has grown in her relationship with him speaks volumes to the other women. Words of praise for him, backed up by the transformation of her life, bring commendation and approval from them.

The Bride's deepening love relationship with Jesus brings her the praise and blessings of those who see striking differences in her.

> *My dove, my undefiled is but one; she is the only one of her mother,*
> *she is the choice one of her that bare her*

These are sweet words of Solomon's own praise given to her. Do you feel joy knowing Jesus looks at you as the chosen one, undefiled, beautiful, and a lily among thorns? He loves it when your face looks toward Him; He delights in your pleasing voice. Do you understand you have ravished His heart? (4:9) Take time to meditate on this and realize who you are to Him.

Judy-6:10 Who *is* she *that* looketh forth as the morning, fair as the moon, clear as the sun, *and* terrible as *an army* with banners?

> *Who is she?*

The royal women now turn to each other and question, "Who is she that is as fresh as the morning?" They are noticing the wonderful changes that have taken place in this new bride of the king. She shines like the dawn, pretty as the moon, bright as the sun. She has a peaceful composure, reflecting much light and pleasantness with eager anticipation of what new opportunities each day holds. The Bride of Christ is a true reflection of her Beloved, and she has the confidence of a whole army waving victory banners.

Meditation Thirty: Read Psalm 27:1,3a. Some other verses that describe the strength of the Bride are Psalm 3:1-3, 18:29-32, and 112:7. List her attributes in your journal. (Whenever you read Scripture, look for additional verses that encourage your strength in the Lord and note those in your journal, too.)

Dixie-6:10 Who *is* she *that* looks forth as the morning, fair as the moon, clear as the sun, *and* terrible as *an army* with banners?

Who is she?

The praise of the queens and concubines mentioned in verse 9 is revealed here. What an astonishing commendation from these influential women! They are stunned by her remarkable transformation in contrast to when she first came to the palace. There was a similar comment in verse 4 of this chapter, where the king describes his bride as beautiful, lovely, and awesome as an army with banners. However, in this verse, the women intriguingly describe her with words of light first. Their use of morning, fair, moon, clear (pure), and sun all speak of the light and glory that shines in and through her now.

Additionally, the king's bride is said to look forth, not with reluctance, but with gladness and eagerness. She is desirous of, and looking forward to, the opportunity of joining Solomon in his work. She has changed much from her earlier attitude.

At the same time, while acknowledging her radiance, these women also recognize the intensity of her determination by using the word "terrible" (Hebrew definition: frightening) and the phrase "as an army with banners." This army is referenced three times in this chapter, once in this verse and also in verses 4 and 11, which point out the incredible metamorphosis that has occurred. Others, who might have been her competitors for Solomon's time and attention, can see the striking changes in her demeanor, and, in a sense, they bow in deference to her. No longer an insecure girl, this new bride has become a confident yet fiercely determined woman sure of victory.

Unlike the uncertain, fearful girl hidden behind the latticed window (2:9), the Shulamite has become a warrior in her spirit, who looks unafraid into the future, transcendent, a fitting helpmate for her husband. So, too, the Bride is becoming a force with which to be reckoned. Learning to have no fear of the enemy or what the future holds, she is valiant and courageous, able with her Beloved to meet every situation and emerge victorious. (Luke 9:1-6, 10:17, 19) Leaping on the mountains and hills of life has finally become part of her triumphant life. (2:8)

When sure knowledge was applied in her daily life, her soul agreed with her spirit rather than opposing it, and significant differences occurred. Nothing could hold her back from dispelling the darkness, advancing, and destroying hell's gates and its power over the souls of mankind. The Bride of Christ is living truth of Jesus' words in Matthew 16:18: "...I will build my church; and the gates of hell shall not prevail against it."

> **Meditation Thirty-One:** You are accepted in the Beloved, a very strong position. (Ephesians 1:3-7, 2 Chronicles 16:7-9, Proverbs 3:5-6) Frequently repeat Philippians 4:13, " 'I can do all things through Christ which strengtheneth me." Thank Him for His grace.

Judy-6:11 I went down into the garden of nuts to see the fruits of the valley, *and* to see whether the vine flourished, *and* the pomegranates budded.

Fruits of the valley

Solomon's bride made the right choices. The result is Psalm 1:3. She's "…like a tree planted by the rivers of water," producing seasonal fruit. What ever she chooses to do now thrives.

It is the same with the Bride of Christ. She, too, has been born with a seed of faith, and shall add qualities which will enhance that faith like excellence, knowledge, self-control, godliness, kindness, and love. (2 Peter 1:5-7) Choosing to learn and embrace the gifts of the Spirit, she will work with these tools to promote maturity in her Christian walk. Then the fruit of the Spirit will show up in her life. (Galatians 5:22-23, 1 Corinthians 12-14)

Dixie-6:11 I went down into the garden of nuts to see the fruits of the valley, *and* to see whether the vine flourished, *and* the pomegranates budded.

Garden of nuts

Solomon's orchards would have included almond and other nut trees, which flourished in Israel. These trees were appreciated for shade and fruit. (Genesis 43:11) The valued almond tree was first to bloom in the spring and produced food, oil, and medicine, and was used for special carved items. Aaron, the first high priest of the Hebrew people, used a staff or rod made of almond wood, which represented his authority over the children of Israel and his position as intercessor. (Exodus 28:1, Numbers 17:1-10)

Almond in Hebrew means "awakening." How appropriate! The Sleeping Beauty bride has been awakened by her Prince Charming, forever changed, and moving into her destiny. As the Bride of Christ grows into her potential, she becomes an avenue of intercession for others. (1 Timothy 2:1) Now her thoughts turn to how she can help others, by prayer and mentoring.

I went

The Shulamite's first initiative is to join in the work of her beloved. She goes to the garden where fruit should be growing. She appraises two things: whether the vine flourished and whether the pomegranates budded. Her statement is one filled with hope, as well as a desire to evaluate the situation.

The Bride of Christ shows much spiritual growth and fruit, but she seeks to know the condition of any areas that have not yet borne fruit. Self-evaluation is always a good idea. Of what does the Holy Spirit remind us in 1 Corinthians 11:31? "For if we would judge ourselves, we should not be judged." Appraising her own development is a way for her to be aware of areas of good progress and those that need careful tending to bring them to a bountiful conclusion.

Judy-6:12 Or ever I was aware, my soul made me *like* the chariots of Amminadib.

My soul

Reflecting on how far she has come, from operating on the soul level to working on a higher spirit level, reveals a truth to her. What a difference! At the soul level, we're thinking on our own, but working on the spirit plane involves the Holy Spirit, Who leads and directs. When we come to Christ, we receive the Holy Spirit and He abides with us forever. He teaches us and reminds us of God's Word. (John 14:16-17, 26)

Dixie-6:12 Or ever I was aware, my soul made me *like* the chariots of Amminadib.

Like the chariots of Amminadib

Do you see the change in the Shulamite's thinking? The chariots of Amminadib were known to be the swiftest, and their drivers gave rapid response to their commander. This reference alludes to this new bride's realization that strength and quick response to her leader had become ingrained before she knew it, "ever I was aware." Now, she is a fierce warrior, not just an initiate in training or a cowering student. This transformation came with her testimony in 5:9-16 as to why her beloved was more than any other and was increased by her soul's surrender to him (6:3). The more we tell others how wonderful our Beloved is, the more we show our trust in Him, the stronger we will grow.

Judy-6:13 Return, return, O Shulamite; return, return, that we may look upon thee. What will ye see in the Shulamite? As it were the company of two armies.

Two armies

The daughters of Jerusalem say, "Return, we want to behold you." What will they see? It will be an overwhelming sight. With the beloved and his bride working together, they will accomplish as much as two armies.

Dixie-6:13 Return, return, O Shulamite; return, return, that we may look upon thee. What will ye see in the Shulamite? As it were the company of two armies.

Return

The daughters of Jerusalem ask her to return four times in this single verse! How desperately they want and need her encouragement. How fervent their plea for her to help them understand what has affected her so drastically! No doubt, they have never seen a queen so fiercely and passionately invested in her relationship with her husband-king and their future. They realize she has begun to move in concert with the plan of her bridegroom, and they are intrigued by this change.

Those who are not as progressed on their spiritual journey need us to remind them, as Judy mentioned in 1:4, to tell them our phenomenal Christ is sufficient, more than enough. He hears, even before we look to Him; He answers in the darkest night. He will always lead us gently toward the fullness of the shining light of God's Presence. How blessed the eternal journey with Him will be!

What will ye see

The daughters of Jerusalem answer their own questions in this verse and in the next several verses in chapter 7.

Two armies

"Mahanaim", meaning two armies is the same Hebrew word used in Genesis 32:2 when Jacob takes his wives, Leah and Rachel, and his children back to Edom to arrange a meeting with his estranged brother Esau. The Scripture states, "And Jacob went on his way, and the angels of God met him. And when Jacob saw them, he said, 'This is God's host': and he called the name of that place Mahanaim," meaning two hosts or bands, physical and spiritual, meeting together and moving in unity. Jacob realized he and his family, servants, guards, etc. were being escorted by this invisible army of angels. (Genesis 32:1-2. See appendices for other evidences of angels' service.)

To the women of the palace, this new queen has become so different. She seems transformed into two armies, fierce and strong when needed. This company of two armies speaks of the integration and accord with which heaven and earth move and work. This understanding of the holy cooperation of humanity with the spiritual realm, and the harmony of their purpose to serve the living God, bring a fortitude and resolve not seen in the ordinary world. The Bride of Christ will be so changed that others cannot help but exclaim she is as strong as two armies. Her transformation is impressive and remarkable to all who have known her.

CHAPTER 7 (7:1-13)

Judy-7:1 How beautiful are thy *feet* with shoes, O prince's daughter! the joints of thy thighs *are* like jewels, the work of the hands of a cunning workman.

Beautiful

These are the daughters of Jerusalem admiring the beauty of the Shulamite. Reflect again on 1:6, when she was shy and said, "Look not upon me because I *am* black, because the sun hath looked upon me…" Now see how far she has come, standing there, allowing them to compliment her. She's like clay, remolded and made into a greater beauty.

Like the Shulamite, the Bride of Christ now has different ways, standards, and motives for what she does. She has reached a higher level of love. "…the path of the just *is* as the shining light, that shineth more and more unto the perfect day." (Proverbs 4:18) "How beautiful upon the mountains are the feet of him that bringeth good tidings, that publisheth peace; that bringeth good tidings of good, that publisheth salvation; that saith unto Zion, 'Thy God reigneth!'" (Isaiah 52:7) "As cold waters to a thirsty soul, so *is* good news…" (Proverbs 25:25) The Bride brings good news of the gospel of peace.

Next, the daughters remind the new queen that the hands of a cunning workman created her. We all have this in common but so often take it for granted. We are created in the image of God. The Trinity said, "Let us make man in our image, after our likeness…", but They didn't just leave us to survive on our own. (Genesis.1:26, 27) They continue to sustain us. (Hebrews 1:3, John 14:16) What a marvelous Creator!

The Bride has been born again and is now being transformed. (John 3:5-7, Romans 12:1-2) From this comes the beauty that the world sees. The change starts from inside and shines through. That's what the daughters of Jerusalem observe in her. That's the beauty we want the world to see in us. (Matthew 5:16)

Dixie-7:1 How beautiful are thy feet with shoes, O prince's daughter!

O prince's daughter

As shown by this title, the observers of the Shulamite see one whose behavior and demeanor fit her exalted station. The bride gains new respect from those around her as her commitment grows. The daughters of Jerusalem give her validation of her new self and endeavors. They have seen the difference in her and proceed to elaborate on it.

Are your behavior and demeanor beginning to match your exalted station? The more you listen to the Holy Spirit and follow His direction, the more you will change and others will see.

How beautiful

The daughters of Jerusalem proclaim her new beauty. Her beloved spoke first of her eyes (6:5); here the spectators speak first of her feet. Why? He looks into her soul; the daughters of Jerusalem see her actions. (1 Samuel 16:7) These ladies-in-waiting have seen the changes in her attitude and have observed her new conduct, which speaks volumes to them. (Titus 2:7-8, 1 Peter 2:12, Ephesians 2:10, Colossians 1:9-14)

This group of admirers recognize that the Shulamite is not the product of her own making. Neither is the Bride the sole creation of her own sculpting; the Lord has used many people to help her. Take a few moments to thank the Lord for sending the ones who have been instrumental in your spiritual growth.

The Bride of Christ is continually being shaped, molded, and filled by God the Holy Spirit. He is her trainer, teacher, and guide in this new life. He deserves the praise for her loveliness. (2 Corinthians 3:18)

Feet with shoes

Slaves went barefoot, while free people wore shoes. The observers make comments about the young bride's beauty, starting with her shod feet, as if greatly impressed with her new state of freedom and her ability to walk comfortably with her husband, the king.

"Feet with shoes" is an odd description, but when joined with Ephesians 6:15, "…feet shod with the preparation of the gospel of peace…" it makes perfect sense. In the Bride's testimony of her Beloved, and promotion of Him as more than any other, she paves the way for her audience to seek Him, too. (5:10-16, 6:1) She is so confident in His love that she welcomes others who want to come closer to Him. Her behavior and words impress people, drawing them to her Beloved. Nothing is more powerful than a life filled with an overflowing love for Jesus and a love poured out in service to Him and mankind.

> **Meditation Thirty-Two:** During the day, express aloud, "I delight to do Your will, Beloved." (Psalm 40:8)

Judy-7:2 Thy navel *is like* a round goblet, *which* wanteth not liquor: thy belly *is like* a heap of wheat set about with lilies.

Wine and wheat

In the Bible, wind, wine, and water are a few of the metaphors used for the Holy Spirit. (John 3:8, Acts 2:1-4, Luke 5:38) Jesus, speaking of the Holy Spirit, said: "He that believeth on me, as the scripture hath said, out of his belly shall flow rivers of living water." (John 7:38-39)

Spiritually, wheat represents Christ, the Bread of life or the Word of God, and there is no lack to all those who desire to hear. Jesus promised, "...I am the bread of life: he that cometh to me shall never hunger; and he that believeth on me shall never thirst." (John 6:35, Matthew 4:4) To perceptive observers, Jesus is the source of all they need to receive, and the Bride will be the storehouse of all that the Beloved Christ has given her.

Dixie–7:1-2 ...the joints of thy thighs *are* like jewels, the work of the hands of a cunning workman. Thy navel *is like* a round goblet, *which* wanteth not liquor: thy belly *is like* a heap of wheat set about with lilies.

Beauty abounds

Superlatives of the bride's features are extravagant because her beauty is exquisite. Her abdomen and thighs are jewels, her navel a filled drinking glass, and her belly bountiful yet beautiful. These aspects represent fertility, which was important in their culture. Onlookers see she is pregnant from her union and oneness with her husband.

For the Bride, these descriptive phrases represent her ability with her Beloved to bring forth others into newness of life in Christ. At the same time, she is no longer interested in self, languishing in her former bed of apathy, but is tenacious and eager to join with her Beloved to accomplish all their will.

Judy-7:3 Thy two breasts *are* like two young roes *that are* twins.

Two breasts

Like two breasts, the Word of God and the Holy Spirit supply the Bride with much to give to others. She is also like a branch of the true vine. Due to the pruning of that branch, she has choice grapes, giving joy and nourishment to all. The work of the branch is to abide in the vine and the Word of God continually, to elevate the power of her prayers. (John 15:4-7) We are called to be aware of others' needs, whether spiritual or material. In the early church, every person's needs were met. (Acts 4:34) The Bride blesses others in her giving.

Dixie-7:3 Thy two breasts *are* like two young roes *that are* twins.

Two

Why the emphasis on "two" and "twins"? The Bride is endowed with more than enough to nurture and nourish new lives in Christ and do as the Lord directed in discipling them. (Matthew 28:19) This teaching involves a several-pronged plan and approach. Matthew 13:1-23 suggests three needy areas the church must adequately address, so the Word can generate a fruitful harvest in a person or a nation: evangelism (spiritual birth), education (spiritual growth), and saturation (physical and emotional support including, if needed, an interval of sustenance or provision to allay the tendency of new converts to worry about their future). When these aspects of ministry are provided to aid possible converts, spiritual growth will occur.

Judy-7:4 Thy neck *is* as a tower of ivory; thine eyes *like* the fishpools in Heshbon, by the gate of Bathrabbim: thy nose *is* as the tower of Lebanon which looketh toward Damascus.

Towers

The Shulamite's neck is long and straight, and reminds the daughters of a strong tower. Her strength is a reflection of her beloved's. He is a strong tower to her, and with him she feels safe. Similarly, the Bride views Christ as her fortress, or high tower, and the one she trusts. (Psalm 144:2)

Solomon's bride has eyes like fish pools, clear and deep and full of discernment in whatever she encounters. Strength is a reflection of purpose. Like a prominent tower, she fleetingly looks back toward Damascus, or the world from which she's come, now realizing the greatness of her future with her king. She's not longing for the old ways but glorying in the new. The Bride of Christ is the same. She delights that her path is as a bright shining light. (Proverbs 4:18, Psalm 119:105)

Dixie-7:4 Thy neck *is* as a tower of ivory; thine eyes *like* the fishpools in Heshbon, by the gate of Bathrabbim: thy nose *is* as the tower of Lebanon which looks toward Damascus.

A tower of ivory

The description of the Shulamite's neck as a tower of ivory attests to her new attitude, a decided contrast to earlier fears. It proclaims and enhances her beauty which emanates from her courage. Trusting him completely, she is lovingly submissive to her husband. In this, she is wisdom and holiness personified. Beautiful and strong in her understanding that, in doing so, she has made the best choice.

Eyes like the fish pools of Heshbon

Heshbon, a southern city sixteen miles east of the Jordan River, had been the resident city of Sihon, a strong Amorite king. The royal pools, formed by a natural spring in the area, were deep and clear. Bathrabbim was a particular city-gate near these pools.

Comparing her eyes to these waters meant the daughters of Jerusalem recognized their queen could now see the breadth and depth of issues and situations she had once been unaware of. She has discernment and the wisdom of how to apply knowledge properly. (Proverbs 4:7, James 1:5-6, Hebrews 5:14)

Tower of Lebanon

The second structure mentioned in this verse is the tower of Lebanon in northern Israel. Towers were often built in the fields to act as storage units for grain and equipment, but they were also intended to be a part of the early warning system of the area. A single watchman atop this tower could scan Israel's border with Lebanon, survey far distances, identify advancing enemies, or spot an approaching storm. This tower and others were safeguards of Israel's protection.

Comparing the Shulamite to such a consequential tower was a great compliment—a testimony to her trustworthiness, strength, and total allegiance to her king. She is unafraid to face her enemies or even the thoughts of her former life in Lebanon. She is on the alert, not only for herself, but for all within her jurisdiction.

The end of a passage listing the spiritual armor of the Christian in Ephesians 6 speaks of the watchfulness in prayer which Spirit-filled believers need to have: "Praying always with all prayer and supplication in the Spirit, and watching thereunto with all perseverance and supplication for all saints..."(verse 18) The command to watch adds the finishing touch to the well-prepared soldier serving in God's kingdom. The Bride is not languishing in her bed or asleep on duty. Sensitive to the enemy's tactics, she stays alert to every possible attack.

Meditation Thirty-Three: Meditate on this verse: "He shall not be afraid of evil tidings: his heart is fixed, trusting in the LORD." (Psalm 112:7)

Judy–7:5 Thine head upon thee *is* like Carmel, and the hair of thine head like purple; the king *is* held in the galleries.

Hair...like purple

Here we get a picture of royalty with the color purple. The bride holds her beloved uppermost in her mind and thinks about what would please him.

Dixie-7:5 Thine head upon thee *is* like Carmel, and the hair of thine head like purple; the king *is* held in the galleries.

Carmel

Mount Carmel, reaching 1,500 feet high in the northwestern section of Israel, rises above all surrounding areas and overlooks the Jezreel Valley on the eastern side and the Mediterranean Sea on its western side, providing far-seeing vantage points to watchmen. The evergreen mountain receives much precipitation during the year, unlike other parts of Israel.

To compare the Bride to this landmark mountain, the site of Elijah's triumph of faith over the false prophets of Baal, speaks volumes as to the changes that have occurred in her. (1Kings 18) She is a powerful warrior woman with such discernment and vision that those who observe her now must remark on it. The queen's companions note her thinking as the excellency of Carmel. (Isaiah 35:2)

Hair…like purple

Some say this refers to her purple ribbon headdress. Spiritually, it makes me think of the nobility of the Bride's thoughts lining up with those of the Lord Jesus: thoughts on things are true, honest, just, pure, lovely, of good report, excellent, and praiseworthy. (Philippians 4:8) It is one thing to know this scripture; it's another to live it. Her admirers see the beauty of her disciplined life, even as it extends to her very thought life, and they comment on how impressive and pleasing it is.

No doubt, when we live in holiness, desiring the Holy Spirit to lead in our thoughts and allowing Him to censor any thoughts that aren't worthy, we bring great delight to Him. (Colossians 1:10) In John 15:26, Jesus taught, "But when the Comforter is come, whom I will send…*even* the Spirit of truth,…he shall testify of me…" This testimony is found in an individual believer's changed behavior, which gives evidence of the indwelling presence of God in that person. John the Baptist expressed it succinctly when he said, "He [Jesus] must increase, but I *must* decrease." (John 3:30) So it is not only appropriate, but necessary that these observers of the Bride see in her those qualities which spotlight this turnaround in her.

> **Meditation Thirty-Four:** Memorize the last of Nehemiah 8:10: "…the joy of the LORD is your strength." The emphasis is on the LORD. Feeling joy as your thoughts meditate on Him and His greatness brings strength to you.

Judy-7:6 How fair and how pleasant art thou, O love, for delights!

For delights

Gazing at his wife, the bridegroom breaks in with this exclamation. How much in love he is with her! We would say "head over heels in love." He can't hold back about how much she pleases him. Yes, she's a beauty on the outside, but he's looking deeper, remembering the diamond in the rough in the beginning of his courtship of her. She's now reached the point where she's truly one with her beloved. Together with the same mind, the same goals, and twice the strength, they can work together with gladness in their hearts. He's still looking at her and, with great pride, says, "She's mine, all mine!"

Dixie-7:6 How fair and how pleasant art thou, O love, for delights!

For delights

In the Septuagint, the Greek translation of the Hebrew Old Testament, this verse reads: "How beautiful are you and how sweet you are, my love!" Her new husband cannot help but interrupt and add his wholehearted praise to those who voice their acclaim of his bride. This speaker is Solomon because he is the only one who uses the title "my love" in this book. Her companions refer to her as "fairest among women" and "prince's daughter" but not as "love." (5:9, 6:1, 7:1) Solomon's exclamation expresses the love of Christ for His Bride. Jesus, too, like Solomon, will regale listeners with His delight in believers who love and serve Him with all their heart. (Revelation 3:9)

Do you believe the Lord Jesus calls you beautiful and sweet? He is Truth; He tells the truth. You must see yourself as He sees you rather than agree with Satan's hateful and demeaning opinion of you.

Judy-7:7 This thy stature is like to a palm tree, and thy breasts to clusters *of grapes*.

Palm tree

The daughters of Jerusalem now reflect on the new queen's stature and how tall and straight she carries herself. She has come to full maturity and has more than enough wisdom to share with those still lacking.

Dixie-7:7 This thy stature is like to a palm tree, and thy breasts to clusters *of grapes*.

Palm tree

Notice that her stature has changed considerably. Having described herself previously as a small lily (2:1), incapable of providing sustenance to anyone, she is now compared to a tall, fruitful palm tree. Her growth reminds me of the description given in Ephesians 4:11-13, 15-16 (NIV) of the fulfillment of the purpose of the five-fold ministry: "And He gave some, apostles; and some, prophets; and some, evangelists; and some, pastors and teachers; for the perfecting of the saints, for the work of the ministry, for the edifying of the body of Christ: till we all come in the unity of the faith, and of the knowledge of the Son of God, unto a perfect man, unto the measure of the stature of the fullness of Christ… speaking the truth in love, may grow up into him in all things…" The Bride has made great strides in her growth and development. Knowing and loving Christ make the difference.

A palm tree is not only unusual in its design but is a sure sign of the presence of abundant water. (Exodus 15:27) In the Christian who has moved into intimacy with the Lord Jesus, there is not only a well of the water of life, but it is ready to flow out as directed by the Holy Spirit. Like the Samaritan woman of John 4, the Bride has drunk from the living water and become a well of water springing up into everlasting life. (John 4:10, 14) She had previously been described as a spring shut up, a fountain sealed, but now she is a site of refreshment and sustenance, a source of life-giving water and hope to others.

Judy-7:8 I said, I will go up to the palm tree, I will take hold of the boughs thereof: now also thy breasts shall be as clusters of the vine, and the smell of thy nose like apples;

I will take hold

"O taste and see that the LORD *is* good: blessed *is* the man *that* trusteth in him. O fear the LORD, ye his saints: for *there is* no want to them that fear him." (Psalm 34:8-9) "How sweet are thy words unto my taste! Yea, *sweeter* than honey to my mouth." (Psalm 119:103) The daughters of Jerusalem have accepted her invitation after embracing the testimony of all that her beloved is. They collectively will take hold of all she has said, wanting their lives to exhibit the differences they have seen in her.

Dixie-7:8 I said, I will go up to the palm tree, I will take hold of the boughs thereof: now also thy breasts shall be as clusters of the vine, and the smell of thy nose like apples;

I will

There is a question to decide in the verses of 7:8 and 7:9. Who is the speaker? Is there more than one? Certainly, in this passage, it could be the group of women continuing to compliment the Shulamite on the beauty of her transformed self. However, the speaker might be the bridegroom or the bride. In analyzing the pronouns used in these two verses, we can see more clearly who the speaker is and learn more about how to study Scripture.

Only two people, Solomon and his bride, have previously used the pronoun "I" in this song. Up to this point, the Shulamite has told much of their love story from her point of view. She has repeatedly used the pronoun "I" to recount the salient moments of their love story. She uses "I" forty-five times in this song, whereas the beloved uses it seven times. The contrast is rather telling in the character of this bride. In the first six chapters, she continually uses "I." She is in the process of transformation. "I" is used about thirty-one times in those chapters. Based on this fact alone, one might think the bride is the speaker because of the use of the pronoun in these two verses.

On the other hand, the bridegroom spoke in verse six. Could he have continued through verse nine? Possibly. Yet look carefully at the other pronouns in verses 7-9: "thy stature," "thy breasts," "thy nose," and "thy mouth."

This reference is to the bride and a continuation of a description of her beauty which her companions began in 7:1. Because her words and changed life have testified to them, the daughters of Jerusalem have been changed. They are now claiming him as "beloved," too.

At this juncture, these ladies reminisce that they had united in purpose as one ("I said"), and had declared their intentions to "take hold" of what she has told them about her beloved. They desire the same life and abundance that she has shown before them. To them, this bride has become, as it were, a vine with clusters of grapes growing up the palm tree, providing all they need to come into a new relationship with their king.

They remark that everything she has told them, every breath she breathes, is like the scent of apples—refreshing, life-sustaining, and vital. Her words have begun to change them, but her life has strongly undergirded her testimony. Had they not seen the difference that intimacy with him had produced in her, they would not desire change in their own lives.

Judy-7:9 And the roof of thy mouth like the best wine for my beloved, that goeth *down* **sweetly, causing the lips of those that are asleep to speak.**

Her testimony

She awakens others with her testimony. How important it is to realize our words may be what someone's spirit and soul are waiting for and hungering to hear. "The mouth of a righteous [person] is a well of life…" (Proverbs 10:11) Sharing our love and praise for Jesus may be the beginning steps to a new life for others.

Dixie-7:9 And the roof of thy mouth like the best wine for my beloved, that goeth *down* **sweetly, causing the lips of those that are asleep to speak.**

Thy mouth

What the Bride of Christ tells observers concerning her Beloved may bring about the beginning of a transformation in them. Those who had been spiritually asleep didn't know Him. More information about Him must be obtained (5:9-6:3). Viewing Him differently now, they awaken to the truth. They are not jealous of the Bride's status, for they recognize her contribution to their new position and understanding. They speak collectively, waking from sleep to a bright new day. (Rom 11:11, 25-27) They are ready to tell others of the One Who is now their Beloved. (Isaiah 60:1, Ephesians 5:14)

Judy-7:10 I *am* **my beloved's, and his desire** *is* **toward me.**

I am his

"All that I am is his," the Shulamite seems to be saying. The Bride says the same thing: "All I am is His." She feels such joy. "I will bless the LORD at all times: his praise *shall* continually *be* in my mouth." (Psalm 34:1) "By him therefore let us offer the sacrifice of praise to God continually, that is, the fruit of *our* lips giving thanks to his name." (Hebrews 13:15)

Dixie-7:10 I *am* my beloved's, and his desire *is* toward me.

I am my beloved's

The first part of this verse is a repeat of 6:3. The bride's response is to the praise coming from the daughters of Jerusalem. (7:1-5, 7-9) The Shulamite explains the changes wrought in her by pointing them to the relationship of love and complete trust shared by her and her beloved. "I am my Beloved's" will become the new and forever-after theme of the Bride of Christ.

His desire is toward me

"Hearken, O daughter, and consider, and incline thine ear; forget also thine own people, and thy father's house; So shall the king greatly desire thy beauty..." (Psalm 45:10-11) Of course, Christ desires His own Bride, for He sees the beauty of her surrendered life. Spirit, soul, and body have been given entirely to Him, nothing held back, and with no reservations or reluctance to trust Him. She is radiant with love for Him. Such a love is what He always wanted, His heart's desire.

Christ delights in you. When you embrace that truth and truly believe He loves you with all His heart, it will transform you. Your love for Him will intensify.

Meditation Thirty-Five: Memorize Song of Solomon 7:10: "I *am* my beloved's and his desire *is* toward me." Quote this verse until you believe it. Repeating "I am my beloved's" is an effective and fantastic way to calm your fears and strengthen you in any situation, "...for in quietness and in confidence shall be your strength..." (Isaiah 30:15)

Judy-7:11 Come, my beloved, let us go forth into the field; let us lodge in the villages.

Come

The bride of Solomon desires to go forth and see if the seeds she's sown have brought forth more fruit. We know, though, that it takes more than a person sowing seeds to produce growth. Paul tells us one sows the Word, another comes along and waters it, and God will give the increase. (1 Corinthians 3:6)

God's Word speaks a lot about being ready. The Bride of Christ must know her abilities and be busy using them, to fulfill the will of God, which includes the Great Commission while she waits for the coming of our Lord Jesus Christ. (Matthew 28:18-20, 1 Corinthians 1:7)

Dixie-7:11 Come, my beloved, let us go forth into the field; let us lodge in the villages.

Fields and villages

"Field" is a term that can refer to land, the world, and people. (Ecclesiastes 5:9, Matthew 13:38, John 4:35) "Villages" probably refer to like-minded people of tribes and areas.

Come, my beloved

Amazingly Solomon's bride now issues the invitation he initially gave her in chapter 2: "Come, my beloved." What a reversal! Her eagerness to go out into the world indicates her conversion, her transformation. She is concerned for those in need, who work in the fields and live in the villages.

"For the love of Jesus" is the motto and motivation of the Bride of Christ. That phrase measures all she thinks, speaks, or does. No longer satisfied with being idle, she intends to be a part of His work and calls Him to join her. Transformation leads to expansiveness of vision and work.

Today, as troubles in the world multiply, and as the days and years seem to speed toward the tribulation as described in the Book of Revelation and other places in the Bible, the Bride will join the Holy Spirit to call for her Beloved to come for her. "The Spirit and the Bride say, 'Come.'" (Revelation 22:17) Christ will respond, "Surely, I come quickly." (Revelation 22:20)

Let us

Note the use of the word "us." Previously, it has been "I," "me," "my," and "you."; now it is "us." What a metamorphosis, indicative of this young bride's new understanding that her life now is a joint venture, a collaboration of heart, mind, and body with Solomon!

The same could be said of the Bride of Christ. Her total change in attitude manifests itself in a desire to extend her borders, to increase her involvement in His outreach. (1 Chronicles 4:10) This is *faith in action*, an important concept akin to the teaching of the type of faith showcased in the book of James. (See Appendix F for more on faith)

The Bride has a vital love and energetic faith in Christ, and believes in His power and Word. Those who love the Lord delight in being a part of His work on Earth.

Judy-7:12 Let us get up early to the vineyards; let us see if the vine flourish, *whether the tender grape appear, and* the pomegranates bud forth: there will I give thee my loves.

Let us see

Have you ever planted seeds in a garden, watered them, and waited anxiously to see some growth? That's the way Solomon's bride is. She's eager to see a harvest to honor her beloved. Her work is an expression of love for him.

"...God *is* not unrighteous to forget your work and labor of love, which ye have shewed toward his name, in that ye have ministered to the saints, and do minister."(Hebrews. 6:10) "Therefore, my beloved brethren, be ye steadfast, unmovable, always abounding in the work of the Lord, forasmuch as ye know that your labor is not in vain in the Lord." (1 Corinthians 15:58)

Dixie-7:12 Let us get up early to the vineyards; let us see if the vine flourish, *whether* **the tender grape appear,** *and* **the pomegranates bud forth: there will I give thee my loves.**

Early to the vineyards

The young bride's priority is to rise early to enjoy the pleasure of Solomon's company and be with him in his work. Nothing is more precious than the time spent with her beloved. What a shift in thinking! Instead of lagging or letting him go to work by himself as in previous times, this bride has learned her lesson. She no longer puts herself first in her choices. His desires are hers now. She wants to engage in what he enjoys. Before, she didn't want to participate in his interests and activities; now, she is captivated by them, because nothing is more valuable to her than being with him.

Her eagerness and energy are equal to the task and present a picture of the Bride of Christ. This is a good yardstick for measuring the quality of our love for Christ. Do we look forward to being in His presence? Do we relish the opportunity to join Him in His activities? Are we more focused more on the interests of Jesus than our own?

Let us see if the vine flourishes

Spring has come again, but this time, the Shulamite finds joy in what gives her husband pleasure, in contrast to her attitude in 2:8-17. Indeed she is transformed. The vine represents her life. This evaluation of her growth will be good. Not only has she matured, but her fruitfulness, both now and in the future, is predicted in the tender grapes and pomegranates to come.

There I will give thee my loves

"Loves" is a Hebrew word for love tokens. The Bride of Christ exhibits such tokens as yielding, strong faith, unwavering trust, quick responsiveness, and, qualities her Beloved treasures, and which indicate her adoration of Him. Intimacy with Jesus only grows sweeter when maturity and wisdom accompany love.

Judy-7:13 The mandrakes give a smell, and at our gates *are* all manner of pleasant *fruits*, new and old, *which* I have laid up for thee, O my beloved.

New and old

The old ways are gone; new ways blossom into life. I have a dear friend who came to the Lord several years ago but was never discipled by the church, so she didn't grow spiritually. A couple of years ago, she went back to church and her studies increased the desire to serve the Lord out of gratitude for what He had done for her. Today she's still in Bible classes and happily serving as a hospice volunteer. It's just wonderful to see her mature and grow in the Lord.

> Back in December 2011, the Lord gave me a dream. In it, I saw additional rooms attached to our home. I kept walking from room to room, wondering why I didn't know they were there all along. I couldn't find the door that led from our home to this new section. The only thing I could think is that doors will open to me in time, and I'll be doing things I never dreamed of, possibly new ministry opportunities. I eventually wrote to Scott McClintock (Dixie's brother), because he interprets dreams. He called and explained that there would be someone as close as a relative to help me. It turned out to be Dixie. This would be the beginning of an increase of my ministry. He said the new bedrooms were to be places of spiritual rest and peace, and my obedience would fill the rooms. (Proverbs 24:3-4) So, fast-forward to a few months later, here I am, helping to write a study on the Song of Solomon. What an honor it is! The Lord has blessed me with this wonderful opportunity to add new fruit in my life.

Dixie-7:13 The mandrakes give a smell, and at our gates *are* all manner of pleasant *fruits*, new and old, *which* I have laid up for thee, O my beloved.

Mandrakes

Mandrakes were common fragrant plants that bloomed in the Spring, announcing the time for harvest in Israel. Ancient people thought that mandrakes were aphrodisiacs, fertility enhancers which stimulated conception, as seen in Genesis 30:14-16. Jacob's beloved second wife, the barren Rachel, desperate to have a son, schemed to obtain mandrakes from her sister Leah. Hence, mandrakes would be an appropriate gift from Solomon's bride to him, since she wants to bear his children. How does this apply to the Bride of Christ?

Our gates

Notice her words, "our gates." By that particular choice, she reminds all who hear her that she and her beloved are one, united in purpose and plan, goals and achievements.

People passing by the massive palace gates could see the gifts left to honor their king. Those who honor their Beloved Christ, after first giving themselves to Him, offer their ministry gifts to Him and need not fear examination by anyone. As David said in Psalm 26:1-3: "Judge me, O LORD; for I have walked in mine integrity: I have trusted also in the LORD; therefore *I* shall not slide. Examine me, O LORD, and prove me… For thy lovingkindness *is* before mine eyes: and I have walked in thy truth."

All manner of pleasant fruits

The NIV uses "delicacies" for "pleasant fruits," and the NLT employs "delights." Either way, they speak of tributes worthy of a king. In some ancient cultures, it was proper for friends and family to lay gifts before the house gate of the newly married. Here, the Shulamite bride sweetly tells Solomon what she has selected as her wedding gifts to honor him, and how she has displayed them for all to see. This is her way of showing her love to him and others. Read Proverbs 24:3-4.

New and old

Like wine, some spiritual fruit has developed and ripened, unlike the "tender grapes" that need more time to mature. Both types of fruit in Christ's Bride bring glory to the Beloved. Each demonstrates her continuing admiration and regard for Him.

Pleasant fruits…laid up for thee, O my beloved

In years gone by, women canned fruits and vegetables from their gardens so their families would have good things to eat in the winter. I can remember many summer days of no air conditioning: my mother leaned over a hot stove, canning the blackberries and wild plums, making pickles, drying apples, etc., for the benefit of her family. She was a dynamic woman, and love was the common ingredient in her labors.

> One Christmas, as a gift, I had a professional calligrapher write and frame one of my mother's favorite quotations, penned by G.V. Owen:
>
> "Kind words beget kind deeds. And so is love multiplied, and with love, joy and peace. And they who love to give, and give for love's own sake, are shooting golden darts which fall into the streets of the heavenly city, and are gathered up and carefully stored away till they who sent them come and receive their treasures once again with increase."*
> *(Life Beyond The Veil, Vol 2, G. V. Owen, p. 67, April 1920)

In Matthew 6:21, the Lord Jesus spoke of laying up treasures in heaven for "…where your treasure is there will your heart be also." I don't think Jesus was primarily teaching about a heavenly bank in which we are to invest, but about the motivation of our endeavors. There is no doubt that there is a heavenly pay-off awaiting those who have been faithful to the leadership of the Holy Spirit in their lives; but the reward is not as important as why or whom they served. When attending church, their motive was to worship the Lord, to sing to and bless Him. When Scriptures were opened, they read to get to know Him. While helping people in need, the love of Jesus was their inspiration.

While baking sweet treats for Vacation Bible School, those who loved the Lord made sure to infuse those cookies with prayer for the children's souls. It is important to remember this life is an occasion to lay up all manner of pleasant fruits to please and honor our Beloved.

Let it not be thought the Christian life is a one-note song. The Lord is a creative God with countless and unsearchable thoughts and designs. Naturally, too, He has enabled His Bride to develop in many ways by the fruit of the Holy Spirit, her abilities, and her spiritual gifts. (Galatians 5:22-23) He also gives her many different and even unusual opportunities. She is unafraid to branch out in her ministry as the Lord leads. One example of that very point is Judy joining me to write this manuscript. A hundred-fold harvest in the Bride's life is not unattainable, but is dependent on the strength of her desire and commitment to Him. (Matthew 13:23) The true depth of her love will determine the magnitude of her harvest to His glory.

What pleasant things in your life, old and new, show to others how much you adore Him?

Meditation Thirty-Six: Before you begin each new activity, repeat the phrase "for the love of Jesus" to increase your focus on Him and help develop the habit of examining motivation for your actions.

CHAPTER 8 (8:1-14)

Judy-8:1-2 O that thou *wert* as my brother, that sucked the breasts of my mother! *when* I should find thee without, I would kiss thee; yea, I should not be despised. I would lead thee, *and* bring thee into my mother's house, *who* would instruct me: I would cause thee to drink of spiced wine of the juice of my pomegranate.

My brother
The Shulamite looks at her beloved in a new way. In a sense, she wishes he had been her brother because of his loving tenderness toward her. He treats her like a lady and has given her a better way of life. Remember chapter 1 where she said her mother's children despised her, making her keeper of the vineyards, preventing her from caring for herself? If she had met her beloved sooner, life would have been different, no doubt easier. She would have had someone to lighten her load, to share all her burdens, one who would understand and help.

What a comfort to know that when nobody else could possibly understand our situation, God does. He not only understands but cares and can do something about it. "Great *is* our Lord, and of great power: his understanding *is* infinite." (Psalm 147:5) Not only that but "…the everlasting God, the LORD, the Creator of the ends of the earth, fainteth not, neither is weary…*there is* no searching of his understanding." (Isaiah 40:28)

I would...bring thee into my mother's house, who would instruct me
The Shulamite would have brought her beloved home. If her mother had known and loved the Lord God with all her heart, soul, and might, she would have taught her children. It would have made a meaningful difference to the girl. In any case, her beloved could have enjoyed the fruit of knowing her early on.

Dixie-8:1-2 O that thou *wert* as my brother, that sucked the breasts of my mother! *when* I should find thee without, I would kiss thee; yea, I should not be despised. I would lead thee, *and* bring thee into my mother's house, *who* would instruct me: I would cause thee to drink of spiced wine of the juice of my pomegranate.

O that thou wert as my brother
What an odd statement, or perhaps not so odd when more consideration is given to her words. She wishes Solomon were as her brother so she could have had the closest ties to him in her early life, without being subject to observers' contempt for any public display of affection. She yearns to have known him for a long time, to have grown up with him, and been able to show affection to him from the beginning. She regrets the wasted years; their time together has been short.

Isn't that a natural thought for one enjoying companionship and love? Why didn't I meet you sooner? Why did I waste all those years when I could have been with you? I've had that very thought about the Lord. Haven't you?

I would kiss thee

In Matthew 26:49, we read of Judas' kiss signaling his betrayal of Jesus in the garden of Gethsemane. This last recorded kiss identified Jesus to the temple guards who, being led by Judas, had come to arrest Jesus, though He had done nothing to warrant their action. How shameful for Judas to turn such a sign of affection into something so despicable. (Psalm 41:9, John 13:18-19)

Solomon's bride has always desired and treasured his kisses. In 1:2, we remember her words, "Let him kiss me with the kisses of his mouth: for your love is better than wine." Things would have been different if she could do over some of the earlier times. She wishes she could make up for a deficit of affection, saying if she had known him sooner, there would have been no delay to shower him with love and attention. She would have taken instruction from the wise on how to be more responsive to her husband. Because Solomon's bride has such strong feelings for him, she is filled with desire and not reluctant to show it.

The attitude and outlook of the Bride of Christ are the same. Those who love the Lord are moved by desire to redeem the time wasted in past trivialities and are not ashamed to demonstrate their love for Christ in their deeds and words. (Ephesians 5:15-16)

I would cause thee to drink of spiced wine

Wine has previously been mentioned several times in the Song of Solomon, with each reference connected to the topic of love. Spiced wine, stronger in flavor and effect, represents how her love has grown and matured.

Judy-8:3-4 His left hand *should be* under my head, and his right hand should embrace me. I charge you, O daughters of Jerusalem, that ye stir not up, nor awake *my* love until he please.

Embrace me

They lovingly embrace each other. The act of their enjoying each other's attentions is a picture of the unity of marriage. The Bride of Christ hears the words "…accepted in the beloved," and to her, these words are a treasure. (Ephesians 1:6) They bring a soothing balm to her heart and heal the wounds of the past. What a phenomenal way to be loved— unconditionally and passionately!

Awake not

This couple does not want any interruptions when they are together. After all, Solomon first loved her. He made the first move in extending his love to her. His words and actions convinced his bride he values her highly, and therefore, wants no disruptions in their precious time together.

It's the same for us when we accept God's invitation for close fellowship with His Son. "God *is* faithful, by whom ye were called unto the fellowship of his Son, Jesus Christ our Lord." (1 Corinthians 1:9) We have to live in this world, but there are exceedingly great and precious promises to assure us we can make it. (2 Peter 1:4) We are to keep our eyes fixed on Jesus "Whom having not seen..." we love and "...rejoice with joy unspeakable and full of glory..." (1 Peter 1:8) So once we open ourselves to the love God extends, how could we allow anything to come between us and Jesus? Let's start our day with our Beloved, allowing no distractions to interfere. If we meet Him in the morning, we'll be with Him through the day, rejoicing at evening.

Meditation Thirty-Seven: Memorize and meditate "...I trust in your unfailing love..." (Psalm 13:5 NIV)

Dixie-8:3-4 His left hand *should be* under my head, and his right hand should embrace me. I charge you, O daughters of Jerusalem, that ye stir not up, nor awake *my* love until he please.

Embrace me

This is similar to verses 2:6-7 and 3:5. There was a custom at marriage festivities for a chorus of maidens to serenade the couple to sleep and awaken them the following morning with a song. Instruction is given to the daughters of Jerusalem not to interrupt the married couple. Not intending to be overly zealous or extreme, this bride is carefully protecting the couple's time together. Their relationship is holy ground and their time together special.

Verse 4 is a spiritual reminder that the intimate relationship between the Beloved and His Bride is also sacred and must be guarded diligently.

Judy-8:5 Who *is* this that cometh up from the wilderness, leaning upon her beloved? I raised thee up under the apple tree: there thy mother brought thee forth: there she brought thee forth *that* bare thee.

Who is this

The daughters of Jerusalem are wondering who is this coming from the wilderness. The Shulamite looks so radiant, confident, and poised they hardly recognize her.

Under the apple tree

Her beloved begins to recall their courtship. An apple tree holds special meaning to them as it was where her mother pledged her to marry King Solomon. What gladness filled their hearts! At first, he was her shepherd and provided everything she needed. He remembers

how he brought her from the vineyards and taught her how to be his queen. He guided her on the right paths and directed her to places where she could safely rest. Early in their relationship, she felt sure he was the right one for her, and that "goodness and mercy" would be with them all their days, a picture of Christ and His Bride walking together. (Psalm 23:6)

Dixie-8:5 Who *is* this that cometh up from the wilderness, leaning upon her beloved? I raised thee up under the apple tree: there thy mother brought thee forth: there she brought thee forth *that* bare thee.

The wilderness

The couple has spent some time in the wilderness, apart from others. We would call this their honeymoon. A superficial view of wilderness in Israel might lead us to question taking a bride to an area we would describe as desert, barren, rocky, desolate. Only the most discerning can understand the desert's potential—its vast beauty, hidden springs of refreshment, and the luxury of solitude in staying at an oasis. The wilderness turned out to be a blessing to them both.

If you feel you're in a barren desert, do not discount it as having no value. It can be the best of times and experiences as you learn to know and trust your Beloved. Every stage of life with the Lord has potential for growth and training if you do not hinder it.

- **The desert can be a place of learning, beauty, and quiet.** Patience and self-control are fostered in the desert. Of course, the sand and heat can be very irritating. If you feel you are in a spiritual desert, it is critical and necessary to watch your attitude and make sure you don't let your soul (thoughts, emotions, will) rule your decisions.

- **The desert can have purpose.** It is a time to draw near to God. "O God, You *are* my God; early will I seek You; my soul thirsts for You...in a dry and thirsty land where there is no water." (Psalm 63:1 NKJV)

- **It is also a place of pledges from the Beloved.** "Therefore, behold, I will allure her, and bring her into the wilderness, and speak comfortably unto her." Although this statement in Hosea 2:14 gives a description of God and Israel as husband and wife, the sentiment, backed by loving regard, is the same between Christ and His Bride.

- **Notice what promises are made to the loved one:** tenderness, gifts of vineyards, and a door of hope, representing abundance and a great future. Additionally, "...I will betroth thee unto me for ever; yea, I will betroth thee unto me in righteousness, and in judgment, and in lovingkindness, and in mercies." (Hosea 2:19)

In the deserts of life, we are removed from the distractions and cares of the world and learn to overcome—to focus on the eternal—as Jesus did in His own wilderness experience. There we find the Lord is our refreshment and our water of life. "Therefore we do not lose heart. Even though our outward *man* is perishing, yet the inward man is being renewed day by day. For our light affliction, which is but for a moment, is working for us a far more exceeding *and* eternal weight of glory..." (2 Corinthians 4:16-17 NKJV) Job understood this precept concerning his future and said, "...He knows the way that I take; *When* He has tried me, I shall come forth as gold." (Job 23:10 NKJV)

- **The desert is the place to obtain power.** On His way back to Galilee after His baptism, Jesus was led by the Spirit into the desert, where the devil tempted Him for 40 days. (Luke 4:1-13) In all that time, He ate nothing. Still, He triumphed. Jesus' desert conquest over Satan's enticements served as the means of releasing power for His ministry. Then Jesus traveled to Galilee, and the power of the Holy Spirit was with Him. (Luke 4:14, Matthew 9:8)

- **The desert is not a waste.** The wilderness experience is for our refinement, training, and preparation to qualify us for promotion, both here and in the life to come. (2 Corinthians 2:14) Those who concentrate solely on desert conditions and its hardships will become weak. Those who steadfastly set their eyes on the Beloved and His promises will come out of the experience as mighty warriors, ready to conquer in their own promised land.

- **The wilderness is not a place of abandonment**. It is not a sign of the King's disapproval. It is not a punishment, nor is it a place of forsakenness. Remember, the Shulamite was not alone in the wilderness; her beloved was there with her, loving, protecting, watching over the one he held so dear. Your Beloved is with you now, no matter what wilderness or desert you think yourself in. He promises always to be with you, the one He loves, His beautiful bride. (Matthew 28:28)

- **Not everyone is in the wilderness at the same time.** Those who asked, "Who *is* this that comes up from the wilderness leaning on her beloved?" hadn't been in the desert at the same time as she. We're all at different places on our spiritual journey with the Lord.

We need to understand that truth, be less prideful and judgmental of others, and seek ways to encourage and be kind to one another. So do not despise your time in the wilderness. It is necessary. "And we know that all things work together for good to them that love God…" (Romans 8:28)

Her beloved

"I *am* my beloved's, and my beloved *is* mine." (Song of Solomon 6:3) The Bride loves Christ above all others. There is none so wonderful and magnificent as her Beloved. If she desired, the Holy Spirit would give her a song of love which she could write and sing to her beloved as David did in Psalm 45:1-8. "He's mine. My heart is overwhelmed! I must sing to my glorious King, the most noble of men, His words touched with grace, whose displays are majestic, whose very Being is robed in splendor. From heaven's mansions, You will come as the all-powerful King of kings, so glorious and mighty, and will secure victory for Your people. Beloved, there is no one like You! I am overcome with Your love and eagerly look forward to being with You forever."

Up

The wilderness experience doesn't last forever. It can bring out the finest in you and be the place that qualifies you for greater authority and governance. (2 Corinthians 2:14) In due season, at the appointed time, things will change. "…he who sows to the Spirit will of the Spirit reap everlasting life." "… let us not grow weary while doing good, for in due season we shall reap if we do not lose heart." (Galatians 6:8-9 NKJV) The Bride of Christ will come out of her own desert experiences tremendously changed, and she will be honored for her love and devotion to her Beloved. Make it your prayer to be of one heart with the Lord Jesus. (Acts 4:32)

Leaning on her beloved

This verse shows the deep relationship between Christ and His Bride. He has been patient, wooed and waited for her, carefully drawing her ever nearer. With every fiber of His being, He has desired a oneness with her that would never diminish and would transcend the heights of love on earth. The Bride has been slower to demonstrate that same high quality of love for Him, but now she is totally enthralled with Him. By learning to lean on her Beloved, the Bride demonstrates a greater trust in Him. Having renounced and rid herself of fears and apathy, the things that retarded the growth of love, she is so different now that it is obvious to others. Being with the Lord on a daily basis is transforming her.

- **You lean because you love.** Submission comes from the Bride's passion for loving Jesus. He is much more to her than an acquaintance or even a friend. Lovers enjoy touching each other. She leans on Him because she enjoys being close to Him, and her passion finds immense pleasure in His company. The way lovers lean on each other is much different than those who need assistance. You don't lean on someone unless you know he's strong enough to support you. The Bride of Christ already knows how strong her Beloved Jesus is and leans on Him because she can, which pleases them both. All are blessed when they give their trust to the Lord Jesus. (Psalm 34:8)

- **The Bride knows she needs Christ's strength**. She does not trust her strength or walk in the pride of self-sufficiency. The Lord is her rock, fortress, and savior, in whom she finds protection. He is her shield, the power that saves her, and He is, most certainly, her place of safety. (Psalm 18:2) Consider Jesus: for Him to have made it through each day in purity and holiness from a little child to adulthood, He had to depend on His Father. (Luke 2:40) In the thirty-three years of His earth life, Jesus daily relied on His Father and, as a result, received all the power, provision, wisdom, instruction, and protection He needed. That's why He was so strong. He had learned to lean on God His Father. (John 8:28-29) Now Jesus' Bride has learned to trust Him, not her own understanding. She is going from strength to a greater degree of strength each day, because she knows where her strength is positioned. It comes from Him. "I can do all things through Christ Who strengthens me." (Philippians 4:13 NKJV, and also see Proverbs 3:5-6, Psalm 37:5, Psalm 84:7a)

- **You have to be very close to lean on someone.** Christ is pleased and encourages His Bride to lean on Him. Imagine He has His arm around her, whispering to her, "I am holding your hand, so don't be afraid. I am here for you—always." (Isaiah 41:13, Hebrews 4:16, 1 Peter 5:7) His Bride would reply, "I love leaning on You, being close to You every step of the way."

- **There's a unique fellowship when two are so close.** There is no space or separation between Solomon and his bride. Their relationship has deepened over time spent together. Those who see them could tell there is extraordinary love between them. Did you know the old hymn *Leaning on the Everlasting Arms* is based on Deuteronomy 33:27? The lyrics declare great joy and fellowship, even peace, when leaning on the everlasting arms and walking with Him. The sweetness of the journey and the brightness of our day result from the blessing of relying on the arm of the Beloved without fear or dread.

- **If you're close enough to lean on Him, you can hear His whisper, and He'll listen to yours.** There is an exceptional delight in the communion and closeness of the Bride and her Beloved. There's no need to shout. A whispered word can be intimate. Do you hear His whispers to you? If not, get closer to Him, and spend more time thinking of Him.

- **She is so close to Him she can hear His heartbeat.** She knows what is most important to Him and wants to be a part of it. He has shown that He is an overcomer and has called her to be one. (Revelation 3:21) Now she has come to such an abiding love for Him, she is more than ready for anything He suggests.

- **They walk in step together.** The prophet Amos in his writing stated, "Can two walk together, except they be agreed?" (Amos 3:3) Christ and His Bride walk together in agreement, of one accord and one mind. His will is hers; she confidently proceeds with Him. (1 John 2:6, 19, Colossians 1:10) Humility and submissiveness are two critical aspects of her harmonious walk with her Bridegroom. Submissiveness is the wisdom to obey, and humility means recognizing that someone more significant and powerful than you is in charge. Jesus was humble and yielded to His Father; these were the very qualities He told His followers to learn from Him. (Matthew 11:29) The Holy Spirit has taught the Bride humility, that leaning on her Beloved is the wise choice. She has listened to His wisdom and applied it, becoming humble and submissive, not prideful and rebellious. His Bride is becoming conformed to His image and to His walk.

As to the second critical part of a harmonious spiritual walk, submission is an uncomfortable subject. It need not be. Who could not be gladly submissive to the One Who loves you so much? He willingly gave His life for your redemption. Our spiritual submission is to Jesus, the Person of the highest caliber, most merciful, and the noblest of character. There is no reason to struggle with submission to the Beloved. On the contrary, to be submitted to the Lord, trusting Him, shows your wisdom.

Some would say you can't learn to be humble or meek or even to love. My feeling is if we couldn't learn, Jesus would not have commanded us to do so in Matthew 11:29, where He said, "...learn of me, for I am meek and lowly..." Furthermore, suppose we could not learn those qualities. Why would the Holy Spirit write "Let this mind be in you, which was also in Christ Jesus...[who] humbled himself, and became obedient unto death..."? (Philippians 2: 5, 8) The Bride's delight is to lean on her Beloved, as was Jesus' desire to do His Father's will. (Psalm 40:8)

- **The Bride trusts Christ, no matter where He leads.** She doesn't know the way; she's unfamiliar with what's ahead, but He isn't. He has been that way before. Her trust in Him is so strong that she doesn't care where He leads her; she wants to be with Him wherever He goes. "Yea, though I walk through the valley of the shadow of death, I will fear no evil; for You *are* with me..." (Psalm 23:4 NKJV)

- **They're going the same way by His direction.** "O LORD, I know that the way of man *is* not in himself; *it is* not in man who walketh to direct his steps." (Jeremiah 10:23) "Commit your way to the LORD, trust also in Him... He shall bring forth your righteousness as the light, and your justice as the noonday." (Psalm 37:5-6 NKJV) What a promise!

- **There are benefits and blessings to walking with Him.** "Surely goodness and mercy shall follow me all the days of my life: and I will dwell in the house of the LORD for ever." (Psalm 23:6) "He who walks with wise *men* will be wise…" (Proverbs 13:20 NKJV) "…whoever walks wisely will be delivered." (Proverbs 28:26 NKJV)
His Bride is not with Jesus because of the blessings. She's with Him because she loves Him. The blessings come as a natural result of their close relationship.

- **Christ and His Bride are so close, His fragrance rubs onto her and hers on Him.**
That aroma is always a reminder of the other person and their love. In the Gospels, there were three times women broke treasured alabaster boxes or flasks filled with costly ointment and anointed Jesus. One was early in His ministry (Luke 7:36-50), another six days before Jesus' last Passover (John 12:1-8), and the final time, two days before the cross. (Matthew 26:2-13, Mark 14:1-9) I like to think the odor of that last heartfelt gift reminded Him that someone loved Him greatly. The fragrance of what we do for Him ascends to heaven with the message of how much we love Him.

- **She loves her Beloved and is loved by Him**. She is confident in that knowledge. She revels in Jesus' love. To her, His love and kindness are more than life itself. "…day by day the Lord also pours out his steadfast love upon me, and through the night I sing his songs and pray to God who gives me life." (Psalm 42:8 TLB) "I shall again praise him for his wondrous help; he will make me smile again, for he *is* my God!" (Psalm 43:5 TLB)

- **She is content in His love and desires no other.** The Bride of Christ is His and only His forever. Oh, such devotion and love for Him! He deserves that and more from you and me.

- **That Christ is your Beloved will be evident to others**. The Bride doesn't care who sees her leaning on Him. She is changed by her experience with Him in the desert; no one recognizes her new self. We "…with unveiled faces contemplate the Lord's glory, are being transformed into his image with ever-increasing glory, which comes from the Lord, who is the Spirit." (2 Corinthians 3:18 NIV) The more we yield to the Holy Spirit, the more we transform into a beautiful Bride for our Beloved.

Who is this?
The Shulamite's companions asked a similar question in 6:10, "Who is this…as terrible as an army with banners?" Her strength and increased confidence have other aspects which are

astounding to them. They sense an extraordinary oneness between her and her beloved, a new unity that will not entertain any creeping division or allow disengagement to intrude.

In contrast, the church of Ephesus in Revelation 2 is described as a wife, but she had forsaken her first love. She had loved Jesus, but her eyes no longer brightened at the mention of His name. She didn't want to talk with Him or about Him. She didn't seek to hear His voice. She had no desire to spend time with Him and didn't look forward to His appearance. There was no yearning in her heart for intimacy with Him. She was attentive to her duties but distant from Him. She was the housekeeper but not His lover. Her work was more important than protecting her relationship with Him. She was always busy but too busy to have time for Jesus. Contrarily, He didn't neglect her. He hadn't forsaken her. He loved her and desired a relationship of closeness with her and sought to re-establish it—hence, the letter of Revelation 2:1-7.

We see a great contrast in the Song of Solomon and Revelation 2. In the Song of Solomon, we see a woman who has learned to love her shepherd-king with all her heart. In Revelation, we see a woman who has stopped loving her Lord by substituting busyness for intimacy. The question is, which person do you want to be?

Others will desire to learn what changed her. "But I, when I am lifted up from the earth, will draw all…to myself." (John 12:32 NIV) Jesus was speaking of the cross when He said, "If I be lifted up…" but this principle is still true today. When we lift Him up, honor Him, live for Him, and exalt Him while demonstrating lives of love and consecration, we will also draw others who want to know Him. What I see spiritually in those I admire causes me to want more for myself.

What do you do if you want to be the one who passionately loves the King? You get to know Him. You study His words, actions, and responses, looking at the Person and character of heart He reveals. You make Him your Beloved. You choose to put Him first in life and learn to lean on Him. Bring every matter, every decision, to Him first. Submit graciously and obey Him. Be confident in Him, His personality, and His love. Trust Him completely. The three R's of the Christian life should be: Relax, let go of tensions and worry and give them to Jesus; Rest in His unfailing love and care; and Rely on Him to guide you. You are not alone in desert experiences. Learn to lean on Him.

> **Meditation Thirty-Eight:** Daily declare and remind yourself: "Today I am leaning on You, Beloved."

I raised thee up

In this latter part of 8:5, Solomon remembers the day of their formal engagement, the pledge, and the covenant of their love made possible by her family's blessing. Christ has

exalted His Bride to be His Queen. (Ephesians 2:6) What a great honor in response to her transcendent love for Him!

Judy-8:6 Set me as a seal upon thine heart, as a seal upon thine arm: for love *is* strong as death; jealousy *is* cruel as the grave: the coals thereof *are* coals of fire, *which hath a most vehement flame.*

Heart and arm

Solomon wants his bride to set a seal on her heart and arm, the emblems of belonging. They have confessed their passionate devotion for each other, a "forever love," as expressed in our traditional wedding vows: "I take you to be my lawful husband/wife, to have and to hold, for better or worse, for richer or poorer, in sickness and health, to love and to cherish from this day forward until death do us part."

God has engraved us on the palm of His hands. (Isaiah 49:16) He says, "...I have loved thee with an everlasting love: therefore with loving kindness have I drawn thee." (Jeremiah 31:3) The Apostle Paul, acting as the father of the Bride, wrote: "...I am jealous over you with godly jealousy: for I have espoused you to one husband, that I may present you as a chaste virgin to Christ." (2 Corinthians 11:2)

Dixie-8:6 Set me as a seal upon thine heart, as a seal upon thine arm: for love *is* strong as death; jealousy *is* cruel as the grave: the coals thereof *are* coals of fire, *which hath a most vehement flame.*

Set me as a seal upon your heart, as a seal upon your arm

It has been conjectured that the young queen voiced this request to Solomon. I disagree. She wouldn't say this to him because she never doubted his love. Remember, she commented in 2:4, "His banner over me was love." Solomon is the one who makes this request of his queen. He wants to be first in her heart. He also wants no doubt or question in anyone's mind about who she is and who she represents. In some sense, he asks for a vow renewal, this time from the depths of her heart, and he receives it from her.

In the same manner, the Bride of Christ has always known she had her Beloved's heart, for early in their courtship, she, like the Shulamite, could declare, "You are mine." (2:16) In all instances, every attitude and conduct have been evidence of Christ's true, constant love for His Bride.

Upon your heart...and upon your arm

What's the difference between the heart and the arm? One is internal; one is external. Both are symbols of your identification. The first only God can see; the other is visible to people. (1 Kings 8:39, 1 Samuel 16:7) Christ wants His seal to be upon our hearts. This is His great desire: His name on our heart, indelibly engraved on our spirit and soul, forever His, and His alone, and His name honored and exalted in all that we do.

> **Meditation Thirty-Nine**: Tell Jesus, "Beloved, You are the seal upon my heart and on my arm."

Love is as strong as death

In Genesis 3, we see that Adam was more willing to die with Eve than for her. When Eve sinned, could Adam have given his life for Eve instead of partaking in the forbidden fruit with her? Would God have raised him from the dead as the reward for love's sacrifice? Sadly, Adam didn't run to the Lord and ask for a plan to redeem Eve, nor did he refrain from sin and disobedience. He didn't refuse sin's temptation to be his bride's savior, but hallelujah, Jesus did!

The Son of God came to Earth to show the world what true love was. Having put aside all of Heaven's glory and humbling Himself by taking on human flesh, Jesus gave Himself as the ransom for the world's freedom from the kingdom of darkness. Jesus taught that love is the foundation and fiber of sacrifice and showed its full measure in His death on the cross for the sins of humanity. (John 15:13) Christ compellingly demonstrated "love is as strong as death" when He endured the cross and ransomed His Bride. (Hebrews 12:2) Father God also showed the power of love and His approval of all that Jesus had done by the resurrection of the Righteous One from among the dead. (Acts 17:31)

Jesus Christ embodied the truth and pureness of God's love for the human race. He personified what the Scriptures teach about love in 1 Corinthians 13 and passages like John 15 and 17. For instance, in 1 Corinthians 13:4-8, which describes the behavior of love, I see the soul of Jesus in His manner toward His Bride. He is patient with her, gentle and kind, etc. Yet this verse in Song of Solomon (8:6) depicts the fierceness of His love for her in every particle of His being and describes it as "a most vehement flame." What person wouldn't want to know such a love?

True love is the basis of all that is from God. His love is of the greatest quality, holy and perfect, strong and vital, capable of the highest degree of sacrifice. The love Christ offers is the same He desires and deserves from His Bride. This kind of love comes not from the weak but the stalwart of heart who give themselves without regard or reservation to their Beloved. They trust Him completely and hold nothing back, knowing what He asks for is the same quality of love He bestows.

Jealousy is cruel as the grave

Exodus 34:14 (NKJV) states: "…you shall worship no other god: for the LORD, whose name is Jealous, *is* a jealous God…" Godly jealousy, a part of true love, professes there is no other as great in my affections as you. True intimate love is exclusive. There is no room for anyone else in the spousal relationship, no place for divided loyalties or wandering eyes. Both partners have a right to expect faithfulness and the conduct becoming it. Neither would do anything to cause doubts as to their fidelity and commitment. Christ and His Bride are genuinely devoted to each other.

Coals of fire

"Coals of fire…a most vehement flame" picture love burning fervently, even fiercely, in spite of the harsh trials of life. The result is a love that cannot be diminished or extinguished. Nothing can separate us from the love of Christ, and we should let nothing come between our Bridegroom and us. (Romans 8:35-39)

The second part of this verse in 8:6, combined with the succeeding verse 7, paints a portrait of true love, as strong as death, but ironically, the essence of life itself. Love will give you the strength to continue when everything in you says, "Quit." It is the greatest of qualities, for among faith, hope, and love mentioned in 1 Corinthians 13:13, only love continues forever. It is eternal. The flames of love never go out. It is jealous, single-minded in its focus, but always holy and pure in its intent for the loved one.

Judy-8:7 Many waters cannot quench love, neither can the floods drown it: if *a* man would give all the substance of his house for love, it would utterly be condemned.

Many waters

This phrase suggests troubles, trials, and difficulties cannot quench love. "Yet in all these things we are more than conquerors through Him that loved us. For I am persuaded, that neither death nor life, nor angels nor principalities nor powers, nor things present nor things to come, nor height nor depth, nor any other created thing, shall be able to separate us from the love of God which is in Christ Jesus our Lord." (Romans 8:37-39 NKJV)

The key to getting through this life and its trials is to keep our eyes looking upward, just as Jesus did. Through the unjust and unlawful trials, false witnesses, beatings, mockings, and the agony of the cross, Jesus never took His focus off His Father. Jesus intended to fulfill His mission of carrying out God's will, because the bond of love between them was so strong. No temptation or trial could separate them. Jesus continued to concentrate on the

One He loved, and in doing so, He set an example for us. Often I sing the song by Wendell Loveless *Every Day With Jesus Is Sweeter Than The Day Before* to remind me to keep my attention fixed on the Lord.

As I get to know Him more, I sincerely appreciate what Jesus went through on the cross to save me. Every morning, I pray this verse, seeking to recognize His presence and to know His will for me: "Cause me to hear thy loving kindness in the morning; for in thee do I trust: cause me to know the way wherein I should walk; for I lift up my soul unto thee." (Psalm 143:8) The Lord walks and talks with me daily, showing me the pathway of life.

It's the same with a husband and wife. Their love is supposed to grow sweeter as the years go by. As affection becomes stronger, you get to know each other better. You must be patient, fair, and honest. In honoring their relationship of trust and fellowship, each should work to make the other one proud. So it is with Christ and His Bride. The sweetness of their relationship increases as He cherishes her in every way, and she delights in doing things that please Him and bring glory to His name. "If you must choose, take a good name rather than great riches; for to be held in loving esteem is better than silver and gold." (Proverbs 22:1 TLB)

If a man would give all the substance of his house for love, it would utterly be condemned

"If you can find a truly good wife, she is worth more than precious gems! Her husband can trust her, and she will richly satisfy his needs. She will not hinder him, but help him all her life." (Proverbs 31:10-12 TLB) When troubles or questions arise, the couple should go together to the Lord for direction. Life is precious, and it matters how we live it.

Dixie-8:7 Many waters cannot quench love, neither can the floods drown it: if *a* man would give all the substance of his house for love, it would utterly be condemned.

Many waters…floods

Many waters, floods, or an avalanche of catastrophes may bring discouragement and momentary despair, but love will rise above it all and prevail. No trouble, stress, or calamity is as powerful as true love. When challenging circumstances intrude or invade, they will not vanquish love. In the beautiful song *Love Can Build a Bridge*, country singer Naomi Judd portrayed the strength of love as a person willing to walk unshod across intensely hot desert sands to share his last morsel with the one he loves. Love sees mountains, still none that cannot be climbed and conquered. Love is not blind to the realities of life but refuses to be stopped by them.

Love is like the rock of Gibraltar, a gigantic stone mountain on the Iberian Peninsula. The frequency of outside forces or troubles falling upon it does not change its composition. Love is more enduring and steadfast than any other entity. (1 Corinthians 13:13, 1 John 4:16)

The quality of love that the Song of Solomon pictures is matchless. It has no equal. No money can buy it. It is given generously, without strings attached. Jesus Christ is the epitome of love. Although "many waters" represent the persecution and troubles of His life in this world, they could not quench His love for His Father or us. Fierce in love's defense, He gave the ultimate sacrifice. The exquisite and intense strength of His passion, His unwillingness to give up or give in, and His adamant refusal to be less than the best describes the character of His love for His Bride. He is teaching her by principle and example what divine love is. He loves her with all His heart, soul, mind and strength. She has seen that in His eyes and actions; she has heard it in His words and tone. Her love for Him becomes stronger by the minute. Christ and His Bride want others to experience this same joy.

Judy-8:8 We have a little sister, and she hath no breasts: what shall we do for our sister in the day when she shall be spoken for?

What shall we do

We read a conversation about a little sister and how to prepare her for marriage. Today, some churches have become concerned about this and are helping to prepare young people for marriage. The New Testament teaches that the older ladies are to instruct the younger how to manage the home, to bear children, and to give no opportunity for the enemy to discredit them. (1 Timothy 5:14) The Apostle Paul emphasized in his letter to Titus, a pastor in Crete, that young women should be serious and to love their husbands and children. (Titus 2:3-5) Then, if some husbands were not believers and did not obey God's teaching, they would see the wives' pure behavior and come to knowledge of the Lord. (1 Peter 3:1-2)

Not fancy hair, gold jewelry, or fine clothes make you attractive. Genuine beauty comes from within; from a gentle, calm spirit. (1 Peter 3:3-4) This loveliness brings glory to God and will never disappear. These are the principles the little sister of faith will have to learn.

Dixie-8:8 We have a little sister, and she hath no breasts: what shall we do for our sister in the day when she shall be spoken for?

The bride uses "we" and "our" in this verse, clearly showing her oneness with King Solomon. Love for Jesus produces that same unity of thought and purpose in the Bride of Christ. She has learned the lesson of John 15:5 (NKJV), "…without Me you can do nothing."

She doesn't want to do anything apart from Him. She continues to foster her dependence on Him, seeking His wisdom. The importance of this quality cannot be over-emphasized. Notice how it is opposite to the independent attitude Israel took with Jehovah. In Isaiah 30:1 and 31:1, God admonished Israel for not seeking His counsel first or bringing their problems to Him.

We have a little sister

Now that Solomon's bride has a vibrant, united relationship with him, the Shulamite notices others around her who need help. Christ's Bride will become aware of those close to her who are deficient in some important spiritual areas. The first and correct inclination of the Bride of Christ would be to bring the problem to her Bridegroom, knowing she can rely on His unlimited knowledge and understanding. It is important to lay every matter at His feet, to seek His grace, knowing we will always receive His best in return. (1 Peter 5:7, Hebrews 4:16) How pleased He must be to know His desire for true oneness with her is coming to fruition.

She has no breasts

The Bride would certainly be concerned for a family member who is in the body of Christ, but not yet of Bride status. This little sister is alive in the faith and should be developing in particular areas, but thus far hasn't progressed. Therefore, she has nothing to offer to anyone else for their growth, for she herself is needy. The Bride recognizes the problem but does not belabor it, immediately desiring a solution from the One she knows can solve this dilemma. It is natural for the spiritually mature person to recognize where help is required and to seek the Lord's direction first. The Bride could pray: Lord Jesus, You are the answer to every problem, every dilemma, puzzling situation, and relationship. You have all knowledge and are the wisdom of God. It makes sense to run to You for help. (Psalm 18:29-30,1 Corinthians 1:24)

In the day she will be spoken for

Immature believers have a future. The Holy Spirit has written, "For I know the thoughts that I think toward you…thoughts of peace and not of evil, to give you a future and a hope." (Jeremiah 29:11 NKJV)

The spiritually mature Bride is willing to provide any necessary work, even remedial training, for this member of the body of Christ. There is no reason to give up on the needy one, just because there has not been much development. Change will take time; growth is a process and calls for patience and perseverance in these matters. When the needy one gets a proper diet and begins to feast on the Word of God: the water, milk, meat, and the Bread of Life, and applies what she learned, she will grow spiritually. (John 7:37-39, 1 Peter 2:2, Hebrews 5:12-14, Matthew 4:4)

Judy-8:9 If she *be* a wall, we will build upon her a palace of silver: and if she *be* a door, we will enclose her with boards of cedar.

Wall or door

Solomon and his bride aren't sure of the little sister's skills, but she will have everything needed to make a successful marriage and bless her husband. By the time the little sister is prepared for marriage, she will have a reputation as a caring, compassionate person ready and able to meet each situation with wisdom.

Believers who are walls can signify salvation or deliverance, while those who are gates or doors may represent people who will offer much praise to the LORD. (Isaiah 60:18b) So, following the Lord's direction, if a wall, the Bride of Christ will offer assistance, even emotional and spiritual healing, to someone in need. She might also provide a refuge, a hiding place for those seeking help, as Psalm 32:7 states of the Lord: "Thou *art* my hiding place; thou shalt preserve me from trouble; thou shalt compass me about with songs of deliverance." On the other hand, if a door, the Bride, with heart fixed on her Bridegroom-King, could teach others of the many ways available to praise Him. (Psalm 57:7, 150:1-6) People would know they could come to her to learn how to move into the presence of God through praise and worship.

The Beloved did the same for her. He freed her from sin, set her foot upon a firm foundation, and gave her a new song, even praise unto God. With her transformation as an example of what Christ's love has accomplished in her, many will trust in the Lord. (Psalm 40:2-3)

Dixie-8:9 If she *be* a wall, we will build upon her a palace of silver: and if she *be* a door, we will enclose her with boards of cedar.

If she be a door

Some Bible scholars think the wall represents a discreet woman and the door a promiscuous one. However, in this passage, I do not believe Solomon, in all his wisdom, would demean this young family member and speak a curse over her by calling her a potential harlot, nor would Christ say that of one of His family. It would contradict His character for the Beloved to speak in such a denigrating manner.

Wall or door

Are you a wall or a door? Before you decide, consider this: the wall goes up first in building construction, providing a larger framework for the smaller door. A wall can exist and function without a door, but a door cannot function without a wall. The door and the wall must be harmoniously and rightly connected. However, a door gives the wall a versatility it would not otherwise have. By its position, function, and movement, the door invites, by offering its users decision-making opportunities and access to what is on the other side of it. See how all these facets speak clearly of the relationship and ministry between members of the body of Christ?

In this verse 8:9, Solomon answers with a strategy to help this little sister, but first, a determination must be made. Is she a wall or a door? Everyone has a purpose in the house of God and the body of Christ by which we can serve the Lord and mankind. (Ephesians 2:10, 19-22) Your life isn't an accident, a happenstance, or a coincidence, no matter the circumstances of your arrival here. God has designed a plan for you, which He will reveal and enable you to fulfill. (Jeremiah 29:11, Philippians 1:6)

Everyone has a different role in this world and needs to find it. Nothing is accomplished until that role, purpose, understanding, and focus come into reality. Part of the satisfaction in living is the assurance that you comprehend your purpose. He wants you to know. No matter your purpose, the Lord is willing and able to make you great in the kingdom if you allow it. The Lord is the builder of the house of our lives. (Hebrews 3:1-6) He will make something wonderful out of your life if you want Him to do so. It's your choice. However, you need to realize it won't be accomplished by self-promotion or fame but by your humility and servanthood. (Matthew 20:26-28)

Silver or cedar

How wealthy the Bride of Christ has become by uniting with her Beloved. All the resources of His kingdom are available to her. She lacks nothing, and her Bridegroom has all the wisdom needed to address any problems or desires that arise. (1 Kings 10:23-24, 1 Corinthians 1:24) She only has to trust Him.

Palace of silver

"If a wall…we will build upon her a palace of silver." Note the use of the word "we" again, this time by Solomon, who is happy to make his bride's wishes a reality. In the same regard, oneness with His Bride is what Christ always desires. He delights when we come to Him with the desire to help a needy fellow believer. Whatever the immature believer's purpose, the body of Christ has the means to enlarge it so maximum utilization and fulfillment are achieved. In verse 10, the Bride equates breasts with towers, so she and her Beloved intend to teach the "little sister…with no breasts" how to become a tower of strength and one who can nourish others in the faith.

If a door…enclose with boards of cedar

Cedar is a strong, enduring wood, knot-free and rot-resistant, ideal for building purposes, and imported to Israel from Lebanon. (1 Kings 5:5-6) Solomon promises his bride that they will supply whatever is necessary to help this little one. Similarly, the Lord Jesus has always been the one Who gives power to the faint and strength to those who have none.

God imparts help when circumstances might cause a person to falter. To that point, in 2 Kings 4:8-17, there is an account of a childless woman who had her husband build a room to house the prophet Elisha whenever he was in the vicinity. In thanksgiving for her thoughtfulness and generosity, Elisha prophesied she would have a son. She received this promise by faith as she listened "standing in the door," and soon after, the prophecy was fulfilled. Her faith was the key that unlocked the door of heaven. (2 Kings 4:15-17) I think doors sometime symbolize people who hear the promise of God and then hold on to that promise, even if their entire world collapses around them. They are not afraid of terrible news; their trust is unshakable in the LORD, and the promise is fulfilled because their faith is unwavering. (2 Kings 4:18-37, Psalm 112:7) This, too, is true of Rahab. She was a strong door of faith, a means for her and her family to be saved from death and to come into the family of God. (Joshua 2, 6, Matthew 1:5, 16)

Walls and doors

Both walls and doors benefit people. That's the key. The Holy Spirit, through the apostle Paul, said it this way: "As we have therefore opportunity, let us do good unto all…" (Galatians 6:10) Whatever our mission, we are here to help people in the name of Jesus and under the Holy Spirit's direction, thereby bringing glory to God the Father. (Matthew 5:16)

Are you laying aside things like your agenda, schedule, pride, convenience, etc., and responding to the Holy Spirit's invitation and direction to serve others? Jesus lived what He taught. He was the servant of God and came here as a servant of mankind, as Philippians 2:7 and Mark 10:45 state. In John 13:4-5, after the last supper with His disciples, Jesus, acting as a servant, washed His disciples' feet. Was there ever a truer incident, apart from the cross, which pictured Jesus' heart of humility, obedience, and His willingness to serve in whatever way the Holy Spirit directed Him?

Members in the body of Christ are to be servants to their King, each other, and the world; we can only accomplish this if we keep His face before us and abide in Him. By our servanthood, we follow His steps and fulfill our purpose. Whether you're a wall or a door, humility is vital to fulfilling your destiny.

In Matthew 18:1-4, Jesus taught that having a high position is not the same as being greatest in the kingdom. In Mark 10:43-44, He specified servanthood as what it takes to be chief in God's realm. Intimacy with Jesus begins it. Being His servant defines your attitudes and work. This transformation will continue, not until death, but until the day of Jesus Christ. So whether we're on earth or in heaven, we will continue to learn, grow spiritually, and serve until that long-awaited, glorious resurrection day comes, after which we will be like Him. (Philippians 1:6, 1 John 3:1-3)

We will build

Notice the emphasis on togetherness using "we" twice in chapter 8, verse 9. In the same way that walls and doors are designed to work together, the body of Christ must do the same. Whatever one's purpose in the kingdom of God, it is essential and crucial to recognize the need for cooperation with others.

Each believer must accomplish what he has been created to do in accord and unity with other members. Oneness in the body of Christ is a major axiom—if not the primary principle—of God's kingdom, with love as its foundation and motivation. In His teachings, Jesus stressed this oneness to His disciples repeatedly. Unity, His earnest desire for His followers, was emphasized four times in the intimate prayer recorded in John 17:11, 21-23. Unity glorifies God and is a commandment, not a suggestion, to the body of Christ. (Romans 15:5-6, 1 Corinthians 1:10, Ephesians 4:3) Oneness is a characteristic of the family of God as it brings peace among believers and fosters rapid and extensive progress and outreach. (Psalm 133:1, Acts 4:32)

Keep in mind that unity does not mean uniformity. Although we all have the same purpose of serving God our Father and bringing others to Him through Christ, we have different roles in accomplishing it. Yours is not the same as mine, and vice versa, but whatever the Lord ordained for us is perfect. Working together is so important. Think of all believers as different instruments in a symphonic orchestra, each having a contribution to make, all combining to produce an excellent result, a magnificent display of musical achievement when submitted to and under the direction of the conductor.

Not all have the same mission, but all are to forward the plan of God, both individually, corporately, and Holy Spirit-directed. (1 Corinthians 3:6) Perhaps the "door" is the person with an evangelistic gift, and the "walls" are the teachers and mentors of the new believer brought in by the gospel message. Both are necessary; both are important. Whatever the case, when we work together, God gives astonishing results. (1 Corinthians 3:7)

In a loving promise to his bride, Solomon says whatever the little sister needs to make her functional and exceptional, they as a couple will offer. King Solomon and his bride will give the little sister what she cannot provide for herself. Today, this is one phase of the work of the Bride and the Beloved in the body of Christ: to mentor, disciple, call back to others, encourage onward, and to do whatever is necessary to bring those represented by the little sister to full maturity in Christ. (Ephesians 4:12-13) In the hands of the Lord, more will be accomplished than the Bride could imagine, and more than she could ever do by herself. (Ephesians 3:20-21)

Judy-8:10 I *am* a wall, and my breasts like towers: then was I in his eyes as one that found favor.

I am a wall

Undoubtedly, the Shulamite knew her beloved had become the door that opened endless possibilities for her to grow. I've discovered that I, too, am a wall. After her retirement, Nema McClintock, a godly woman, a "door", was directed by the Lord into a ministry of writing and sending scripture cards to enlighten and lift discouraged souls. Each December, working on an old manual typewriter, she would type thirty 3x5 index cards with Scriptures, Bible or personal stories, and decorate them with stickers. She included a written promise to continue sending more scripture cards each month for a year. One particular year, Nema had ten people on her list, which required monthly typing of three hundred cards. That's love!

God is always ahead of our prayers, already working, just waiting for a willing laborer. Eventually, someone else would need to continue this card ministry. Nema invited me to join her in ministry many years ago. My "spiritual mother" showed me the cards of encouragement that she and her Beloved had put together. In time, Nema's mantle of service transferred to me, just like Elisha did after Elijah. (2 Kings 2:1-15) I have a copy of all 365 of Nema's cards. I continue this encouragement ministry, creating cards as the Holy Spirit directs.

> The fact that the wall is bigger than the door means the ministry will spread farther. A customer of my husband Tom's car repair business was diagnosed with cancer and would have to drive many miles to Chattanooga, TN, for long outpatient treatments. This customer asked Tom if he would drive her to the hospital, keep her truck at his garage during the intervening hours, and return for her in the afternoon. Week after week, this was the routine they followed.

> The sick woman's nephew was also a customer and told Tom he didn't think his aunt had received salvation. After Tom related this story to me, God directed me to set apart specific cards with the plan of salvation on them. I decorated them and sent them to the nephew. His aunt allowed her nephew to read them to her. Before she died, the nephew said she was reading the cards herself, and we believe she accepted Jesus as her Lord and Savior. Interestingly, the cards got in when people couldn't, for she had been hurt in the past and wouldn't allow anyone on her property except her nephew. Secondly, because of Tom's kindness, she accepted the cards. Love opened the door to salvation.

Another opportunity came when an elderly man from my church returned home from spending a long day at the hospital with his ailing wife. He found my booklet of cards in the mail, sat, and read them immediately. His testimony was: "I was washed by the water of the Word and refreshed." Praise the Lord!

When my son was in the Navy, I sent him Scripture cards to read, and he, in turn, passed them on to encourage others. The cards were a gentle reminder that God was wherever they were, whether in the Mediterranean or off the coast of Africa. Scripture cards have also been sent to military personnel in Iraq, pastors' wives in Africa, a Russian orphanage, and evangelistic outreaches in Germany. These are just a few of the many wonderful accounts of how God continues to work through this card ministry and how this "little sister" became a wall.

Dixie-8:10 I *am* a wall, and my breasts like towers: then was I in his eyes as one that found favor.

A wall and towers

What resolution and certainty! Solomon's queen knows her purpose and feels firmly established like a wall. The bride no longer focuses on self, but on others and how she can serve them. The contrast between her comments about herself in 1:6 and here is remarkable. You can sense her confidence and assurance. She understands that she has much to offer. "My breasts like towers" represent how much she has to give, more than she had realized previously. Has it occurred to you that you also have much to give in service to the Lord and an eternity to cherish Him? Ask the Holy Spirit to teach you about this. Feel your Bridegroom's pleasure in your increasing desire, knowledge, and wisdom.

Towers

Walls and towers protect people and aid in warnings. Selfish people don't minister to anyone but themselves. Those who are spiritually mature understand that they have a mission to be a tower, to help others, as the Lord directs. (Galatians 6:10) God has ordained their good works, and they are to complete them. (Ephesians 2:10) It is so important to live a life fulfilling the opportunities to love and to serve. Jesus said the same thing to Peter in John 21:15 (NKJV): "…do you love Me?…Feed my lambs." Ultimately, we must remember we are ministering to the Lord when we help others, and it is our privilege. Be a tower! (Matthew 25:31-40, Colossians 3:23-24)

In Solomon's time, a wall could not be easily moved. The steadfastness of your faith needs to be like an immovable wall. In Psalm 62: 1-2 (NKJV), King David penned, "Truly my soul silently *waits* for God: from *Him* comes my salvation.

He only *is* my rock and my salvation; *He is* my defense; I shall not be greatly moved." Later, in verses 5 and 6 of Psalm 62 (NKJV), David speaks with increased confidence: "My soul, wait silently for God alone, for my expectation *is* from Him. He only *is* my rock and my salvation: He *is* my defense; I shall not be moved." In Psalm 16:8, David wrote, "I have set the LORD always before me; because he *is* at my right hand, I shall not be moved." Notice the difference in the words "not be greatly moved" and "not be moved." The first phrase shows his honesty, and the second emphasizes his increasing determination. From these verses, we understand that faith must be nurtured by meditating on who God is, His character, and past works. Then, in trials and tribulations, our trust and expectations in the Beloved remain strong and steadfast like a tower, accompanied by peace and joy. (Isaiah 26:3, Philippians 4:6-7, Romans 15:13)

I was in his eyes as one that found favor

In Matthew 20:20-23, one day, the mother of James and John came with them to Jesus, seeking to gain a high position for her sons in His coming kingdom. Jesus answered them by saying, "…to sit on my right hand, and on my left, is not mine to give, but it *shall be given to them* for whom it is prepared of my Father." It is my thought that Jesus declined their request because the privileged, right-hand position had already been designated for His Bride. In Psalm 45:9, it is written of the Messiah-King, "…at thy right hand did stand the queen in gold of Ophir."

If my speculation is true, this would be the epitome of honor, blessing, and favor from God the Father to the Bride of Christ. For as the Lord said in the books of Romans and Hosea, "…I will call them my people, which were not my people; and her beloved, which was not beloved." (Romans 9:25, Hosea 2:23) To elevate one to the highest level who, before her transformation, was categorized as an enemy of God and a sinner, is truly amazing grace and great favor! (Romans 5:10, 8) At the appointed time, Christ Jesus will proclaim to the world His love for His Bride by having His enemies bow down to her. "Behold, I will make them of the synagogue of Satan…come and worship before thy feet, and to know that I have loved thee." (Revelation 3:9) During a discussion with a friend, I was asked what one word described how I felt in my relationship with the Lord, and I replied, "cherished." That's how the Bride feels, and that feeling will increase the more she is with her Beloved.

Meditation Forty: Study the virtuous woman in Proverbs 31:10-31. In your notebook, list the attributes the Bride of Christ has in common with her.

Judy-8:11 Solomon had a vineyard at Baalhamon; he let out the vineyard unto keepers; every one for the fruit thereof was to bring a thousand *pieces* of silver.

King's vineyard

Solomon had a vineyard he had leased to keepers. Jesus' vineyard was and is the world. He sent His disciples out to preach the gospel and directed them to look and see that the fields were ready for harvest. "…the one who reaps draws a wage and harvests a crop for eternal life, so that the sower and the reaper may be glad together." (John 4:35, 36 NKJV) The Apostle Paul said it this way: "I have planted, Apollos watered, and God gave the increase." (1 Corinthians 3:6)

The fruit thereof was to bring a thousand pieces of silver

Jesus stated we are to love Him first and foremost, more than anyone or anything. He said "…whoever does not bear his cross and come after Me could not be My disciple. (Luke 14:27 NKJV) In the succeeding passage (Luke 14:28-30), He gave the example of building a tower. First, the builder must count the cost to determine whether he can finish his project. Generally, you don't want to start something if you can't see it through to completion. When missionaries go to a mission field, they proceed by faith, believing God will provide what they need. Jesus promised: "Verily I say unto you, There is no man that hath left house, or brethren, or sisters, or father, or mother, or wife, or children, or lands, for my sake, and the gospel's, But he shall receive an hundred-fold now in this time, houses, and brethren, and sisters, and mothers, and children, and lands, with persecutions; and in the world to come eternal life." (Mark 10:29-30) You can never out-give the Lord.

Dixie-8:11 Solomon had a vineyard at Baalhamon; he let out the vineyard unto keepers; every one for the fruit thereof was to bring a thousand *pieces* of silver.

King's vineyard

Solomon liked gardens and spent much time in them. He wrote that he planted vineyards, gardens, orchards, and all kinds of fruit trees. "I made myself water pools from which to water the growing trees of the grove." (Ecclesiastes 2:4-6 NKJV) In recalling the past, the Shulamite recounts the rare, fine quality of the produce of the king's vineyard, in which he allowed others to participate in the work. He relied on their help, as he did the shepherds under his authority in chapter 1. The royal fruit produced in his vineyard was precious, costing a thousand pieces of silver. People who understood and desired the value above all else paid the price to obtain it. Indeed, it was a great tribute to the vineyard's owner. Similarly, three women who poured their very costly ointments on Jesus at different times throughout His ministry expressed their resplendent praise for Him. Their extraordinary gifts and extravagant offerings were a display of the highest tribute they could show their Messiah. (Luke 7:36-50, John 12:3, Matthew 26:2, 6-13)

Judy-8:12 My vineyard, which *is* mine, *is* before me: thou, O Solomon, *must have* a thousand, and those that keep the fruit thereof two hundred.

My vineyard

The Shulamite now has her own vineyard and is delighted to work it. She tells her beloved Solomon she has done it all for him from a heart of gratitude, filled with joy for all he has done for her. Solomon's bride gladly shares her delight with others so that they might know a better way of life. I wonder what specifically she would tell those around her. She might encourage them not to worry, saying, "Remember we'll have everything we need for today and all our tomorrows. The king will see to it."

The Bride of Christ also has a heart of gratitude for her Beloved. A better life begins with thanking the Lord for His goodness and trusting Him for the future. (Matthew 6:31-33)

Dixie-8:12 My vineyard, which *is* mine, *is* before me: thou, O Solomon, *must have* a thousand, and those that keep the fruit thereof two hundred.

My vineyard

The thought the Shulamite confessed in 1:6 was "…mine own vineyard have I not kept." Look how she has changed! She relishes the thought of Solomon seeing the results of her work and fruitfulness, and she wants to bless him and those who helped her with it.

The Bride of Christ also can discern her progress portrayed in this verse. You can almost hear the satisfaction and delight in her voice as she regards her life and the rewards of it, all to glorify her Beloved, the One Who was instrumental in her extraordinary transformation. She also wants to bless those who helped her achieve her purpose. These gifts express her thanks and appreciation. It is important to acknowledge those who have given encouragement and support. The Lord provides and directs them at the right time and place to minister to our souls and aid in our transformation. Our appreciation shows that their obedience to the Lord was important, not only for them, but to us.

Judy-8:13 Thou that dwellest in the gardens, the companions hearken to thy voice: cause me to hear *it*.

The companions hearken

The Shulamite is well-taught and has learned much. She's usually found in the gardens with companions listening to what she says. She speaks with great wisdom and holds their attention. Her beloved Solomon wants to hear her, too, and tells her so.

Cause me to hear

Prayer is our conversation with Jesus, our King. We are encouraged to "Pray without ceasing." (1 Thessalonians 5:17) This means talking with our Beloved throughout the day, including Him in everything we do. He loves us and longs for that involvement. The Lord does not slumber or sleep. (Psalm 121:4) He's watching over us, patiently waiting for us to wake up and say "Good morning," and begin a lovely conversation with Him.

In stark contrast, some may quickly read a few Scriptures and offer prayers for family and friends at mealtime, perhaps bowing their heads with a few words of thanks. Too often, prayerful conversation is very short. He wants to hear our voices speak words of love, praise, and faith. They thrill His heart.

Dixie-8:13 Thou that dwellest in the gardens, the companions hearken to thy voice: cause me to hear *it*.

Thou that dwellest in the garden

Because there have been so many previous references to his work in the gardens, one might think this is the bride speaking to Solomon. However, Solomon is the speaker because the next verse is his lovely bride's response to his request, and in it she calls him "beloved." Till now in 8:13, Solomon's bride has shown an increasing passion for gardening and fruit-bearing, which had previously been solely his interest. (Song of Solomon 7:11-13) She's called a dweller in the gardens because she is now comfortable spending time there. Her beloved's passion has become hers.

Cause me to hear

The voice of His Bride has such attractive tones to Christ. He loves to hear her. He encourages her to tell Him her thoughts and desires. Of her, He might repeat the words spoken in 5:16: "To Me, her mouth is most sweet; yea, she is altogether lovely."

Here, we find another difference between the body of Christ and the Bride. The Bride *loves* to be with Him, think about Him, and talk with Him. To her, prayer is not a chore or duty, nor is it a religious ritual. She enjoys their conversation as much as He does.

Judy-8:14 Make haste, my beloved, and be thou like to a roe or to a young hart upon the mountains of spices.

Make haste, my beloved

I used to sit on the porch at the end of the day before my husband Tom came home from work. Being home all day, I missed his presence and couldn't wait to hear his car coming down the hill. At last, I'd see his sweet smile, and when he'd see me, he'd say he missed me, too, and wondered if I'd be waiting for him.

The Bride of Christ is anxiously awaiting her King's appearance. She will urge, "Hurry, my Beloved, and come to me." His reply, "Surely I come quickly…Even so come, Lord Jesus," she would respond as the Apostle John did in Revelation 22:20. (See also v. 17)

Dixie-8:14 Make haste, my beloved, and be thou like to a roe or to a young hart upon the mountains of spices.

Make haste, my beloved

Solomon longs to hear her voice. She immediately responds "make haste, my beloved"—no waiting, hesitance, or reluctance. She lets no time lapse between Solomon's desire and her answer. "Make haste, my beloved," is the call of a woman in love. His every wish is her pleasure to fulfill.

The Bride of Christ's desire is for Jesus, and she knows His desire is for her. (Song of Solomon 7:10) She encourages Him to join her quickly. Their oneness is now her primary focus, and she nurtures it. He has captured her heart forever. Lovingly she invites His nearness and the prospect of their intimacy. (Revelation 22:17) This is not last on her list but first, and He is honored by her passionate, deep love. The Beloved and His Bride are truly one in every way, consumed by their love for each other.

Meditation Forty-One: I start my day by saying, "Thank You, Beloved, for always being near and caring so deeply about me and my day. Thank You for hearing my cries and concerns for others and answering me when I need direction in our work. You're never too busy to respond, and hearing Your voice is the happiest time of my day. I love You, Beloved. Amen." (Judy's prayer) Finish your love letter to Jesus (Meditation 1) Read it aloud to Him.

CONCLUSION

Our purpose in writing this book is to exalt our Lord Jesus Christ and to help you consider the book of the Song of Solomon, not as a marriage manual or a historical account, but solely as a study of Christ and His Bride—His beauty of character and actions, her development and transformation, and their love that initiated and colored everything they did. We hope the desire for a deeper and richer relationship with our Beloved Jesus has welled up in you. Like the Shulamite maiden, we pray that you are willing to let go of fears, apathy, and all the soulishness that would hold you back from becoming His in every way. A glorious, present and eternal reward awaits those who respond to the stirring of the Holy Spirit.

The first step in becoming a member in the body of Christ and the family of God involves receiving the truth: God gave His greatest gift, His only begotten Son, Who volunteered to come to Earth to be the Savior and Redeemer of the world. (Philippians 2:5-11, Isaiah 9:6, 6:8, John 3:16, Matthew 1:21) No one else could have done it. It cost Jesus everything, including His life and, for a short time, His Father's fellowship (but not His love). Jesus had to trust His Father's promises to Him, in order to fulfill His mission on Earth.

However, God did not put an equally exorbitant price on the salvation and eternal life He offered mankind through Jesus. No, it was and is presented as a gift free of charge. It is given to all who will humble themselves, repent of wrongs done, believe Jesus paid the penalty for their sins by His death, and accept Him as Lord of their lives. This act includes believing God raised Jesus from the dead, by which God assured everyone that Jesus' holy life and sacrifice, being your substitute, taking your place on the cross, paying the penalty for your sin, were acceptable to God the Judge. Jesus paid in full the needed price of atonement, thereby purchasing your forgiveness. (Acts 17:31, Ephesians 1:7, 4:32, Colossians 1:14, Psalm 86:5, 103:3, 1 John 1:9)

Jesus' death and resurrection brings salvation and the gift of eternal life to you, if you will receive Him and what He did for you. "For with the heart one believes unto righteousness, and with the mouth confession is made unto salvation." (Romans 10:10 NKJV) Eternal life is given to the person who understands and acknowledges salvation cannot be purchased, earned, or worked for; it must be received by faith. (Ephesians 2:8-9, John 3:15-16, 10:28, Romans 6:23, 1 John 5:11-13) "Jesus as Lord" becomes the primary, underlying principle and motto by which a believer should live the rest of his life here.

APPENDICES

Appendix A

Dixie–5:2 I sleep, but my heart waketh: *it is* **the voice of my beloved that knocketh,** *saying,* **Open to me, my sister, my love, my dove, my undefiled: for my head is filled with dew,** *and* **my locks with the drops of the night.**

Dreams

Think how many people in the Bible were instructed, encouraged, received promises, and were warned of danger through dreams. Abimelech, Gentile king of Gerar, saved his life and that of his family by believing the dream God gave him. (Genesis 20) Jacob came to believe in the God of his fathers through a dream (Genesis 28:10-22), and later, from another dream, received instruction as to how to increase financially. (Genesis 31:1-13) Joseph, a young son of the aged Jacob, had two dreams which contained prophecies of his future. (Genesis 37:5-11) No doubt, that Word from God sustained him through the thirteen years of slavery and imprisonment he suffered in Egypt. (Genesis 37:2, 37:12 - 41:14) God gave the ruler of Egypt prophetic dreams which Joseph interpreted, therefore, great promotion came to Joseph. Because Pharaoh believed the interpretation, it resulted in the sparing of the nation of Egypt and others from extinction, and ultimately saved the founders of the nation of Israel. (Genesis 41)

In Judges 7:9-15, God gave a dream to a heathen enemy soldier. Gideon, a man of Israel, overhearing an enemy soldier recounting the dream and its interpretation, learned his men would win the battle against the host of Midian—and they did. King Solomon received two dreams in which the Lord made appearances, and gave instruction and warnings to him. (1 Kings 3:5-15, 9:2-9) A heathen king, Nebuchadnezzar of Babylon, received prophetic dreams which Daniel was able to interpret. (Daniel 2, 4) Daniel himself received dreams and visions from the LORD. (Daniel 7) So did Joseph, the virgin Mary's husband-to-be, and the wise men from Babylonia who sought the Christ Child. (Matthew 1:20, 2:12-13, 19) Joseph, Daniel, and others were also given the ability to interpret dreams. (Daniel 1:17)

The naysayers who want to dismiss any possibility of a supernatural message from the Lord through dreams will propose that a dream can be a product of what someone eats, etc. Isaiah 29:8 (NKJV) agrees: "It shall even be as when an hungry man dreams, And look—he eats; but he awakes, and his soul is still empty; or as when a thirsty man dreams, and look—he drinks; but he awakes, and indeed *he is* faint, and his soul still craves…" However, to dismiss every dream as insignificant makes no sense, given the many prophetic dreams of believers and the Biblical examples listed previously.

In November of 2004, I received what I term to be my first dream from the Lord. In actuality, it wasn't the first, but the first I recognized as from the Lord. In the dream, it was Halloween. I had gotten a small bag of scripture-wrapped candy to give children, even though we never had any come to our house. In the dream, two children came to our door. Surprised by their knock, I felt bad because I hadn't put the candy in a pretty basket so it would look nice, and the children were having to wait for me to find the treats. I not only found the original bag of candy, but also another bag of candy, three or four times bigger than the first one. I had much more candy than I thought. The children were so happy to receive from such bounty.

The interpretation given by my brother: when your ministry begins, perhaps unexpectedly, you will have more than enough to give to others. Opportunity may present itself in the near future. You will feel unready for it, but you will have more than is necessary to meet their desire. Don't worry about presentation. It's not a pretty presentation that's important, but a heart desirous of giving. You will have what they want, and they will be glad to receive from you. Now eight years later, writing my fourth book, teaching the Bible in an online study on the Gospel of Mark (www.lambtalk.net), and getting to sub occasionally as a Sunday School teacher, I see how the Lord has been fulfilling this dream through me.

I had the honor of contributing to a wonderful book by a close friend, Mari Fitz-Wynn, *God's Whispered Dreams: Messages, Meanings, and Miracles*. I wrote about dream interpretation in it.
(Available at www.faithjourneypublishing.com)

Appendix B

Judy-5:9 What *is* thy beloved more than *another* beloved, O thou fairest among women what *is* thy beloved more than *another* beloved, that thou dost so charge us?

- **My Jesus is higher than angels.** "For to which of the angels did God ever say, "You are my Son; today I have become your Father?..."" (Hebrews 1:5 NKJV)
- **My Jesus made the world.** "All things were made through Him, and without Him nothing was made that was made." (John 1:3 NKJV) "...Thou, Lord, in the beginning hast laid the foundation of the earth: and the heavens are the works of thine hands..." (Hebrews 1:10) "Who hath measured the waters in the hollow of his hand, and meted out heaven with the span, and comprehended the dust of the earth in a measure, and weighed the mountains in scales, and the hills in a balance?" (Isaiah 40:12)
- **My Jesus guides me with His eyes.** "I will instruct thee and teach thee in the way which thou shalt go: I will guide thee with mine eye." (Psalm 32:8)

- **My Jesus always knows where I am and what I'm doing.** "O, LORD, You have searched me and known *me*. You know my down sitting and my uprising… and are acquainted with all my ways." (Psalm 139:1-3 NKJV)
- **My Jesus has feelings and is moved with compassion.** "So Jesus had compassion *on them*, and touched their eyes; and immediately their eyes received sight, and they followed him." (Matthew 20:34)
- **My Jesus watches over me.** "…he…shall neither shall slumber nor sleep." (Psalm 121:4)
- **My Jesus comforts me.** Jesus knows what it's like to need comfort, emotional encouragement, and prayer. When He was at Gethsemane, He wanted that support from His friends, but they failed Him. God sent His angel to comfort Jesus. (Luke 22:43) Jesus, following in His Father's example, was a comforter, too. As He prepared to leave this world, He prayed that the Father would give another Comforter, the Holy Spirit, to abide with us forever. (John 14:16) "Blessed *be* God, even the Father of our Lord Jesus Christ, even the Father of mercies, and the God of all comfort; Who comforteth us in all our tribulation, that we may be able to comfort them which are in any trouble, by the comfort wherewith we ourselves are comforted of God." (2 Corinthians 1:3-4)

Appendix C

Dixie-5:9 What *is* thy beloved more than *another* beloved, O thou fairest among women what *is* thy beloved more than *another* beloved, that thou dost so charge us?

My Jesus is extraordinary in His attributes. He provides His strength to help me. (2 Chronicles 16:9) Jesus thinks about me all the time, (Psalm 40:5), encourages me, and urges me to come to Him when I need forgiveness or help. His door is always open. (Hebrews 4:16) For me, He is the Way back into the garden of God. Do you realize how extraordinary that is? What Adam and Eve lost through disobedience and sin is regained in Jesus Christ. They were banished from the garden where fellowship and communion with the Lord had been the norm. Now, through Christ, we are invited to enter the garden of God and savor that fellowship and communion again, to know *all* the blessings of joy with the Lord Jesus. With Him are pleasures forever. (Psalm 16:11, Song of Solomon 6:3)

Appendix D

Dixie-6:4 Thou *art* beautiful, O my love, as Tirzah, comely as Jerusalem, terrible as *an army* with banners.

A warrior example

In my mind, the warrior Caleb was a Bride type in the Old Testament. In Numbers 13 and 14, Caleb, at the age of forty, was selected as part of a group of twelve men sent to spy out the land of Canaan. All twelve observed giants, and walled, fortified cities there, but unlike the ten fearful spies, Caleb believed more in God's spoken Word than the obstacles viewed in the land. He didn't view the conditions as insurmountable, but as mountains to be leaped over. He refused to doubt; his banners were flying high. In the strength of the Lord, the Israelites would be victorious.

Unfortunately, the children of Israel were not willing to trust the Lord, so they failed to take the land God had offered them. Forty years later, after the older generation had died (except for Joshua and Caleb), their children lifted banners of faith and became the conquerors of the Promised Land.

Even when Caleb was in his eighties, he had not lost that great confidence in the Lord and His Word. After much of the land of Canaan had been conquered and allotted to the different tribes, Caleb asked Joshua to give him the area that he had surveyed forty years earlier and that Moses had promised him, even though it still had some giants living there. In Joshua 14:5-15 and 15:14, Caleb reminds Joshua of what the Lord had said to them through Moses. In this powerful passage, note how many times Caleb refers to the Word of the Lord.

Caleb's confidence and determination, heard in his declaration of "…I wholly followed the LORD my God," are the same as the Beloved sees in His Bride. (Joshua 14:8) She has hoisted banners of love over Him, and now there is no stopping her. Knowing Him, His character, and His life intimately—and, therefore, trusting Him completely—finishes the foundation for a new way of thinking for her. She is ready to advance and win in the contest of life. With Him, she can conquer all things. (Romans 8:37) The Bride has learned to focus on the goal, as Jesus did. (Hebrews 12:2) He has shown her by example how to overcome, and now she personifies the same.

Appendix E

Dixie-6:13 Return, return, O Shulamite; return, return, that we may look upon thee. What will ye see in the Shulamite? As it were the company of two armies.

Armies

Similar to Song of Solomon 6:13, in 2 Kings 6:14-17, the prophet Elisha was aware of and made strong by the knowledge of the presence of an accompanying army of angels protecting him and his servant from the king of Syria's forces. This union of man with the angelic realm was also seen in Jesus' life: (Mark 1:13, Luke 22:43, John 1:51, 1 Timothy 3:16, Matthew 28:2, 5, Acts 1:10-11); with His disciples after Pentecost (Acts 5:19, 8:26, 12:7); and with saints through the ages. (Luke 16:22, Acts 10:3, 22, 27:23, 30-31, Revelation 2:1, 22:16)

Appendix F

Dixie-7:11 Come, my beloved, let us go forth into the field; let us lodge in the villages.

Living faith

Faith can be dead or alive. Which it is depends on what comes afterward. Dead faith is to believe something but never act on it. In contrast, living faith is to know you have received the Word of God and then apply it to the situation. Two examples of living faith are Abraham and Rahab. Having believed the Word from God that his son, Isaac, would be the first of a multitude of his descendants, Abraham was later instructed to sacrifice that same son to God, but he knew the Lord was obligated to keep His Word and, therefore, would have to resurrect Isaac. He was not afraid to trust the Lord. That's how strong Abraham's faith was. (Genesis 15:4-5, 22:1-19, Hebrews 11:17-19)

In Joshua 2:1-24 and 6:22-25, Rahab, who had heard about the God of the Hebrew people and the great miracles He had done (which had happened forty years before), believed "… the LORD your God, he *is* God in heaven above, and in earth beneath." (Joshua 2:11) Therefore, she protected the Hebrew spies, choosing service to the true God over loyalty to a heathen king. Abraham's trust and Rahab's faith were active, alive, not dead, because what they believed was shown in their actions supporting that belief.

The Bible is full of examples of living faith. The woman with the issue of blood in Mark 5:25-29 is a picture of dynamic faith. "When she had heard of Jesus, came in the press behind, and touched his garment. For she said, If I may touch but his clothes, I shall be whole." Note three parts to her healing: hearing, believing, and touching His garment. If she had not reached out and touched the fringe of His prayer shawl as evidence of what she believed, she would not have received her healing. Living faith is shown in an action.

Another example of active faith is the Syrophoenician woman, who had a young daughter tormented by an unclean spirit to the extent that the girl could not get any rest. That concerned mother had heard a Jewish Healer was in the area, and she found Jesus and fell at His feet, desiring Him to cast the demon out of her daughter. She believed the mercy of God would trump borders, ethnicity, gender, religious affiliation, and any other limitations. She was correct. Her pursuit of God's mercy resulted in the healing of her daughter. She heard, she believed, and she pursued. She had living faith. (Matthew 15:21-28)

In Acts 9:10-19, the Holy Spirit directs a disciple named Ananias to go to a certain street and a particular house where he would find Saul of Tarsus, a zealous persecutor of Christians. Saul had been blinded by an encounter with the resurrected Jesus on the road to Damascus three days earlier. The Holy Spirit's instructions were for Ananias to lay hands on Saul and heal him of blindness. This and other specific information constituted words of knowledge from God to Ananias. (1 Corinthians 12:8) Despite his fears about possible dangers, Ananias followed the Holy Spirit's command, thereby demonstrating his faith was alive.

Recently I was discussing this topic with a friend who was ill and believing God for healing without going to the doctor. We both had already realized that, through this testing, the Lord wanted to promote her to higher level of faith in Him. The Lord had given her several instances of encouragement and words of support during her six days of illness, such as "Rise and be healed," and, on the next day, "Today is the day of salvation." Within twenty-four hours, she was healed. She asked the Lord, "Am I to go back to work (a strenuous job)?"
He asked, "Are you healed?"
She answered, "Yes, Lord."
He asked, "Why are you waiting?"
Since we had just finished a discussion of living faith versus dead faith, she said, as she got up to go to the phone: "My act of faith will be to call my work and get off the sick list."

That's what is meant by having living faith. A short time later, the Lord gave her words of commendation for her faithfulness to believe Him. An example of dead faith is given in James 2:15-17, concerning the possibility of a destitute church member seeking help from church leaders. They prayed for him but gave no help, in contrast to the instruction we're given in Galatians 6:10. Their faith was dead because they failed to be God's hands of compassion to that needy brother. Romans 10:17 (NKJV) states, "…faith *cometh* by hearing and hearing by the Word of God." Truth must be heard and believed, yes, but then it must be acted upon to become living faith.

Appendix G

Dixie-8:9 If she *be* a wall, we will build upon her a palace of silver: and if she *be* a door, we will enclose her with boards of cedar.

No matter if a wall or a door in the Lord's house, we are privileged to be His servants. (1 Corinthians 6:19, Ephesians 2:19-22, Hebrews 3:6) Following the Lord's lead, the apostle Paul also claimed the title of servant. (Romans 1:1) So did James, the Lord's brother and head of the church in Jerusalem (Galatians 1:18-19, 2:9, James 1:1, Acts 15:4, 13, 19), the apostle Peter (2 Peter 1:1), Jude (Jude 1), and John. (Revelation 1:1) These men and others felt honored to be known as servants of their Lord.

ABOUT THE AUTHORS

DIXIE MCCLINTOCK was a career mathematics and physics teacher for thirty years and retired early to become a caregiver for her mother. For more than ten years, Nema, Judy, and Dixie met weekly for a Bible study. God richly blessed, and now Judy and Dixie continue learning more from the amazing Word of God.

JUDY RUSK has been a happy homemaker for many years. Judy and her loving husband Tom have two sons and three grandchildren. Throughout her life, she's had the opportunity to study the Bible and learn to apply it. Judy says her prayers have been answered because "…not one word has failed of all the good promises [God] gave…" (1 Kings 8:56 NIV) The Lord has extended her the privilege to co-author this book.

ABOUT THE BOOK

Have you ever been dazzled by the Beloved? Is there an eagerness in you to know Him better? Would you like to be awakened or renewed to the realization of Christ's wondrous and overwhelming love for you? The Lord Jesus wants you and every believer to be part of His Bride. This is His desire. We have written this book with the expectation that through it, you will more clearly hear His song of love to you, as we have. We wanted to share what He has shown us thus far. Neither of us is a Bible scholar, but we know and love the Author of our faith, the Lord Jesus Christ, our Beloved.